WAR CYCLES - PEACE CYCLES

Richard Kelly Hoskins

The Virginia Publishing Company

LYNCHBURG, VIRGINIA

Published   by

The Virginia Publishing Company
P. O.   Box 997
Lynchburg, Virginia 24505

Printed in the United States of America.

Library of Congress Catalog Card Number 85-060212

Also by Richard Kelly Hoskins

OUR NORDIC RACE, 1958

INTRODUCTION

In the Spring of 1980 I was asked to speak at a financial seminar in Washington, D.C. At that time gold had just traded at $850 an ounce. Other commodities were reaching fantastic heights. During the seminar speaker after speaker rose to comment on unending inflation.

This flew in the face of history. When my time to speak arrived I told the audience that based on the prior three economic cycles since this country was founded, we could expect lower commodity prices, higher stock markets, and then - a 1929 type depression.

The example I used which made it all inevitable is the example below:

If there is only $10 in existence, and
you lend it to someone under condition that he repay $11,
and if he agrees to this,
he has agreed to the impossible.

A usury contract impossible to fulfill has been made. Another fish has been caught. If you understand this you can dispense with reading this book. You already understand usury.

The audience at the seminar was not satisfied. That afternoon most of them met in a hot crowded meeting room for a question and answer period. After almost 3 hours we had to call a halt. I promised that I would elaborate on their questions and put it down in a book. After 5 years this book is the result of that meeting.

Money is simple. The same things occur throughout history time after time. It is like a car going around the block. One time it may be green, another time orange, another time black. After the 16th time it doesn't make any difference what color the car is - you will recognize it.

The same goes for money. There may be some little change each time an economic event comes around - but after 15 times you learn to recognize what it is. Once we grasp how simple the system is, it becomes easy to make an accurate educated guess what will come next. What is happening now has happened before - and will happen again.

TABLE OF CONTENTS

ILLUSTRATIONS

SECTION I
BABYLONIAN ECONOMIC SYSTEM - 2000 B. C.

Chapter 1

THE FIRST DEFAULTS

Archaeologists digging in the ruins of ancient temples, or ziggurats, in Babylonia have discovered extensive evidence of the economic system practiced by the priests of Baal. Instead of finding money (or coins) as we know it, we mostly find clay tablets representing promises to pay - or IOUs. Along with the clay tablets has been uncovered the secret of their economic system, a system in some respects more efficient than our economic system today.

People only borrow when they are in need or if they are greedy and think they are getting a bargain. In Babylonia after a bad crop year, the farmers would be forced to go to the priests of Baal for a loan to buy seed for the following year. Let us say a farmer named Seth was one of those who needed money for seed. The temple priests were most accommodating and graciously allowed Seth to borrow 10 talents under condition that he repay 11. His land, livestock, wife, children and he himself served as collateral.

In that day there was little money in circulation. The sudden appearance of 10 talents in circulation allowed Seth and all the other farmers to buy seed and plant great fields of grain. They also bought cattle and sheep and many other necessary things. Here we have a situation of a debt of 11 talents coming due while there are only 10 talents in circulation with which to pay.

We can imagine that Seth was panic-stricken after having paid back 10 talents and finding that he still owed one more, and that there was no way to pay because there was no more money in circulation. He could offer the priest thousands of bushels of grain in payment, but the contract he signed was due to be paid in TALENTS - not grain. Cattle? Seth had herds of cattle, pigs, and flocks of sheep - these were also turned down. The contract was to pay in TALENTS - not sheep and pigs. Seth had gathered up the only 10 talents in circulation to pay down on his 11 talent debt and now there was no money to be had. Land, corn, cattle, sheep and pigs had no value as payment against his debt. The contract he had signed stated that he was to pay "talents" only, and there were no talents in circulation.

Chapter 2

DEFAULT & PROHIBITION OF USURY

Now arrives the moment of truth - default - bankruptcy. Since Seth could not pay his debt of 11 talents when there were only 10 talents in circulation, he must forfeit his collateral. His livestock went first, his lands next, then his children were sold into slavery as well as his wife, and then he himself became a slave. This is where most slaves came from - debt. Besides Seth and his family, there were tens of thousands of Babylonians who could not pay debts of 11 talents when only 10 talents were in circulation. By the thousands they were herded into captivity. The priests of Baal reduced a large part of their fellow countrymen to slaves and the "system of interest" spread wherever Babylonian armies marched or Baal priests practiced their religion.

Prohibition

The God of Abraham, Isaac, and Jacob saw how His people "Israel" were adopting the practices of the Baal priests. They were lending 10 talents and demanding payment of 11 talents when there were only 10 talents in circulation. They were reducing their own people to slavery just like the heathen Babylonians, in violation of God's express law against such practices:

Thou shalt not lend upon usury to thy brother; usury of money, usury of victuals, usury of anything that is lent upon usury.

Unto a stranger[1] thou mayest lend upon usury; but unto thy brother thou shalt not lend upon usury...
Deuteronomy 23:19, 20

Prohibition

When the "interest system" was again creeping in - this time from Egypt, it was commanded to be written:

He that putteth not out his money to usury, nor taketh reward against the innocent. He that doeth these things shall never be moved. Psalm 15:5

Prohibition

Once more the Babylonian system of interest was rampant in Assyria, Babylon, and Greece, causing ruin and despair wherever it reached, and so God placed prohibition upon prohibition:

He that hath not given forth upon usury, neither hath taken any increase, that hath withdrawn his hand from iniquity, hath executed true judgment between man and man...Hath given forth upon usury, and hath taken increase: Shall he then live? He shall not live; he hath done all these abominations; he shall surely die, his blood shall be upon him.
Ezekiel 18:8,13

1. Heb: "zûwr". In Hebrew the word "stranger" has two separate, distinct meanings. The words "zûwr", "nokrîy, & "nêkâr" refer to "racial aliens." The words "gêr" & "tôshâb" refer to racial kinsmen living in foreign lands. The above usage of "stranger" permits one to lend at usury to a racial alien while forbidding the use of usury to a racial kinsman.

3

There were two more prohibitions:

Prohibition

Ye exact usury, every man against his brother....let us leave off this usury. Nehemiah 5:7,10

Prohibition

He that by usury and unjust gain his substance, he shall gather it for him that will pity the poor.
Prov. 28:8

Those who would like to profit from "the system" turn to Luke 19:12-29 to justify their conduct. This is the parable of the ten talents written in 30 A. D. where the Lord comes and supposedly asks for His money with interest. Through the centuries our ministers have told us that the Holy Bible is without error. Every other mention of interest in the scripture is to forbid it. This one does, too - if one reads the scripture as our grandfathers were taught to read it.

In this example the Lord left money with different servants. All prospered but one. That one was asked to give an account. He replied by saying that he feared the Lord because he was "an austere" man - meaning a "harsh" man. Everyone knows that the God of Israel is not "harsh" - but gentle and long suffering. This proved the servant a liar. He then said "thou takest up that thou layest not down, and reapest that thou didst not sow." This was calling his Lord a "thief"! God is not a thief! It proved the servant twice a liar. Out of his own mouth the servant proved that he was worthless by not doing anything with the talent entrusted to him. Next, he was caught twice in lies. Then his Master asked him why he did not add insult to injury by putting the money at usury (a forbidden act) so that the servant could then call his master a "usurer", too. (Masters are responsible for their servants' actions). After being called a liar and a thief by a worthless servant, the Lord instructed that the money be taken from him and given to a productive servant.

Every verse in the Bible dealing with usury condemns the practice. This is the one single example that modern day apologists for the System try to twist into their service. Thomas Aquinas of the Catholic Church and Martin Luther of the Protestant Church agree that the "Parable Of The Ten Talents" does not remove the prohibition against the use of "interest".

Chapter 3

EARLY BANKS & BANKERS

Since the earliest times there have been banks and bankers. The type of bank which was approved operated simply to bring a person with money together with a person who needed money and together they became partners in a Joint Venture business enterprise. For this service banks charged fees. The other kind of bank which was disapproved operated on the Babylonian principle of lending 10 and collecting 11. The one was necessary, natural, and orderly; the other unnatural and disorderly. The reasons the disorderly "interest system" has been forbidden to faithful Christians are obvious. If you borrow 10 and are forced to pay back 11, sooner or later the usurer will take your property.

Ancient Money Contracts

The example used earlier of Seth borrowing 10 talents and having to repay 11 talents is straightforward and easily understood. But to elaborate just a little:

Suppose Seth goes again to the lender and borrows 10 gold talents and agrees to repay interest each year of 3 1/3 talents, and also agrees to repay the 10 gold talents whenever the Baal priest asks for it. Each year for three years Seth pays 3 1/3 talents. At the end of three years there is no more gold in circulation and Seth must ask for a loan in order to pay the interest he had agreed to pay (or forfeit his farms, children, etc.).

The lender then has a choice: he can lend Seth gold talents with which to pay interest or he can give him a clay tablet which the lender says is worth 3 1/3 talents and keep his gold. Understanding money is just common sense. Which would you do? You would give Seth a clay tablet and keep the gold. This is the reason for the clay tablet mentioned earlier. It was a loan substitute for gold. The citizens of Babylon treasured their clay tablets. They are found in great quantities today wherever excavating is being done in the ruins of Babylon.

We have mentioned the Temple banks - they were big ones. There were also government banks, and private banks such as the Igibi Bank which flourished in 575 B. C.[2] These banks offered almost every service offered by banks today including the use of checking, savings, letters of credit, and the Babylonian form of paper money - the clay tablet. The banks kept the gold... naturally.

In ancient Egypt a canal had been dug from the Nile all the way to the Red Sea. Boats coming from India could stop by barges tied up by the side of the canal and get a loan - day or night. At night these loan-boats were well lit so that they could be seen from a long way off. They are the ancestors of the drive-in window in today's banks. There is nothing new under the sun.

Persia Conquers Babylon

The relationship between nations follows almost exactly the relationship followed between individuals. If one nation desires something another nation has and doesn't have the required payment - the money can be borrowed. If interest is required, as it usually is, trouble is just a matter of time.

Babylon had a neighbor to the north - Persia. In the course of trade Babylon graciously made loans which enabled Persia to buy things she ordinarily would not be able to buy. The loans were made at standard interest rates for the time, 33 1/3%, payable in gold. Persia kept her part of the bargain as best she could. She borrowed extensively and was required to repay double the amount in three years. After paying back the original loan, Persia, like Seth earlier, found that there was no more money left in circulation and that she still owed Babylon's bankers the interest on the loans.

The king of Persia had other problems resulting from this Babylonian loan. Interest on the loan drained Persia of money. Commerce came to a virtual halt except for barter. There was no gold for taxes so the king could not pay his retainers. King

---

2. Ency. Brit. 14 Ed. Banks, p.67

Cyrus of Persia needed gold. Babylon had the gold Persia needed. Persia went to war against her creditor and conquered Babylon in 536 B. C. - and confiscated Babylon's gold. She also adopted Babylon's usury system. Usury between nations inevitably leads to war.

Greece Conquers Persia

As Persia spent the confiscated Babylonian gold, there was an instant flash of economic activity. New cities were built, industries were financed, armies outfitted, and palaces were built. The flood of wealth sent Persian merchants to Greece. The Greeks needed Persian wares so they borrowed with the promise of returning the loans plus interest.

A case in point: in 412 B. C. Sparta borrowed 5,000 talents from Persia to build warships. This loan like all the others was at standard rates. Seven years later, in 405 B. C., Lysander of Sparta used these ships to destroy the whole Athenian fleet which was attacked while they were drawn up on a beach. This event made Sparta "number one" in Greece - all on borrowed money.

Let's look at this transaction in a little more detail. If the Spartans repaid the Persians' loan monthly, the payments would have come to 153.19 talents monthly for 7 years. At 33 1/3% the total repaid would have come to 12,857.96. A tidy profit - if that much money could actually have been found in circulation to meet the payments.

Chances are the Spartans needed the entire 5,000, and everything else they could get together, to prepare for the coming war. If this is what happened, the debt would have looked like this:

Spartan Debt To The Persians @ 33 1/3%

5,000.00	borrowed
6,666.65	owed at end 1st year
8,888.84	2nd
11,851.79	3rd
15,802.39	4th
21,069.85	5th
28,093.13	6th
37,457.51	7th year

7

In that day 1 talent was a substantial sum. Five thousand talents was enough to buy an entire navy. Thirty seven thousand talents was an impossible figure. "The borrower is servant to the lender." Sparta was forced to use the navy she had borrowed the money to buy - she couldn't allow the unpaid debt to continue to mount. When she won the war, she transferred the payments of this horrendous debt to Athens - and Athens instead became the servant of Persia. The Persians certainly felt themselves the real winners. Greeks were killing Greeks - and their 5,000 talent loan had brought home wonderful riches. It was these loans that drained Greece of money and paved the way for unending war.

336 B. C. - Alexander The Great

Philip II of Macedonia died. Philip had conquered Greece and placed her under his rule. His son, Alexander, inherited the throne. Quickly putting down army discontent, he inspected the treasury. It contained the equivalent of a measly $120,000, not even enough to pay his army. In addition, he owed $1.5 millions.

Alexander had no choice. He had to have money to pay his army and to pay his debts. Greece was bare of money. Persia was rich. She had the money she had taken from Babylon and from her interest charges to Athens and other Greek cities over the years. The pressing need for money forced Alexander to invade Persia. Leading his matchless Grecian phalanx against the Persians, he won magnificent victories and gained an empire - and $440 million in gold from Darius' banks and temples.

Rome Conquers Greece

The Grecian empire encompassed most of the known world. A model Greek city was built in each conquered country to demonstrate the superiority of the Greek culture. Each city contained a temple. Each temple was also an interest bank which made loans. Gradually the gold in the form of interest payments returned from the people to the Greek temples scattered all over the empire and gradually depression also set in.

Greek traders established cities in the southern and northern parts of Italy. In the middle was the young vigorous Roman federation. The Greek traders traded extensively with their

Roman neighbors - much of it on credit - lending 10 gold coins under condition that 11 be repaid. The Romans were hard put to pay their ballooning obligations to the Greeks and at the same time maintain their armies which were needed for their incessant wars. Choosing to gain by war what she could not gain by peace, Rome turned on Greece, conquered her, and confiscated her wealth concentrated in the Greek temples and the municipal and the private banks.

Basic Rules

The basic rules covered thus far on which all economics and understanding of national and international events are based are these. First, the act of lending at interest is forbidden:

Thou shalt not lend upon usury to thy brother. Deu.23:19

Next, the act of going into debt is forbidden:

Owe no man anything but to love one another. Rom. 13:8

and finally, if once these laws are broken, other laws come into play:

The borrower is servant to the lender. Prov. 22:7

No man or nation wishes to be a servant or slave. When it is discovered that the interest loan is a trick and there is no way to repay the debt, both men and nations will turn on their lenders.

A loan must be accompanied with bribes to keep the rulers of the stronger nation friendly. Babylon was active in the internal affairs of her neighbors. Persia was always active in the internal affairs of Greece.

In spite of bribes, in time the "system" itself generates a "desperation level" that bribe money will not fix.

Chapter 4

TAXES - TO START MONEY MOVING

"Interest requires a heavy tax so that money will not be hoarded but circulated to pay interest." - Hoskins 4th Law of Interest.[3]

Taxes!   This was one of the most brilliant inventions of the classical age. This is where "share the wealth" taxes started. While there have always been taxes, the specific reason for these heavy taxes was to milk the rich and start money circulating again. Everyone paid them.* The rich in Athens groaned, but they paid. The rulers spent it as fast as they could get it. It worked. Commerce and trade broke out of stagnation - then blossomed. It required rigidly enforced collections to break loose the tightly held money. No holdouts were allowed since the holdouts plus interest could in time result in owning all the money again through use of The System.

This universal taxation, whose benefits were discovered long ago in Greece, is essential to the usury system. Through the years men have spoken against taxation. Everyone who has paid taxes has wanted to do away with them, but what happens when taxation is abolished? The usury-bankers end up with all the money, and none is left in circulation. The only thing that has kept the usury system operating through the ages is taxation. In spite of its beneficial effects, the biggest and most modern buildings in the blighted debt-ridden downtowns of the world are still banks and insurance companies. Both are active in usury in slightly different ways and have cornered the larger part of the wealth of the world.

People who talk against taxation haven't thought the matter through. The only time heavy taxation is not needed is when there is no usury system.

3. See Appendix I, "Hoskins' 7 Laws Of Interest".

* Note: Today, special taxes such as the "inheritance tax" are used to force owners to sell their businesses and land to corporations owned by the international usurers. A businessman may have bought his business for $50,000. He dies and it is valued at a million. The son is often forced to borrow heavily to pay the inheritance tax. When he cannot meet payments, he is foreclosed. This is the only way the usurers could ever hope to capture most family-held property passed down from generation to generation.

Rome's Debt Solution - Conquest!

The first war with Carthage gave Rome 3,200 talents in tribute and the second war returned 10,000 talents. This money was spent on her debts. In a short time Rome was hard up again and was forced to conquer Greece. The Greek wealth lasted Rome for a while and then, like Greece, Persia and Babylon before, Rome was forced to conquer and conquer and conquer. After Greece came Syria, and then Carthage again. By 14 A. D. she had conquered what would be modern-day northern and southern Italy, Sicily, Greece, the immense coastline of North Africa, Turkey, Algeria, Spain, Egypt and France.

By 98 A. D. Rome had added Morocco, England, and most of Scotland, and by 98-116 A. D. Arabia, Mesopotania and Armenia. It was becoming expensive to conquer and the returns were scant. As long as there were nations to conquer and gold to be won, Rome was a vigorous expanding empire. When the Roman legions were at last reduced to wandering over the hot barren sands of Arabia and the equally empty barren steps of Russia, Rome had reached the end of the line. There is never enough gold to satisfy the demands of usury.

Chapter 5

ROMAN GOLD SUBSTITUTE - WAR BORROWING

Men seldom go into debt freely. We have seen how The System demands that new money be borrowed into existence in order to pay 11 for 10 when only 10 exists. This will work for that class of citizen who is always in debt, but it will not do for that solid type of citizen who for business or religious reasons will not borrow or go into debt. This type of individual must be forced to borrow new money into existence for the good of society as a whole. This is most easily done in wartime. It then becomes a "patriotic" measure.

The ideal war is the kind that results in conquests with light casualties. If such wars are not available, one must make do with what one has. Spain was such a case. Rome waged a long continuing war with her which lasted for generations. Whenever money got scarce as interest payments took money out of circulation, the Spanish War would be taken off the back burner and heated up. This provided the excuse to levy new taxes, the payment of which required private Roman citizens to borrow new money into existence from their friendly bankers.

Problem Wars

A problem occurred in 54 B. C. when Crassus, the great Roman financier, took an army into Syria to see if he could expand Roman holdings. In that day a leader had to pay for the privilege of conquering a province. If he were victorious he had a lease on his conquests for five years. That is, after the expenses of using the Roman army were met. Everything above the military expenses that could be milked from the conquered land belonged to the general. After five years of such exploitation the province reverted to Rome. A man could get rich or he could become poor depending on how well his campaign went before the conquest, and how successful the tax collections were afterwards.

Crassus was a good general, but he ran into a nation he couldn't handle. He and his army were destroyed by the Parthians. This involved Rome in never-ending wars with this nation. It was a running wound which helped bleed Rome of her manhood, but offered a perpetual excuse to borrow continuously more and more money into existence.

Thus, the Romans' debts grew larger and larger while more and more Roman boys marched away forever.

Herman - 16 B. C. - 21 A. D.

The second of the problems was that of the Germans led by Herman. Herman was a German serving in the Roman army when he learned of the coming Roman invasion of his native German lands. Using the cloak of official business to travel extensively beyond the Rhine, he aroused the scattered German peoples who formed a confederation to fight the coming invasion.

When Roman preparations were complete, the Roman legions wound their way across the Rhine into the forests of Germany. It was in the Teutoberg Forest that Herman and his warriors waited. When the time was right, the attack was made. The battle lasted three days. When it was over, the Roman legions had been annihilated. The monument to Herman commemorating this great victory still stands at the site of this battle. The victory stiffened the Germans and from that time onward they pressed against the Empire whenever an opportunity arose.

The Roman Peace (25 B. C. - 175 A. D.)

Rome found herself at war in Spain, Syria, and Germany. This was too much even for Rome. The attempt to wind down the military adventures ushered in the period called the Roman Peace. This "Peace" was not completely free from war, but it was quieter than the years preceding it. It also turned out to be the villain in the destruction of the Roman Empire.

Peace or no peace the Roman armies still must be fed, housed, and armed. To do this taxes were farmed out to the various provinces. The provinces in turn farmed them out to the various cities. The cities farmed them out to the individual citizens, industries, and farms which surrounded them. This meant that a certain tax was due on a certain date based on the amount of money needed by the empire - and it must be paid. There was no way out of it.

The central government did not borrow money as a rule. This left the individual Roman citizen holding the bag. The average Roman had very little money, and so in order to pay these taxes, he was forced to borrow from private bankers. Borrowing 10 pieces of silver and having to repay 20 over a period of time became an impossibility and so the farmers threw their hands up and abandoned their farms to their creditors. They weren't making enough to pay the interest on their debts which they had incurred to pay taxes, and so they came to town and became part of the Roman mob. This was the origin of the Roman mob - debt-ridden and bankrupt Roman farmers. His farm was sold to a new debt-free immigrant for the remainder of the money owed on it.

Roman Welfare State

Welfare in a usury society is always designed to aid the welfare of The System, and only incidentally, the welfare of the individual. Rome was no exception. The bankrupt Roman farmer arriving in town found three possible avenues open to him:

1. He could join the Roman army - a relatively care-free life.
    There was freedom from responsibility, and certainly there
    was freedom from taxes. Of course, the soldier would be
    called on to build the Roman roads and fortifications and
    help with the maintenance of the walled cities. Too, there
    was always the never-ending training and actual fighting
    required periodically in the life of a soldier.

2. He could go as a colonist to the new lands in Africa, Spain,
    or France which were open to settlement. Unfortunately, the
    tax followed him to the new land and often this made the new
    land unprofitable to work even before the plow had been put
    into the ground.

3. He could stay in Rome and go on the welfare lists. This
    allowed him to eat, and also served the needs of the state.

As mentioned before, the overriding need of Rome in the
"peace phase" was to increase the money supply. New conquests
had stopped. There was no captured gold arriving to pay interest on debts. Most native Romans were deeply in debt and
couldn't borrow new money into existence. New debt-free immigrants had taken over the borrowing function from the native
Romans.

A bankrupt man is a debt-free man so the bankrupt Roman mob
was placed on the welfare lists - the dole. With this government
handout the recipients could buy goods on credit worth many times
the amount of the "dole". As long as merchants received
payments, both debtors and creditors were happy and the money
credit supply expanded - benefiting everyone.

Roman Taxes

The dole helped the mob to increase the money supply. This
was good, but the dole money had to come from somewhere, since
the central government did not borrow. It came from increased
taxes farmed out to "the provinces". This made the taxes on
surviving merchants and farmers heavier than before. At this
stage a number of things started happening.

First, it was so difficult to make money and pay taxes that

men quit their businesses and joined the mob in Rome. Consequently, laws were passed prohibiting men from leaving their occupa-
tions.*

Declining Birth Rate

Next, since money was so hard to come by and.expenses were
so high, there was a great reluctance among the people to have
children.**

By 65 A. D., the usury contract had swept the heartland of
Rome clear of Romans. Tombstones show that 90% of the population
bore non-Roman names or had names that had been "Romanized". Due
also to voluntary childlessness, of 400 families of senators
under Nero all trace is lost a generation later.[4]

There were more Romans in Gaul and North Africa than there
were in Italy. Lack of money caused Rome to resort to force to
collect tax levies. The imperial cities were assessed taxes and
the shortfall was made up by "Curiales" - officeholders in
charge. In former days this office was much sought after. After
the imperial tax quota was filled, whatever was left over could
be kept by these tax collectors. Now it was impossible to collect the needed tax quotas, much less hope for "surplus" taxes.
Because of usury there were 25 pieces of silver owed for each
piece of silver in existence. To make good the shortfall of
government taxes in these conditions was to seek ruin. If the
Curiales didn't have the required tax on due date, they had to
borrow the needed tax money into existence themselves. Men
refused to serve. Curiales had to be appointed.

A commentator on this period in a complete quandary over how
the 10 for 11 system works made the following comment: "Yet
there was still plenty of money about, and thanks to a highly

---

* This is the situation that exists in some of the communist countries today.

** The difficulty in making ends meet is the reason for the declining birth rate
in Europe, the United States, and the Soviet Union. This was the beginning of
the great population reduction of the Roman Empire. The size of cities declined
so drastically that the soldiers rebuilding the walls around Roman cities had to
build them only one-third to one-fourth the length that they had previously been.
The Roman people were being taxed so heavily they refused to have children. If
they had children, there would not be enough for everyone to eat. In Greece and
parts of Italy, people became so desperate that they exposed their female babies
to the weather to die.

4. Tenney Frank, An Economic History Of Rome, p. 206, New York 1962.

developed banking system loans were available at a rate of interest which rarely exceeded 6%." The writer obviously did not understand that at this time the Romans were so heavily in debt that it made absolutely no difference whether rates were 100% or 1%. The borrower would have equal difficulty in qualifying for a loan or having any chance whatsoever of repaying the loan if once obtained.

The rich bought up land to form estates. As early as 367 B. C. laws had to be passed limiting the acreage owned by the wealthy to 1,250 acres.[5] It had gotten so that there was none available for the small farmer. The "Licinian Law" was passed requiring interest paid to be deducted from capital.[6]

This was the same as doing away with interest. None of these reform laws lasted long. In 326 B. C. slavery and the death penalty for non-payment of debts was abolished - everyone was becoming a slave.

The remaining Roman and Greek farmers deserted the land en masse and moved to the cities. In 135 B. C. Tiberius Gracchus crossing the formerly rich and productive province of Etruria had the impression that the land was empty. In 124 B. C. he tried to distribute land in order to get the Roman Mob back to their farms. He was killed in a riot. In 121 B. C. his brother Gaius did the same and was assassinated. By 100 B. C. there were only 2,000 landed proprietors in all of Italy.[7]

Abolition Of Slavery

In the process of conquering the world, Rome brought in millions of slaves. Many were Greek. Many were slaves sold to the Romans by their masters in other lands in payment for goods and taxes. These slaves living throughout Rome were, because of their slavery, denied the opportunity to become consumers and borrow money like the rest of the Roman population. As the decline of native population continued, the authorities were forced to free these slaves so that they could in turn borrow new money into existence. Slavery can never exist over a long period in a usurious society. The slaves are always freed to borrow

---

5. Jean-Philippe Levy, The Economic Life Of The Ancient World, Chicago, 1964, p.54

6. Levy, p. 55.

7. Levy, p. 70.

money.

Eleven free men can borrow more money than a master with ten slaves. The System of Usury itself decrees that slaves be freed, so that they can do their part in borrowing money into existence. It was along about 200 A. D. that slavery started to disappear.[8]

I have never encountered a case in history where slaves were freed en masse for humanitarian reasons. First usury causes high prices (inflation), then heavy debts, a landless people, lower birth rates and declining population, and finally immigration of new peoples needed to borrow money into existence and pay taxes, or slaves are emancipated to achieve the same object.

Thus we have newly freed slaves in many cases receiving treatment and privileges which in former days would have been reserved to Roman citizens only. It is always so. A debt-free potential borrower is of far more value than a heavily indebted native citizen. The Roman financial community welcomed these freedmen with open arms and treated the debt-ridden native Roman with scorn. As an added source of revenue "Roman Citizenship" could be purchased for a reasonable sum. Nothing was denied them. Everything could be bought - if you had the money.

---

8. Rostovtzett, The Decline Of Rome 3rd Century, p. 24.

SECTION II
JUDAISM, ISLAM, & CHRISTIANITY

Chapter 6

SAMARITANS

To understand economics one must understand the religious
rules under which economics operates. Economics operates differently under different religious systems.

Samaria was the land settled by Israel after they came out
of Egypt. Israel later sinned greatly against God and was punished by being conquered by the Assyrians in 721 B. C. It is
estimated that in excess of 3.5 million Israelites were deported
into lands to the north on what is now the eastern border of
modern-day Turkey. From there they spread all over the world in
the 700 years before Jesus was born. Settlers were brought in to
live in the vacant cities. The Bible describes the advent of the
Samaritans in this manner:

...The King of Assyria brought men from Babylon....and placed them in the cities of Samaria instead of the Children of Israel...They...know not the manner of the God of the land... Then the King of Assyria commanded...carry thither one of the priests whom ye brought from thence...and let him teach the manner of the God of the land...Howbeit every nation made Gods of their own...unto this day...they fear not the Lord, neither do they after their statutes...which the Lord commanded the children of...Israel...as did their fathers so do they unto this day. II Kings 17:24-41

Here we have a racially alien people brought in by the Assyrians to occupy the lands vacated by Israel in Samaria, marrying the few Israelites still living there, practicing the worship of the Lord God Jehovah, but at the same time keeping their old gods, and not obeying the laws of God. This is the reason the prophet Jeremiah in 599 B. C. issued this warning:

I have seen the folly in the prophets of Samaria, they prophesied in Baal, and caused my people Israel to err. Jeremiah 23:13

Israel was ordered to have no dealings with Samaritans. Jesus instructed his 12 disciples as he sent them forth:

...Go not unto the way of the Gentiles, and into any city of the Samaritans enter ye not: But go rather to the lost sheep of the house of Israel. Matthew 10:5,6.

Ecclesiastical writers point out that according to Biblical definition - Samaritans did not LOVE the Lord. The word LOVE is defined by the Bible as follows:

And this is love, that we walk after his commandments.
2 John 6

Judah
Shortly after the Israelites of Samaria were taken into captivity and their lands and cities given to alien races brought in from Babylon, the Israelites of Judah were also conquered.

These Judean Israelites were taken as prisoners into the cities of Babylon. The vacant lands of Judah were occupied by alien nomadic races who were called Jews because they lived in Judea. They adopted the religion of the Israelites, with certain modifications as the Samaritans had done in Samaria. These "Samaritans" living in Judah called themselves "Jews".

Seventy years later Nehemiah returned with less than 50,000 Israelites to rebuild the wall of Jerusalem. This made Jerusalem a tiny island of Israelites living in a sea of Jews. In time they too were called "Jews" because they lived in Judea. The Bible tells us that "many of the people of the land became Jews; for the fear of the Jews fell upon them." Esther 8:17.

It was in dealing with these Judean Samaritans (not Israelites) who called themselves Jews that Jesus said;

Ye believe not, because ye are not of my sheep, as I said unto you. My sheep hear my voice, and I know them, and they follow me. John 10:26,27

With the advent of Jesus the Israelites living in Galilee and Jerusalem became Christians. This left a mass of Samaritan Judeans who called themselves "Jews". These were not "adam" people who could "blush rosy".

Jewish Beliefs

It is next to impossible to make a Christian convert of an educated Jew. All that is needed for a possible convert to revert to Judaism is for an educated rabbi to talk to him for 10 minutes.

Jewish rabbis are often highly educated people. They have gone to school perhaps twice as long as a Christian minister and are conversant with Biblical law - which they call the "Torah". Most can speak and read Hebrew.

The first thing that he can do when talking to a Jew who is considering converting to Samaritan Christianity is to open the Christian Bible written in the original Hebrew. He can then point to the word "man". Time after time he can point to the word "man". The "convert" reverts to Judaism.

To see what the rabbi saw - take "Strong's Exhaustive Concordance" and look up the word "man". Then, turn to the Hebrew section in the back of the concordance to locate the word for "man" which is "adam". You will find that the word "adam" (man) is used hundreds of times throughout the Bible. Under "man" locate the verse "In the beginning God created man", or "adam", as an example.

The word "adam" is not just another name like John or Bob. "Adam" is the Hebrew word meaning "to turn rosy", or to "blush red". A better translation of the above verse "In the beginning God created man" would be - "In the beginning God created 'he who blushes red'." The hundreds of uses of the word "adam" in the Bible refer each time to "he who blushes red". Very few Jews can "blush red". The rabbi merely shows his wavering charge that the Christian Bible was written for those who turn "rosy" or "blush red".

For the few Jews who "blush red" because of mixed marriages with those who can, the rabbi can point to the passage:

A bastard (mixed-breed) shall not enter into the congregation of the Lord; even to his tenth generation shall he not enter into the congregation of the Lord. Deu. 23:2

All modern day Jews, except the very latest Christian converts, are the result of mixed marriages. They are told that the Christianity of the Bible is the Christian's religion. He is shown what he believes to be conclusive proof, right out of the Christian Bible, and then he is told that Jews have their own holy books called the Talmud written by Jews for Jews.

Talmud

The "Jews" say that when Moses was on the mountain receiving the ten commandments written in stone, God spoke to him about the day-to-day problems of his people.[1] These "instructions" given by God to Moses mark the beginning of the "verbal traditions" handed down from generation to generation. They have been added to by countless rabbis through the centuries and now are contained in 66 large books. Since these verbal traditions deal

---

1. Pirke Aboth. 1.1

with immediate problems, the Jews state that they are more important and receive precedence over the "statutes, laws, and judgments" contained in the Christian Bible. The Jews know and quote
the "Torah" (the Law) but they obey the interpretations of the
Torah contained in the Talmud.

Some of the problems discussed by their ancient teachers are
of such antiquity that no one really knows what they are about.
The total content is immense and so varied that it is difficult
to find two Jews of different schools who agree on anything. For
this reason you find Jews split into many different sects, often
in active conflict with each other. At the same time they consider themselves a nation against the world. Their spiritual
homeland is still the Talmud regardless of the political subdivision they might be living in at any certain time.

The Rise Of Islam

The Islamic phenomenon occurred with unbelievable rapidity
and took the Christian West by complete surprise. One moment
there was no such thing as a Mohammedan - and the next, Islamic
armies turned the skylines black with their numbers and were
hammering on the gates of western cities.

The Prophet of Islam - Mohammed - arrived late on the
scene. Excluded from the Christian religion by being "non-
Israel" and "non-adam", and rejecting the Jewish religion as
being entirely too materialistic for the aesthetic Arab, he
blended his version of God, Moses, Jesus, the prophets, angels,
and paradise into the "Holy Koran". This most holy of all books
to Islamic peoples is open to all upon conversion. The seed fell

Note: While it is rare to convert a Jew to Christianity it is frequent that
Christians are converted to a form of Judaism. Often this is done without the
convert realizing it. It is done by the utilization of the law contained in
the Torah and transposed by Talmudic reasoning into something similar to the
following. "Jesus didn't really create the bread to feed the 5000. In that day
most of the people carried their food with them. The multitude was touched by
Jesus' teaching and shared their food. This was the real miracle - the sharing.
It was as great a miracle as if he had actually created bread." Or "Jonah wasn't
really swallowed by a whale. He was held up by dolphins and brought to land. It
was doubtless done by the will of God and is no less a miracle ." This type of
logic is called the Judeo/Christian Ethic. The Christian Bible is not the final
authority and there are no absolutes in this logic. All agree that the Bible
says "Owe no man anything but to love one another" - but the Judeo/Christian
convert learns to add "Unless you can advance God's cause by going into debt."
Or "Thou shalt not lie" - "unless you do great harm by telling the truth". Or
"Thou shalt not commit adultery" - "unless you run into a situation where there
are consenting adults and no one can be hurt." In this way the Christian law of
right vs. wrong is made of no effect. A "Judeo/Christian" convert has been made.

on fertile ground.

Mohammed died in 632 A. D. Within five years his followers swarmed from the desert and conquered Syria, and in seven years, Egypt. In 70 they were in Spain, and in 100 years they were contending for the rule of the West in the heart of France. The chivalry of Christian Europe turned them back at Tours, by the slimmest margin.

Not until 721 A. D. did Islam start its prohibitions against interest with the writings and practices of Hazrat Imam Abu Haneefa.[2] At that time they started to practice the prohibitions contained in the Holy Qur'ran - the same ones that the Christian religion had long maintained.

From that early time until the later conquest of Arab lands by Christian powers their history of interest is similar to that of the Christian West. They have alternated between periods of orthodoxy and periods of apostasy.

Most Arabs and their converts took as natural the prohibitions against interest, that it was Allah's will that they march against the Christians[3], and that it was their right to have ownership of Jerusalem. Their Qur'ran had ordered the first two and promised them the third.

Christian Beliefs

All religions have "beliefs", and "laws" to go by. Judaism has its beliefs, Islam has its own, and Christianity is no different.

Christians believe that Jesus is God. He said "My father and I are one". He was here before the earth was made. He made the earth. When He was born into the world, He returned to the same world He created in the beginning. The Bible has no "new" and "old". Jesus obeyed the "old" while adding the "new". It is all part of a continuing story.

2. Dr. Nejatullah Siddiqui, Banking Without Interest, page ix, Islamic Publications Ltd., Lahore, Pakistan 1976.

3. The Koran exhorts Muslims to "kill off" Jews, Christians, and other non-Muslims. In the Book of Repentance alone there are 16 such directives: 5, 9, 12, 14, 20, 24, 29, 36, 41, 44, 73, 81, 86, 88, 111, & 123.

The Christian Bible is particularly insistent on one subject
- the Law - the thing that makes it different from other
religions. This Law is said to be placed here for our protection. If we follow it, we are safe. If we disobey, we suffer.
The following gives an indication of the extreme importance
placed on this one subject by the Christian Bible:

Keep my commandments and do them. Lev. 25:18

Remember all the commandments of the Lord. Num. 15:39

Keep my commandments always... Deu. 5:29

Keep all my commandments to walk in them and my statutes...
1 Ki. 6:12

Keep my commandments and live... Prov. 4:4

We know him if we keep his commandments. 1 John 2:3

If ye love me, keep my commandments. John 14:15

This is the love of God that we keep his commandments.
1 John 5:3

Till heaven and earth pass, one jot or one tittle shall in
no wise pass from the law, till all be fulfilled. Math.
5:18.

Whosoever therefore shall break one of these least commandments, and shall teach men so, he shall be called the least
in the kingdom of heaven. Math. 5:19.

As we can see, not a thing has changed between the Old and
New Testaments in regard to obeying God's Law. It is with reason
that God said "I am the Lord, I change not...," and "Am I a man
that I should repent (of what he had said)?"
To ensure that his people would have every opportunity to
live safely and be able to protect themselves, God fixed it so
that HIS people would always know the correct thing to do:

I will put my law in...their hearts; and will be their God, and they shall be my people. Jer. 31:33

For this reason it is assumed that all "Christians" know the Law, which is why to this very day the Christian government authorities maintain that "Ignorance of the law is no excuse".

Those who freely give their obedience to God and willingly do all in their power to obey his Law receive "Grace". This is not a new thing that came with Jesus. David, the beloved of God was a murderer and an adulterer. He "repented" and returned to the obedience and safety of God's Law, and in return he received the grace of forgiveness. If there is no "repentance", there is no "grace".

It would seem that the above is simple and clear enough, but not to those who are looking for an excuse to break the Law.

The Bible says "..sin is the transgression of the Law." 1 John 3:4. "For all have sinned and come short of the glory of God." Rom. 3:23. If we admit that we are sinners, we also admit that we are under God's Law. To avoid the penalty that goes with sin, each Christian must seek God's "grace" of forgiveness.

This part is fine, but we are also expected to do as David did and "repent". This means we must stop doing whatever it is that we are doing wrong and start obeying God's Law. Some people don't like this.

If one wishes to continue breaking God's Law and does not wish to repent, he must brazenly flout the Law, deny its existence, or deny that he is covered by it. The Samaritan teaching helps with its "grace" argument. It is done so that offenders can keep on "doing their thing".

Several of their favorite quotes are: "For ye are not under the law, but under grace," Rom. 6:15; and "Wherefore, my brethren, ye also are become dead to the law by the body of Christ." Rom. 7:4.

The two traditional counter-arguments to this "Grace and everything goes" business is to quote the same Paul who made the above statements in the first place: "Do we then make void the law through faith? God forbid: yea, we establish the law." Rom. 3:31. Or, the prophet Jeremiah who was endorsed by Jesus:

**Will ye steal, murder, and commit adultery, and swear false-
ly....and say, We are delivered to do all these abominations? Jer. 7:9,10.**

This is precisely what they want to do. They want to
"steal, murder, and commit adultery" and say that they can do it
all through "grace". This is especially true of the modern
Judeo/Christian crowd. Most Christians do not bother to answer
them. The rule has been simply to obey the words and commandments of God and Jesus, along with Moses and the prophets and
those disciples who were personally taught by Him. The writings
of all others not endorsed by Jesus (such as Paul himself) are
accepted as long as their teachings are in agreement with the
teachings of Jesus and those personally endorsed by Him.

To Christians everywhere God's Word contained in the Christian Bible is recognized as the true word of God. Through the
ages it alone has been the arbiter of right and wrong. Its
teachings are considered infallible.

Chapter 7

THE CRUSADES

The Arabs took Jerusalem. The more zealous of them abused
Christian pilgrims, robbing, killing, and denying them access to
the Holy Tomb. Their cry from the Holy Land had been heard.
Pope Urban II, himself a Frenchman, crossed the mountains from
Italy to France. There in the heartland of Christendom he spoke
these words to the faithful who flocked to hear him.

"An accursed race,...estranged from God, has invaded
the lands of the Christians in the East...and has depopu-
lated them by fire and steel and ravage. These invaders are
Turks and Arabs...they have torn down the churches of God
everywhere, or used them for their own rites...The invaders
befoul the altars with the filth of their bodies...

"Even now the Turks are torturing Christians...What
shall I say of the ravishing of the women? To speak of this
is worse than to be silent. You in France, have heard the

murmur of agony on the borders of Spain...

"On whom will fall the task of vengeance unless upon you, who have won glory in arms? Come forward to the defense of Christ...enter upon the journey - whosoever shall offer himself to go upon this journey, and shall make his vow to go, shall wear the sign of the cross on his head or breast...

"Take up your arms, valiant sons, and go. Better fall in battle than live to see the sorrow of your people and the desecration of your holy places.

"...Lo I see before you, leading you to His war, the standard bearer who is invisible - Christ."

There was silence for a moment; than a shout "Dieu le veut!" (God wills it!) The shouts became a roar. Steel whispered as hundreds of swords slipped from their sheaths. The Crusades had begun![4]

Templar, Hospitallar, Teutonic Knights

The Christian cross of the Crusaders carried all before it and a Christian kingdom was established in the Holy Land. The ensuing conflicts with the irate Moslems surrounding the Holy Land gave birth to three hard core groups of fighters. These tough soldiers stood out from the rest of the crusaders by being hardier, tougher, more devout than anyone else. They were the Knights Templar, Knights Hospitallars, and the Order of Teutonic Knights.

The best known was the Order of Templars founded in Jerusalem in 1118 by two French knights. This order quickly gained recruits and fame. In fact, it gathered an immense following throughout Europe. This order in the beginning was a military police for the Holy Land, but quickly took its place in the battle line and as guards on the frontiers. To be a knight of

---

4. Harold Lamb, The Crusades, Doran & Co., Inc., Garden City, N. Y., 1930, p. 39.

Note: "Judeo/Christians", a cult unknown 30 years ago, have brought into question who is entitled to rule the Holy Land. This is one question our Crusader ancestors were quick to settle. The promise to Abraham in Gen. 17:8 states: "I will give unto thee, and to thy seed after thee...all the land of Canaan, for an everlasting possession." The question of knowing who the children of Israel are after a lapse of 1700 years when all genealogical records had long since been destroyed was done by checking the promises and proofs contained in the Bible. Abraham had been promised that his descendants would be as many as the

the Templars you had to be of noble blood. You also had to give up all worldly possessions when you enlisted and become a pauper. The order was strict. Members were bound by vows of implicit obedience to their masters, ordered to keep silent at meals, and required to sleep in their clothes to be instantly ready for combat. It was a celibate organization. Temptations of the world had little hold on these warrior-priests. Their amusement was Bible study, training in arms and tactics, and lion hunting. This last pastime depleted the lion population of the Holy Land.

If a hot-headed brother struck a blow against another brother, he was required to fast for 40 days. An argument was punished by having the offending parties eat together on the ground for a month. Anyone actually raising a weapon against a fellow Templar or deserting in battle was publicly humiliated by being driven from the order. These men were reasonably certain that they would die with their swords in their hands and be buried in the Holy Land. This did not deter the stream of volunteers. Hundreds appeared on the roads of Jerusalem - the white mantles with the red cross of the Templars, the black mantles with the white cross of the Hospitallars. They were the flower of the Christian armies.

Fantastically brave, a Templar was never caught with his back to the enemy. Odds of five to one against them on the battlefield were usual and their successes phenomenal. In 1125 at the Battle of Hazarth, King Baldwin lost 24 knights while the Turks lost 2,000. Again in 1191 at Joffa two crusaders were killed along with 700 Turks.[5]

When on rare occasions knights of the order fell into the hands of their enemies, they were immediately slaughtered without mercy. The Mohammedan leader, Saladan, who with overwhelming numbers achieved a victory over the Crusaders, went through the ranks of the captives man by man to search out every Templar and

"stars in the sky". That could include the Saracens and certainly the Christians, but not the Jews who have always been few in number. Israel was promised that they would be "many nations". The Christians were many nations. The Saracens were eliminated since they recognized no nation but "Islam". The Jews had no nation at all at the time of the crusades - much less "many". God said that Israel would "bear His name". The Christians did. The Saracens and Jews did not. God said that "No bastard (mixedbreed) shall enter the congregation of God". (Both Mohammedans and Jews were mixed-breeds). True Westerners were and are the only pure-bred race in the world. The list of "proofs" is endless. (See footnote p. 116.)

5. Encyclopedia Britannica, 14th Ed., Tactics, p. 44.

Hospitallar knight. He could have ransomed these men for large amounts, but he didn't. He had them cut to pieces in front of his army - every last one of them. In the eyes of the infidel their blood was worth more than their money.

Other Christians who because of age or infirmity couldn't go on the Crusades did what they could for The Cause. Many gave gold outright, or left their property and their money in their wills to the Templar organization to outfit other fighters and to supply them with arms and munitions. The Templar and Hospitallar organizations became immensely rich, although its individual members had nothing.

The Arabs despised the sign of the cross. To them the cross meant "Crusader." Today many Christians wear the cross as a sign that they are brothers in spirit to the crusaders of old. The red cross signified Templars*, who came mainly from France, but who had chapters in every Christian nation. The white cross signified the Hospitallars, who came mostly from Norman stock in southern Italy** and from the northern countries. The black cross signified the Teutonic knights from Germany.

Fratricidal Warfare In The Holy Land

The Templars and Hospitallars became the champions of the Christian West - the human wall that held back the fanatical hordes of Islam from the sacred tomb of Jesus. They also became rivals. This rivalry spurred by competition and jealousy caused them to commit the tragic sin of fighting each other. This violated the scripture about shedding Christian blood:

Thou shalt not avenge, nor bear any grudge against the children of thy people. Leviticus 19:18

Support cooled from the devout. Through the years Christian historians have pointed to this tragic event - Christians shedding Christian blood - as being the basic cause for the loss of the Holy Land.

To compound their error, in their strivings with each other,

---

* The modern day masonic Templars have no connection with the Crusader Order of the same name.

** The Normans in Southern Italy were a branch of the same Normans who invaded England in 1066. These people were descended from Norsemen who had settled in France a few generations earlier.

both organizations made allies of neighboring Saracens in order to gain advantage over their Christian brothers. This was a complete turn-about. In earlier Crusades the heathen inhabitants of Jerusalem and other cities and towns in Palestine were killed or driven away in obedience to the Biblical command:

> Thou shalt consume all the people which the Lord thy God shall deliver thee; thine eye shall have no pity upon them: neither shalt thou serve their gods; for that will be a snare unto thee. Deuteronomy 7:16

> He that sacrificeth unto any god, save the Lord only, he shall be utterly destroyed. Exodus 22:20

> ...Ye shall drive out all the inhabitants of the land from before you...And ye shall dispossess the inhabitants of the land, and dwell therein: for I have given you the land to possess it...But if ye will not drive out the inhabitants of the land from before you; then it shall come to pass, that those which ye let remain of them shall be pricks in your eyes, and thorns in your sides, and shall vex you in the land wherein ye dwell...It shall come to pass, that I shall do unto you, as I thought to do unto them. Numbers 33:56

> ...Ye shall make no league with the inhabitants of this land; ye shall throw down their altars." Judges 2:2

These very strict commandments were given to Israel so that they would not mix with strangers and "learn their ways". They were constantly reiterated by these warrior priests and were the reason the Crusaders were so unyielding and so firm in their dealings with the former Islamic inhabitants of the Holy Land. The first Crusader arrivals, however, refused to share their large estates conquered from the enemy with later arrivals.

> "...Ye shall divide the land by lot for an inheritance...the more...the more inheritance...the fewer...the less." Numbers 33:54

This refusal to share the land caused most of the later

arrivals to return home once the campaigning was done, causing a shortage of both workers and warriors. This need for workers for their new estates caused the crusaders who remained to become tolerant of neighboring Muslims. These "strangers" became allies of one side or the other in the struggle between Templars and Hospitallars. The Muslims moved back into Christian·Palestine, and became "thorns" by encouraging the fratricidal Christian warfare. This effectively neutralized Christian strength at a time of growing Islamic power. It also turned away many Christian recruits who became disgusted with this further evidence of disobedience to God's law in dealing with "zûwr-strangers".

In the course of combat between the competing Christian forces, prisoners were taken. Saracen "strangers" (allies of one side or the other) took their share of Christian prisoners and ruled over them as their masters, to sell, kill, or ransom as they saw fit. This caused a tremendous revulsion among those who knew the prohibiting law:

Thou mayest not set a stranger (Heb: "zûwr")* over thee, which is not thy brother. Deuteronomy 17:15

The crowning blow to the Christian cause came from its champion, Richard the Lion-Hearted. Richard had great admiration for his opponent - Saladan. In an attempt to negotiate a peace which the fragmented Christian effort could not win by war, he offered his sister's hand in marriage to the infidel ruler's brother with the recommendation that the two rule Palestine together. This was stupid in the extreme. It alienated what was left of the Christian support from the West and added yet another Law violation to the long list already committed:

Ye shall not give your daughters unto their sons, nor take their daughters unto your sons, or for yourselves. Nehemiah 13:25

---

* (Heb.) "zûwr" - stranger, a racial alien vs. "gêr" - stranger, a racial kinsman living in a different political jurisdiction. i.e. Frenchman, Germans, and English crusaders were (Heb.) "gêr" strangers. The Saracens were "zûwr" strangers.

A daughter may:

> ...marry to whom they think best; only to the family of...
> their father shall they marry." Numbers 36:6

> ...Separate yourselves from the people of the land, and
> from the strange (zûwr) wives. Ezra 10:11

This offer of Richard humiliated the entire Christian West.
The thing the Christian people in the Holy Land obeyed strictly
were the laws prohibiting racial interbreeding.*

There is a Saracen story which has survived the years that
illustrates this point graphically. The Arab writer telling the
story complained, "They (the Christians) are an accursed race,
and they will never intermarry with another..."[6]

In his story it seems that an Arab-raiding party attacked a
Christian convoy killing all its defenders. Counted in the loot
was a beautiful Christian girl. She was well treated and given
to the ruler of a Saracen city. He had one son by her and he
then died leaving this young son as ruler and his mother as the
actual power behind the throne. In this position the former
captive girl had more wealth and power than she ever dared dream
of.

She then did something which is natural and normal by Christian standards, but which completely bewildered the Saracen
writer who judged by Islamic standards. She deserted both the
city she ruled and her son and made her way back to a small
Christian village in the Holy Land where she met and married a
poor Christian shoemaker. This made no sense at all to the story
teller. How could anyone wish to trade a position as the ruler
of a city to become wife to a humble shoemaker?

The young Christian woman was obeying the laws of her religion as all well-instructed Christians would do in the same
situation.

---

* To finance his army Richard had borrowed heavily from the Jews ("The Borrower
is servant to the lender.") and in the manner of servants had adopted many of
the beliefs of his masters.

6. Harold Lamb, The Crusades, p. 348, Doubleday, Doran & Co., Inc., Garden City,
New York, 1930).

> We have trespassed against our God, and have taken strange (zûwr) wives of the people of the land...make a covenant (an agreement) with our God to put away all the wives, and such as are born of them. Ezra 10:2-10

Even Abraham, the father of our entire Israel race, sinned in this respect. He took a Midianite wife who bore him a son "Midian." Obeying God, Abraham gave gifts to all his mixed-breed children and their alien mothers and sent them away. (Genesis 25:1-6) The Arab story teller could not understand that if Abraham, the father of all Israel had to do this painful thing, his Christian descendants could do no less, if the race chosen by God for Himself was to survive.

Phinehas' Priesthood

This Christian taboo against racial-interbreeding is always enforced by "public opinion," but it is also enforced by something else a good deal more lethal - religious sanctions. If Saladan had been foolish enough to have allowed his brother to have taken Richard's sister as his wife, he would have fallen under the shadow of the Christian's "Covenant of Phinehas," the agreement which is always in effect where devout believers reside.

> ...and the people began to commit whoredom with the daughters of Moab...one of the children of Israel came and brought...a Midianitish woman...when Phinehas...saw it, he rose up from among the congregation and took a javelin in his hand and he went after the man of Israel into the tent, and thrust both of them through...and the Lord spake... saying, Phinehas, the son of Aaron the priest, hath turned my wrath away from the children of Israel...that I consumed not the children of Israel...Behold, I give unto him my covenant of peace...and his seed after him, even the covenant of an everlasting priesthood; because he was zealous for his God, and made atonement for the children of Israel. Numbers 25:1-13

A Christian breeding with a "stranger - Heb: zûwr (racial alien)" would have exposed Saladan's brother and his bride to the very real probability of being executed* by any one of the many Christians with whom he came in contact. Or death could have come from one of his own subjects, since Mohammedan and Jewish Law also forbid intermarriage.**

This foolish offer of Richard's served notice that he was fighting for his own glory and knew or cared little for God's Law which he was sworn to uphold. As a consequence, Christian reinforcements virtually ceased and monetary aid dried up. When Richard at last deserted the cause which he helped lose and departed for England, he was captured by another Christian prince and held for ransom as if he were no more than an infidel himself. In spite of the stories of Robin Hood robbing the rich to pay his ransom, the people of England took a long time raising the money to buy his freedom.

In the days following, the Saracens became more and more powerful and the followers of the Cross weaker. In only a few short centuries from the date of the founding of the crusaders' Christian kingdom in Palestine, the banner with Christ's cross was pushed into the sea by the rising crescent of Islam.

It wasn't until 1917 that Allenby marched into Jerusalem and placed Palestine under the British flag with its three Christian crosses. He did in a few months what centuries of effort were unable to do earlier. Once more ignorant Christians neglected to clear the land of its heathen population and even allowed others to immigrate. Once again;

> **Those which ye let remain of them shall be pricks in your eyes, and thorns in your sides, and shall vex you in the land wherein ye dwell... Numbers 33:55**

In 1948, the Christian West gave the land away again. The object of the crusades that had cost millions of Christian lives was casually given away without a thought!

---

* The mark of Phinehas is said to be **P, +P, or ꟼ** .

** Islamic and Jewish law both forbid "interfaith" marriages. The Jewish Talmud book of Eben Haezar (44,8) states that marriage between Christians and Jews are null. In either of these religions if the partner becomes "converted" the marriage is allowed. In spite of these prohibitions U.S. News & World Report of Apr. 4, 1983 reports that at least 40% of Jews marry outside of their faith and that studies show that 7 out of 10 of the children of mixed marriages are raised as Jews. This would be expected since the Christian religion is the only religion that forbids both interfaith and inter-racial marriage and the mixed-breed offspring are not accepted "even to his tenth generation". Deu. 23:2.

Chapter 8

THE SAMARITAN CHURCH SPREADS TO ITALY

The Normans completed their conquest of southern Italy in 1060. They then passed over into Sicily and commenced a crusade against the Saracens there. These Saracens were a mixed breed race - dark skin, dark-eyed, and coarse-featured. The war dragged on until 1090. The Saracens came to the Christians with the proposition that if they would be allowed to live in peace, they would submit. Immediately a great controversy arose among the Christian warriors. Peace that allowed both Saracens and Christians to occupy the same land was forbidden by God.

Thou shalt make no covenant with them...They shall not dwell in thy land, lest they make thee sin against me. Ex. 23: 32, 33.

But of the cities of those people, which the Lord thy God doth give thee for an inheritance, thou shalt save alive nothing that breatheth: but thou shalt utterly destroy them...that they teach you not to...sin against the Lord your God. Deuteronomy 20:16-18

Be ye not unequally yoked together with unbelievers...what part hath he that believeth with an infidel? ...Come out from among them and be ye separate. 2 Corinthians 6:14-17

But the Norman leaders were war-weary. They made peace with the Saracens and let them remain in peace. Later the Normans recruited them into their army and moved back to mainland Italy to fight other Christians. The Saracen soldiers from Sicily were awarded lands in southern Italy as spoil and remained there. In fear of the Catholic Church they professed Christianity and became Samaritan-Christians. "The Word", however, went through the "Saracen filter" and became "Samaritan". "...into any city of the Samaritans enter ye not." This is how the "Christ professing" Samaritan Church of the Saracens was planted in Italy.*

Today, Italy's Samaritans are prominent not only in politics and business, but in the hierarchy of the Roman Catholic Church itself as well as the mafia. Most southern Italians and Sicilians cannot "blush red" and they act differently from the Italians who can. Many still speak an Italian dialect with a Saracen accent. The "other Normans" who invaded Christian Britain and lived among their own kind have flourished, while their brother Normans who invaded southern Italy and Sicily learned the ways of the inhabitants, and as a consequence have been bred out of existence.

The southern Italians and Sicilians absorbed a large number of Jews from Spain and elsewhere. The Jewish population of Sicily alone was reckoned at almost 10% in the early 1400's. Because of this it is almost impossible to tell the difference between the two peoples by observation since they have become closely related by blood. On December 31, 1492 the Jews were deported. Many left for Constantinople and the Pale (see p. 86). Many others had concealed their identity earlier and remained as secret Jews (see Maranos p. 55).

---

* During the period 1130-1138 Sicily was backed by the papacy against other Christian states. The pope in Rome was Anacletus II. He was the son of a rich converted Roman Jewish banker. His sister was married to Philip II of Sicily. Both the spiritual advisor of the king of Sicily and his wife were Jews. This has been given as the reason for his erratic and un-Christian-like actions.

SECTION III

TALLIES - TEMPLAR WEALTH

Chapter 9

TALLIES & T-BILLS

When the crusaders first left their homelands in Europe for the crusade to the Holy Land, they took with them almost the entire circulating supply of gold and silver coins. This left western nations, England in particular, with no money.

In the year 1100 A.D. Henry I, 4th son of William the Conqueror, ascended the throne of England. Finding the treasury empty and his needs great, he cast about for a source of income. Having wise advisors he soon hit on a plan. The plan, with a few refinements, remained in effect for the next 726 years - and can be reinstated tomorrow. He issued "tallies".

A tally was a stick about nine inches or so long with each of the four sides about 1/2 inch wide. On two of the sides, the value of the "tally" was carved into the wood. On the other two sides, the amount was printed in ink.

The tally was then split in half lengthwise. One half remained in the treasury and the other half was given to soldiers

for their pay, to farmers for wheat, to armorers for armor, and
to laborers for their labor.

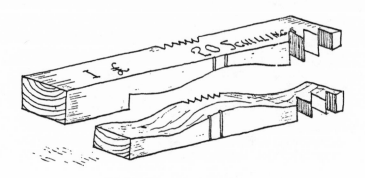

TALLY STICK

At tax time, taxpayers were required to bring in one half of
a tally to pay their taxes. Woe unto the man who did not have
the required number of tally sticks. As a consequence, these
intrinsically worthless sticks of wood were in great demand.
Gold and silver coins were fine if you traveled abroad for a
crusade or something, but at home if you did not have your tax-
tally at tax time - you were done.

Upon receipt of a tally the treasurer would immediately
match the presented half with the half stored in the treasury.
THEY HAD TO TALLY - which is what gave it the name. Counterfeiters lost their heads! Actually, it was practically impossible to
counterfeit a tally. The wood grain had to match - the notches
had to match - and the ink inscriptions had to match. This could
only come about if both pieces came from the same split tally
stick.

There you have it! An inexhaustible source of revenue for
the government. The means were available to make tallies as long
as there were trees. There was a demand as long as the government required the tallies for taxes. The system flourished as
long as tax-evaders and counterfeiters were punished and they
always were. For 726 years the system flourished.

Interest In England

Government "tally" money and "usury" money cannot exist side by side. Tally-money makes usury-money look bad because it stays constant, while usury-money expands and contracts. The advent of usury-money spelled the death of the tally.

The process started in 1694 when the Bank of England was chartered. This new type of interest-bank was permitted because of a promise made by the Pretender to his financial backers before he became King, and before he had access to the privilege of issuing the potentially inexhaustible supply of wooden money. When the Pretender became King, he kept his promise to his usurer bankers. The days of tally-money were numbered.

At that time there were about 14 million pounds in tally-money in circulation. In 1697 when the capital of the Bank of England was increased, 160,000 pounds of this new money was paid for with tally-sticks. The irritation of having usury-money and tally-money circulating at the same time ended when Parliament abolished the use of tallies for taxes in 1783.

Circulation of tallies continued in the back country of England until 1826. In 1834 the treasury tallies were burned by allies of the Bank of England. The furnaces which heated the House of Lords were used. The fire blazed up and burned down both houses of Parliament.

Tallies were thought to be extinct until a casual discovery in the Chapel of the Pyx in 1909 uncovered 1,300 more Exchequer Tallies. You can now see them in British museums.*

The T-Bill

The government has the right to make money. It can do so whenever it chooses. In the United States the government has authorized its Treasury to create Treasury Bills. These bills are created out of thin air, but they are no less real than the wooden tallies of our ancestors.

The Trillion Dollar Question

The government doesn't need to borrow money from the banks of the Federal Reserve and have a debt of over a trillion dol-

---

* The use of tallies was universal in western Europe. Research your older encyclopedias for more complete information.

lars. It can make money instead. All it has to do is MAKE IT -
T-Bill tallies in denominations of $1, $5, $10, $20, $50, $100,
and $1000. Then it can spend them for needed government ser-
vices, and tax them out of circulation again. Our ancestors did
it for almost three-fourths of a thousand years.

The reason it isn't done is that the trillion dollar debt
pays interest. Tallies don't. If the debt were paid off with T-
Bill-Tallies, someone would be deprived of over 100 billion
dollars a year in interest! Where would bankers' profits and the
politicians' campaign funds come from if this were stopped?

Everyone meets congressmen who pretend not to know what to
do about the trillion dollar debt and the 100 billion dollar
interest. Suggest to them that they take a hatchet, walk in the
woods, and find a tree...

T-Bills are modern-day tallies. They are created money.
They are not usury any more than a wooden tally was usury.

First Entry Of Jews Into England
The tally sticks were a wonderful invention. They were
freely accepted - in England. The King of England, however, had
to have gold or silver to do business in France. A Frenchman or
Italian wasn't thinking about taking an English "wooden tally"
in exchange for his goods. They required "hard money," the very
thing that had left the country to pay for the crusades. The
frugal Englishman who owned precious coins kept them.

In an attempt to solve this problem King William (Rufus) in
1087 opened the doors of England to the Jews under the condition
that they lend at "interest," a thing forbidden to native Christians, and that further, the King get half the profit. Every
effort was to be made to obtain the needed gold and silver in
payment for loans instead of wooden tallies.

1096 A.D. - First Crusade
The Jews became the King's valued unofficial tax collectors.
As fast as their usury brought a debtor into bankruptcy, the King
got his share.

Other conditions found their way into the relationship between the King and the Jews. Whenever a Jew was converted or
died, his estate escheated to the King. The Jews could only live

in the town which contained an ARCHA[1], an office in which every transaction with the Christians was recorded by government agents to make sure the King got his cut. In practice this worked the same way as it had in every other country. Ten pounds lent at 20% would require repayment of 20 pounds in a little more than four years.

10	pounds borrowed				
12	owed end of 1st year at 20%.				
14.4	"	"	" 2nd	"	
17.28	"	"	" 3rd	"	
20.74	"	"	" 4th	"	

If the loan were due in "tallies" there was some slight chance that it would be paid. If it were due in gold or silver, there was virtually no chance that the loan would be paid since almost all gold and silver had vanished from England. The debtor lost all. The King chuckled with glee as he got half. The debtor's choice was then to rot in debtors' prison or put himself into indentured slavery for seven years to work off his debt. The Jews were estimated to have owned one-fourth of England, a never-ending source of wealth to the King who made money on every transaction or whenever a Jew was "converted" or died, in which case his entire estate went to the crown.

In England the main irritant with the Jew was usury, the thing that caused problems from the first. It was the system he practiced. The people learned to hate the Jew because the Jew meant slavery - economic slavery.

The feeling against Jews had risen so high that in 1218 Stephen Langton, Archbishop of Canterbury, required them to wear an oblong white badge so that Englishmen would know who they were and what they did.

In 1269 they were prohibited from hiring Christian helpers while working as artisans, merchants, or farmers since the Law states:

Thou mayest not set a stranger (zûwr) over thee, which is not thy brother. Deu. 17:15

---

1. The Jewish Encyclopedia, England, p. 165.

The Church added its own prohibitions forbidding Christians to work for Jews, and with promptings from the Pope in Rome, the Jews were also prohibited from taking interest. If they could not take interest, their usefulness to the King was destroyed.

Jews Expelled

On July 18, 1290, the Jews were deported from England; 16,000 left. This handful was all there were. This deportation was forced on the king by a combination of religious authorities, and nobles, with the wholehearted support of English freemen. Since the King was in debt to the Jews and was their "servant" - "The borrower is servant to the lender" - an agreement was worked out so that they were allowed to carry away portable property such as British money and silver and gold art objects that they had accumulated. In exchange, the King received houses, lands, and castles obtained by their usury contracts. All these escheated to the king. Once more England was stripped of her floating supply of gold and silver.

Chapter 10

TEMPLAR WEALTH

As mentioned before, many devout Christians left their estates to the Templars in their wills. In every country in the West, from Denmark to Ireland, from Spain to France, local Templar organizations over the years accumulated wealth. Their skill at arms made them the natural traders of the day and their honesty made them trusted bankers.

A merchant in England might ask the Templars to transfer a certain amount in gold to Paris to cover a business deal. A Templar courier would take a "gold deposit receipt" to the Paris Temple. This piece of paper allowed the merchant's Paris business contact to collect the agreed upon amount of gold. Sometimes he did collect - sometimes he only collected the paper "gold deposit receipt" - which was as good as gold. He could use this paper receipt as paper money if he chose. Merchants anywhere would accept it. Any settling up by actual transfer of gold between the London and Paris Templar Temples could be done at a later date. Interest-free loans were made to kings and merchants, and trade was largely in their hands. The Templars were the wealthiest organization in existence in every country. This wealth was the reason for the Templars' downfall.

Templars Destroyed

The people of France forced their King to expel the Jews in 1306, just 16 years after they had been expelled from England. As in England, the French King was in debt to the Jews and was their "servant". Consequently, the same sort of agreement was worked out as in England earlier. They were allowed to take almost the entire floating supply of coins with them in exchange for their extensive property holdings.

This made the King a gigantic property holder but left France with little money with which to honor foreign commitments. What was left of the remaining supply of gold and silver money was in the hands of the Templars.

To get the Templars' gold, the Templars in 1307 were charged with heresy by Pope Clement V, a French Pope. Templar leaders were seized and imprisoned. Their property was confiscated. The cash went into the empty coffers of King Philip of France. Their lands were seized by the Catholic Church. In every Christian country the word went out to seize Templar wealth.

It was in this way - without being convicted or even heard - the noblest of the Christian orders was extinguished. Noble knights bearing scars of a score of battles with the infidel in the Holy Land begged bread or hid in the forest. Those who gave to these unfortunate men were excommunicated. The Grand Master, Jacques de Moley, was burned at the stake.

In recent years there have come certain detractors who accuse this organization of taking "interest". One of the best replies to this charge is found in Thomas Parker's book "Knight Templar In England", p. 71:

". . . had there been any grounds at all for a belief that the Templars engaged in usurious activities, such a charge would surely have been included in the indictment drawn up against them at the time of their arrest and trial."

The lesson to be gained from this tragic occurrence is that to survive, it is not enough to have a noble cause and to be pure and righteous. If you are wealthy while the government is poor, the government will find a way to take your wealth. In the process of seizing your wealth they may also liquidate you to prevent future claims.

The problems associated with the violation of our Common Law descend to the present day. The priestly tribe of Levi was to receive no land but was to live on the tithe from the other tribes of Israel. Even though their motives were good, the wealth accumulated by the Knights Templar priesthood was in violation of this rule and aroused the jealousy of powerful enemies. The accumulation of wealth by this priestly organization caused their destruction.

The great wealth in land and gold accumulated by the Roman Catholic Church through the centuries has constantly brought it also into conflict with national governments, and has caused its destruction in many lands.

In England, the Queen is head of the Anglican Church. Much of her wealth was confiscated from the Catholic Church. This has been a never ending source of irritation to her subjects. Her opponents maintain that if she is to be "of Levi", she should obey the rules of Levi. If she is to be of "herself", she should abdicate as head of the Anglican Church and be "of herself". There is no "grace" without "repentance". The "Law" applies to everyone - especially "the king".

SECTION - IV

ABOLITION OF USURY IN THE WEST

Chapter 11

CANON LAW ON USURY

In early days all Christians belonged to the Catholic Church. The Catholic Church had many rulings on the subject of usury. These rulings were incorporated into canon law. The laws started with the Bible, were added to by laws of ancient Rome, added to again by the Orthodox Church of the Eastern Roman Empire at Constantinople and were improved upon extensively during the 1100s, 1200s, and 1300s, when some of the finest ecclesiastical thinking took place.

At that time there were two types of courts. Civil courts tried civil cases. Ecclesiastical courts tried offenses against Divine Law such as crimes of heresy, sacrilege, adultery, perjury, and usury. Usury was considered a violation of scripture, against the natural law, and therefore against God Himself. It was forbidden by both the Divine and Canon Law.

Prohibitions against usury were not only directed against

those who took usury, but against their families, those who refused to denounce them, and those who had any part in drawing up contracts whether or not they were lawyers, notaries, or judges. Penalties were directed against those who rented houses to usurers which allowed them to pursue their trade and the rulers who allowed them to reside within their territories. This included priests who did not enforce the Church's edicts against these offenses. A priest was not allowed to receive their offerings. The old excuse that "the money has committed no sin" would not stand in an ecclesiastical court. If a usurer brought offerings to a church and disappeared, the church was required to restore the money to the victims from whom the usurer had exacted the money.

In 1179, the Third Lateran Council laid down the three prime penalties for manifest usurers:

1) They were deprived of Communion.
2) Their offerings were refused.
3) They were denied Christian burial.

This law was interpreted to mean that the offender was not even to set foot in church during divine services. Pope Alexander III stated that if the usurer did not cease his activities he was to be excommunicated and cut off from all intercourse with other Christians.

In 1212, the Council of Paris decreed that the property of a usurer was to be confiscated by the King upon the usurer's death and distributed to the poor. The usurer was denied the right to will anything to his own family since the fruits of a robbery were not to be the object of a gift. Once the charge of usury had been established, the ecclesiastics must undertake to make restitution to those who had been defrauded. Servants must leave the employ of a usurer or suffer the same penalty as their master. This same council declared automatically excommunicated any minister who granted Christian burial or accepted offerings from these outcasts.

The Council of Lyons in 1274 stated that if a stranger who was a foreigner was accused for one month and had not been removed from the territory, the whole territory fell under an interdict.

A wife of a usurer had no right to anything that he might give her. It was considered better that she leave him and beg bread than for her to receive support from her husband. After being excommunicated for one month, the sacraments were to be refused to his wife and family if they remained with him. All the faithful must within a month denounce a creditor or face excommunication. A cemetery where a usurer was buried was placed under an interdict and no one was allowed to enter until the body of the offender was removed and disposed of elsewhere.

Lawyers were not only forbidden to draw up usurious contracts, but they were also forbidden to defend usurers. Clement V at the Council of Vienna in 1311 and 1312 declared that any public official, whoever he was and whatever rank he held, was to be excommunicated if he had anything to do with drawing up a law compelling debtors to pay usury, or denying them the right to recover usury. Any such law drawn up was decreed to have no force since it was in violation of the law of God.

Another type of law forbidden was a law prohibiting usury past a certain percent. The reason for this was that it would lead the unthinking to believe that usury at a percent less than the prohibited amount was all right. The Council of Vienna affirmed the law that those who proclaimed that usury was not sinful were to be punished as heretics. The decree was not only against usurers, but against anyone who encouraged the practice of usury by stating that it was not a sin against God.

The basic church teaching was that anyone who paid usury could seek restitution. Borrowers could always demand the return of usury. Not only is the usury not owed, but the usurer could not receive or keep it without committing sin.

The most interesting thing about these opinions is that the Church forbade usury simply because it was forbidden by the Bible.[1] So far as I have been able to ascertain, there was no real understanding of the economic benefits that accrue to a society that is free from the usury contract - such as the absence of wild economic booms and devastating collapses, bankruptcies, and unemployment. It does show the spiritual maturity of our grandfathers who, without knowing the reason for prohibition of usury, still enforced the divine law of God - and profited

---

1. Medieval Studies, Vol.1, 1939, Vol.II, 1940. Pontifical Institute of Medieval Studies, Toronto, Canada.

mightily in doing so. Usury almost completely disappeared from the Christian West.

Chapter 12

THE RENAISSANCE

The universal prohibition of interest unleashed the mighty Western Renaissance. Usury had acted as a rope which had been strangling the West. As soon as it was banned, the West broke forth into a flowering which could not have been imagined earlier. Italian merchants became wealthy enough to travel to China with their goods. Spanish and Portuguese explorers were financed and uncovered continents with which to trade. Money for the development of inventions became available. The Michelangelos, Rembrandts, Shakespeares, and Newtons were supported by the growing wealth of the West, and they did their thing - and made it profitable. This was an era free of interest!

Circulating Money

"Tallies" were a very important part of the economic system of the Middle Ages. Anyone who had the power could issue them. The Hansiatic League was a confederation made up of scores of independent German cities. They had the power to issue tallies - and they did. So did virtually every county and large city in Europe.

The hard pocket money was gold and silver coins. Many of these coins were in poor condition, being worn, clipped, and some counterfeited. This seemed to make as little difference then as it did in Roman days. People cheerfully accepted them in payment for goods and services. Why not? The government accepted a clipped coin as readily as a full weight coin for taxes. Not so the foreign merchants. When they made a transaction, they wanted payment in full weight gold coins. Thus we have two kinds of coins - "discount coins" for the citizens and "trade coins" for the merchants.

Paper money of large denomination was simply a gold deposit receipt. A bank had, in the manner of the Templars, taken in a store of gold and issued a paper to that effect. The paper bore the stamp and guarantee of the bank. The gold belonged to whoever presented the paper. Few people will carry around five pounds of silver coins or two pounds of gold coins in their pocket when a piece of paper which is light and portable will serve the same purpose. Of course, the peasants always wanted their one or two coins in hand instead of a piece of paper. They still do. Since "interest" was not present, there was no compelling reason to issue more "gold certificates" than there was gold reserve. It was to everyone's advantage to keep the system honest.

In addition to gold deposit receipts there were other kinds of large denomination money. It might take the form of a deed to a house, a business, a ship or some other sort of debt-free equity which had an accepted value in the market place. To make this "paper money" more readily acceptable, it was often guaranteed by a bank that had investigated and found that this boat or that house was indeed worth so much money on a certain day and in public recognition of that fact attached their seal for a small fee. This deed was used as paper money and had worth. It was not a mere "promise to pay".

Buying Joint Venture

If a man wanted to buy a boat to go into the fishing business and didn't have the necessary money, but had a good deal of experience, chances are he could work out a deal. He would go to a bank and ask for money, say 500 pounds. Upon establishing the fact that he had 20 years experience, the bankers might risk some of their investors' money with him. The bank would buy the boat and hire him as captain with a salary. At the end of the first year he could be given the option to buy 10% of the business. If he took up the option he would then own 10% of the business and get 10% of the profits. The bank would get 90% for their investors. The second year he might buy another 10%. He would then own 20% of the business and get 20% of the profits. If the bank thought he was doing a poor job, they might fire him and hire another captain. He would still get 20% of the profits since he owned 20% of the boat. If the boat sank, insurance covered it.

The bank got a fee for its services. That's all. Not a large fee either.

Another way to handle the same boat contract was on a "rental" basis. The bank's investors would buy the boat and "rent" it to the buyer. The buyer kept all the profits and paid rent to investors. There might be an option to "buy" the boat.

The type of contract which could be drawn was limited only by the imagination. One thing - it had to be fair! No one will go into a contract which doesn't seem fair to both sides - especially if the deal is being watched by the Christian community.

In the way illustrated above, in ten years the buyer could own his own ship without having to put up any money of his own. Of course, the 10 year contract is given only as illustration. Practically there were no such contracts that went past 7 years:

At the end of every seven years thou shall make a release (cancellation of debts). And this is the manner of the release: Every creditor that lendeth ought unto his neighbor shall release it (cancel the debt); he shall not exact it of his neighbor, or of his brother, because it is called the Lord's release. Of a foreigner (Heb: zûwr - "racial alien") thou mayest exact it again but that which is thine with thy brother thine hand shall release. Deut: 15:1-3

The House Buyer

If a man wanted to buy a house, the same sort of business arrangement could be made. He might have 10 pounds of his own for a down payment. He would go to the bank and ask for a loan for the balance. The bank would send out an appraiser to find out if the house was really worth the discussed purchase price of perhaps 100 pounds. If it was, a deal could be struck. The man by putting up his 10 pounds might own 10% of the house and the bank 90% by putting up 90 pounds.

The buyer also paid rent. He received 10% of his own rent because he owned 10% of the house and the bank received 90%. The next year he bought another 10%, and owned 20%. He then received 20% of the rent. The bank owned 80% and received 80% of the rent. Each year the bank allowed him to buy more of the house. In time he owned it all. If he failed to pay the rent, he was evicted and another renter/buyer installed. He still received 20% of the rent because he owned 20% of the house. Being kicked out did not deprive him of what was already his.

Of course, the contract might specify that any new buyer/renter could have the option to buy his 20% share also. What is fair or not fair is much easier determined when one does not have wild market swings brought about by interest-caused inflation or deflation, i.e., the house being worth 100 pounds this year, 200 the next year, and dropping to 50 the year after. In that day they had nothing comparable to the booms and busts that are the rule today. It is said that the price of bread remained the same for four centuries in the Hanseatic League.

Determining Usury Contracts

In a no-interest contract there is always risk for both partners. If the risk factor is all on one side, the church determined whether it was a usury or non-usury contract. The usury contract makes one side risk-free and eventually ruins the borrower as it was designed to do. The no-interest contract shares the risk. Both parties rise or fall together. This is one of the oldest rules of Canon Law in determining whether or not a contract was a usury contract - "equal risk".

Early Bank Failures

For many years the private bankers did most of the business for merchants and kings - practically all of which was interest free. Problems could and did arise in a private banker's dealings with kings. If the king politely requested a private banker to make a loan to him, the private banker did - or came under his displeasure. The problem was compounded if the king rode off to war and got himself killed. In these cases the debt was seldom paid and the private banker was ruined. On other occasions the private bankers might allow good merchant customers to borrow from him to cement their relationship. If the merchant wasn't able to repay, the banker was in trouble. During one forty-two year period following the expulsion of the Jews from England and France, the following Italian banks were ruined for lack of specie to honor their obligations:

1304 - Francosi Company
1312 - Macci
1315 - Frescobaldi
1320 - Cherchi Bianchi
1343 - Peruzzi Co.
1345 - Acciaiuoli
1346 - Bardi

The banking houses of Bardi and Peruzzi of Florence failed when Richard III of England went bankrupt following the 100 Years War with France. Wooden tallies were fine at home, but gold was needed for foreign wars. Kings and their governments could make wooden tallies, but they couldn't make gold. They ruined many private bankers by their forced loans to obtain it.

The existence of the non-usurious private banks was further endangered by the arrival of Marano usury bankers from Spain starting in 1492. These people quickly made alliances with local rulers desperate for cash. Soon the combined activities of ruler preference and usurers siphoning off the floating money supply put most of the private bankers and many of the merchants out of business. It also brought on depression and unemployment.

The failure of a bank was a serious event. The repercussions went far beyond the individuals involved. Trade treaties between cities and countries could be jeopardized, and entire manufacturing industries shut down if the financing of the operations ceased.

To prevent powerful merchants and princes and newly arrived usury bankers from putting undue pressure on private banks, the cities of Europe took over the banking business by establishing "municipal banks".

Chapter 13

THE MUNICIPAL BANK OF AMSTERDAM

The most famous of the city-run banks was the great Bank of Amsterdam. This interest-free bank was established in 1609. Since half of Europe's commerce was carried in Dutch ships, Amsterdam had need of such a bank. This was the largest and wealthiest bank in the world.

Its main purpose was to facilitate and expedite trade. It did not make loans for its own account. If a captain had a ship's cargo and no crew, he might come to the Bank of Amsterdam. The Bank might locate investors who would be willing to invest the needed money to hire a crew for 20% of the profits of the voyage.

If a captain needed a cargo, he might lease his ship to bank investors for the length of his expected voyage and hire himself on as captain with a bonus of 15% of the profits. The bank got a moderate fee for arranging these deals. If the ship was lost at sea - like the other such contracts - it was insured.

Chests of gold would come in the front door of the bank in the morning and leave by the rear door that evening. Gold was considered a commodity to be traded. It could be stored for future use, or it could be used for the backing for gold deposit receipts. Municipal banks were large, powerful, efficient operations. Their advent pushed private banks into the background - for a time.

The Age

The four centuries lasting from the 1200s through the 1500s is a most misunderstood period. The "establishment", with reason, wishes to portray the period as being one of poverty, tyranny, dirt, and backwardness.

Such was hardly the case. The greatest display of a nation's wealth, "cathedrals" were built all over Germany, France, and England during that period. The "skilled" labor was mostly volunteer. Thorold Rogers, Professor at Oxford University in the middle of the last century wrote: "At that time a laborer could provide all the necessities for his family for a year by working 14 weeks." The rest of the time was his to do as he pleased. Many parts of Europe were so prosperous during the 14th century that hundreds of communities averaged between 160 to 180 holidays a year. Some labored for themselves; some studied; some fished; others volunteered their labor to build these massive structures. Lord Leverhume, writing at the same time, said, "The men of the 15th century were very well paid."

While today one may find a few score visitors at one of the great cathedrals, Cobbett in his History Of The Reformation states that our ancestors had the wealth and leisure for 100,000 pilgrims at a time to visit Canterbury and other shrines. This from a land that contained 1/10 today's population.

This same William Cobbett recorded in his Rural Rides that when he viewed Winchester Cathedral he said, "That building was made when there were no poor rates; when every labouring man in England was clothed in good wollen cloth; and when all had plenty of meat and bread...."

This was an age peopled mostly by those who had repented. Most neither took usury nor gave it. There was no pressure of "due bills". As a consequence the lands were with material and spiritual wealth. The municipal banks, the creation of the people, fought usury banks tooth and nail. It was not until the advent of Napoleon, the hatchet man of the usury bankers, that municipal banks were shut down permanently.

SECTION - V

RETURN OF USURY TO THE WEST

Chapter 14

RETURN OF USURY TO THE WEST
Maranos

The Saracens conquered Spain as they had Sicily. They conquered the Jews who lived there among the Christians. These Jewish captives easily adopted the religion of their conquerors and became honored and respected members of the Mohammedan community and married freely into their ranks.

The Arabs pushed on over the Pyrenees Mountains into France where they fought a large Christian army at Tours. They lost this hard-fought battle and were forced back into Spain.

The Spanish Christians had not surrendered when the Mohammedans swept through Spain, but waged a holy war against the Infidels from strongholds left to them in the mountains. These wars lasted for centuries.

Over the years the Spanish Christians gradually beat the Mohammedans back and re-conquered the land of Spain. Again, as in the case of Sicily, many of the Saracens and Jews remained. This again presented the Christian rulers with the problem of the conquered aliens. The law still required:

> **Ye shall drive out all the inhabitants of the land from before you....if ye will not drive out the inhabitants of the land from before you.... those which ye let remain ....shall vex you...Num. 33:52-55**

> **Now give not your daughters unto their sons, neither take their daughters unto your sons, nor seek their peace or their wealth forever. Ezra 9:12**

To keep their industries and estates provided with workers, efforts were made to "convert" these aliens into "Samaritans" and bring them into the Christian community. This caused the other prohibition to be violated:

> **A bastard shall not enter the congregation of the Lord: even to his tenth generation shall he not enter into the congregation of the Lord. De 23:2**

About 250,000 of these Jews who had lately been Mohammedans easily switched their faith to Jesus. These new converts were called "Maranos". In time all restrictions were removed from these new converts and they were accepted into the Christian congregation of God with open arms.

In spite of holy and canon law, some Maranos married into grandee families, the highest families socially in Spain. The Catholic Church had long had restrictions against such things. The 2nd Council of Orleans in 533 A. D., Clermont in 535 A. D., and Orleans 538 A. D. all prohibited intermarriage of Jews and Christians. Violators were excommunicated (Concil. Aurel. ii. can19; Mansi, viii. 838; can. 13; Mansi, ix15). The canon law was based on scripture:

I am the Lord thy God, which hath separated you from other people. Lev. 20:24

So shall we be separated, I and thy people, from all the people that are upon the face of the earth. Ex. 33:16

...when they heard the law, they separated from Israel all the mixed (mongrel) multitude. Neh. 13:3

Many of these new converts became priests. Some even became bishops and archbishops. The Law forbidding such things was forgotten:

...when the tabernacle is to be pitched...the stranger (Heb: zûwr, racial alien) that cometh nigh shall be put to death. Num. 1:51

Thou shalt appoint Aaron and his sons, and they shall wait on their priest's office: and the stranger (zûwr) that cometh nigh shall be put to death. Num. 3:10

I have taken your brethren the Levites from among the children of Israel:...thou and thy sons...shall keep your priests office...and the stranger (zûwr) that cometh nigh shall be put to death. Num. 18:6-7

...let them make them broad plates for a covering of the altar... To be a memorial unto the children of Israel, that no stranger (zûwr), which is not of the seed of Aaron, come near to offer incense before the Lord. Num. 16:38-40.

They went in and stood beside the brazen altar*...and the Lord said unto him...set a mark upon...the men that sigh and that cry for all the abominations...And to the others he said...Go ye...and smite...but come not near any man upon whom is the mark...and begin at my sanctuary. Ezek. 9:2-6.

---

* This is the origin of brass plates on altars in Christian churches. Their presence or absence is public proclamation of church beliefs.

From 1449 on the Maranos took over "high society" and finance. Some were confidants of the king. The Maranos became powerful and arrogant. They owned and ran Spain. They also became indiscreet by letting it be known that they were not really Christians. The King formed the Inquisition to investigate the matter. Their findings came like a thunderbolt. The Maranos were holding Jewish religious services while pretending to be Christians. This had been going on for generations. The reports had been true.*

Blue Blood

Based on the "prohibition" of bastards (mixed-breeds) the Spanish at long last attempted to right matters by instituting the "limpieza de sangre" test, or test for "purity of blood".

The Jews were considered "bastards" for two reasons. First, they could not pass the "blush test" since they were kinsmen to the dark-skinned Turko-Finns who had immigrated into Spain from southern Russia over the prior five centuries. Next, they had interbred extensively with their former Mohammedan rulers, another group closely affiliated with, and kin to, these same Turko-Finns.

The Spanish test "limpieze de sangre" to determine who was a mixed-breed and who wasn't was easily administered. It was merely a form of "blush test". One simply raised one's sleeve where there was no sun-burn and if the blue veins were visible - it meant that one was a "blue blood". If you were a "blue blood", you were neither a Marano, Moresco, or other mixed breed. This was all there was to the world renowned test of "blue blood".

In 1492 the Maranos were expelled from Spain. Many went to Arab countries and became violent anti-Christians. Some went to Spanish and Portuguese possessions in the New World. Others went to Holland where, according to the Universal Jewish Encyclopedia, p. 433, "The return of the Maranos to Judaism in a free Holland signified the casting off of the oppressive shackles..." (Meaning

---

* "We have discovered thousands of 'underground Jews' in Portugal... descendents of Medieval Portuguese Jews who... converted to Roman Catholicism in the 15th century while secretly believing and practicing Orthodox Judaism... In Majorca, a Spanish island to the east of the mainland, there are an estimated 30,000 descendants of the Medieval Spanish Jewry who have not been assimilated into the general Catholic population, although the Majorican maranos are formally Catholic." The Jewish Voice, Dec. 1983, p. 10, Phoenix AZ 85001.

58

Christianity). Still others went to England where they pretended to be Spanish-Christians. An Englishman didn't know the difference.

The history of the Mohammedans closely parallels that of the Jewish Maranos. Presented with the option of conversion, expulsion, or death, many naturally chose conversion. The Jewish Maranos were expelled in 1492 and the Mohammedan "Morescos" were expelled in 1502. By 1510 Spanish authorities reported to the Pope that all "strangers" had been expelled from Christian Spain.

This myth was exploded with the "Moresco Revolts" that devastated Granada between 1568 and 1570.[1] Spanish landowners wanted to keep Mohammedan laborers to work their lands. Consequently, it was only a question of time before the mixed descendants of Christians and Mohammedans formed a "Samaritan" population that worked its way into the government and church. They changed the outlook of the land, the church, and the complexion of Spain's population.

The "Christians" of southern Spain "did it their way". As in the case of Sicily and southern Italy, much of Spain was lost to her Christian conquerors and much of the population resembled their kinsmen to the east - the Saracens.

Chapter 15

KILLING THE KING

In 1647, Oliver Cromwell was fighting a civil war in England and needed guns and supplies. To get them, he borrowed money at interest - and England was right back into it again.

Cromwell contacted Jewish moneylenders in the Netherlands who were willing to make loans. There were two conditions. The first was that Jews be allowed into England. This was agreeable to Cromwell. The second condition was more delicate. The loans must be guaranteed. If large loans were made to Cromwell's government and King Charles II came back to the throne, the loans

---

1. Encyclopedia Brittanica 14th Ed, Spain, p. 133.

would be repudiated in an instant. The lenders would lose their money. In other words, as long as Charles lived, no loans could safely be made.

Copies of letters are in existence recommending that Charles be given a chance to escape. His recapture would turn public opinion against him and would provide an excuse for his trial and execution.[2] This is in fact what happened. An opportunity was presented to Charles. He tried to escape, was recaptured, tried, and beheaded - "Regicide", the killing of the king.

This is one of the earlier incidents in Western history of loan guarantees being insured by the murder of a ruler, although the practice was common in the ancient world. Regicide is an integral part of the usury contract and is found wherever the contract itself is found. The list grows long as the years go by.

Louis XV of France was done away with in precisely the same manner 150 years later. Like Charles II of England, he had been deposed as ruler. The real power lay in the revolutionary government which had borrowed from the international bankers and was servant to them. In spite of this, however, no big loans could be made to this government as long as the king was alive and could possibly nullify them at a later date. Louis was given a chance to escape. He was given a large conspicuous coach too heavy for his horses to pull rapidly, which would attract attention. There were two elegantly dressed gentlemen riding in advance, displaying gold coins to a hungry population. All this in time of revolution. Louis almost reached the border before he was captured. It made good copy for the newspapers. Returned under guard, he and his queen were condemned to die. They died well. The loans to the new revolutionary government were safe. Regicide!

Napoleon Bonaparte was defeated and sent into exile. While he was gone from France, Jacob Rothschild negotiated large loans for the Bourbon[3] who had replaced him as the ruler of France. Napoleon returned to France and was defeated again at Waterloo.

---

2. "Will grant financial aid as soon as Charles removed. Charles should be given an opportunity to escape. His recapture will then make trial and execution possible. The support will be liberal but useless to discuss terms until trial commences." (Letter by E. Pratt to Oliver Cromwell). David Astle, Babylonian Woe, p. 118, Harmony Printing, Ltd., Toronto, 1975.

3. Encyclopedia Britannica, Rothschild, 14th Ed. p. 574.

V - RETURN OF USURY TO THE WEST

A near thing for the safety of the loans. Once more he was exiled on a more distant isle. He died. A great monument was built in Paris for his body. A few hairs of his head were taken and recently analyzed.[4] They contained arsenic. Napoleon had been poisoned so that he would never return and repudiate the loans made to the new government.

During the War Between The States, France tried to get her foot in the American door by sending Maximilian to Mexico as king. Mexico was the economic territory of the American northeast banking cabal. This new king of Mexico was very popular with the Mexicans. In spite of this, when he was captured by the rebels he was not imprisoned or ransomed and sent home, he was shot. He would never return to repudiate any of the loans made to Mexico's new rebel rulers.

There was a hue and cry in the newspapers of the northeast banking interests to execute the president of the vanquished Confederate States of America. For two years he was kept in a dark, wet, cold cell in the side of an earthen bank in Fortress Monroe. He was an ill, broken man when put there. He should have died and was expected to die. When it was apparent that there was no way the ravished and occupied South (which was ruled by blacks) could ever revolt, he was released. As a precaution, laws were passed preventing him from ever holding office. Other laws were passed preventing white men from voting in the South. These laws were enforced by an occupying army. There was no way that the ex-president or the citizens he had represented could return to power to repudiate carpet-bagger loans. Jefferson Davis was one of the fortunate few. He remained alive in spite of the nearly successful effort made to kill him.

Nicholas II was Tzar of Russia. The communists took over. The lenders in New York made loans to the new communist government. To prevent him or any of his family from regaining the throne and repudiating the loans, the entire family was shot - even the little children. The loans were secure.

Adolph Hitler was ruler of Germany. Germany lost the war. Losers are borrowers. Hitler knew he was earmarked for a "show-

---

4. Ben Weider & David Hapgood, The Murder of Napoleon, Congdon & Lattès, Inc., N.Y. 1982.

case trial" and so he killed himself. "Ex-post-facto" trials were held for all the rest of the members of his government who might be looked on as his heirs. They were liquidated with few exceptions. Even the idealist, Rudolph Hess, who tried to end the war between Christian nations by flying to England was locked away permanently in Spandau Prison by mutual consent of the victorious lenders. Occupying armies keep watch over the sanctity of the loans. The puppet government of today's Germany owes its existence to the occupying armies and leaves Hess in prison without a word of protest. The post-war German loans were guaranteed at Nuremberg. There is no one left alive who can rock the usury boat. Mussolini, the Italian leader, was executed for the same reason.

The real rulers of Japan were the military leaders. They were executed and the army and navy banned to keep any other military figure from arising to renounce the post-war loans. To this day Japan has no army or navy worthy of the name. Her puppet government owes its power to its country's conquerors and keeps the country that way.

Vietnam had a ruler. His name was Ngo Dinh Diem. American newspapers say that the Americans had him executed. He will never return from the grave to repudiate the recent loans made to the Vietnamese - North or South.

Loan guarantees to nations involve regicide. There is little doubt that the recent assassinations and attempted assassinations of rulers here in America and elsewhere are connected with loan guarantees. The evidence will come to light in future years. It almost always does. Seldom do things happen by accident where usury is involved.

Cromwell's Loans

Charles I was beheaded January 9, 1649. Cromwell held meetings to discuss readmission of the Jews. Immediately a distinctly hostile spirit emerged among the Christian merchants and clergy who united in opposition. To prevent an adverse vote, Cromwell dismissed the Council.

To change public opinion, Manasseh ben Israel, a large book publisher and a leader of the Holland Jewish community, published a book Hope of Israel in 1650. This book was given wide publicity among the "fundamentalists" of the time - the Puritans.

V - RETURN OF USURY TO THE WEST

This book advocated the entry of the Jews into England because it was said the Messiah could not come until the Jews were in ALL lands. England, it was maintained, was the only country which did not contain Jews. If the Jews were admitted, the Messiah might be expected.[5]

The Puritans bought this story. They forgot all about the Biblical injunctions forbidding strangers to enter the land. Still, the larger part of the population of England was still against the admittance of the Jews. Cromwell took it upon himself to allow entry of the Jews quietly. He got his loans. "The borrower is servant.." By 1655 there were a considerable number of Maranos in England, secret Jews posing as Spanish Catholics.

In 1655 England went to war with Spain. The Jews posing as Spanish Christians had to openly declare themselves "Jews" in order to avoid confiscation. This was also the year in which Charles II of England entered into negotiations with these same Amsterdam Jews against Cromwell to secure financing for his return. In 1655 and 1656 a horde of Jewish refugees from the Polish Ukraine arrived in Holland putting further pressure on Manasseh ben Israel to force England open to immigration.

In 1660 Charles II came to the throne. In addition to the loans which he had contracted with the Amsterdam Jews he borrowed heavily from the local goldsmiths. In 1672 he repudiated the loans to the local goldsmiths, causing a general suspension of specie payment. Charles was disliked.

Sometime about 1684 William III of Orange obtained a loan of two million gulden from Antonio Lopez Suasso,[6] an Amsterdam Jew. This aided the Dutchman to capture the English throne in 1688. The Jews again had an English ruler who was obligated to them since "The borrower is servant..." This was the third in a row.

Between 1700 and 1750 the Jews working their usury system in England increased their capital from 1.5 million to over 5 million pounds.[7] In 1870 the University Test Act allowed Jews to enter English universities. In 1890 complete equality was granted to Jews in England. It had taken a long, long time.

5. Jewish Encyclopedia, England, p.169

6. J/E, p. 169

7. J/E, p. 169

Chapter 16

THE MISSISSIPPI BUBBLE

It was called the Mississippi Bubble because the Mississippi River region was then owned by France and formed part of the company in which the initial speculation centered. It is called a "bubble" because most of the financing was done on borrowed money. When time came to pay there was more money owed than there was in existence so there was the panic and collapse which always takes place. The Mississippi Bubble is unique in that it was so big and that it took only four years from beginning to end.

John Law, the man who started the plan, was born in Edinburgh, Scotland. He studied math, commerce, and political economics in London, and banking operations in Amsterdam. In 1705 he got the idea of starting a National Bank in Scotland just like the Bank of England. Paterson, another Scotsman who has been given the credit for founding the Bank of England, opposed the idea of a competing usury bank and had the plan halted in the Scottish Parliament. Law took his idea to France.

While Britain was occupied with the Bank of England, France was a fertile ground for something like it. On May 20, 1716, Law obtained a patent to establish the "General Bank" with 6 million shares at 4.17 livres per share. Buyers of the stock could put up one-fourth hard money and three-fourths government IOUs. This gave the bank 4.2 million livres in gold and 12.5 million livres in government IOUs. With this money in the bank (one-fourth hard money and three-fourths IOUs), Law was then given permission to hand out banknotes to anyone who wanted to borrow money into existence.

Everyone in France seemed to need money so they came to the General Bank, left their personal IOUs, and took away freshly printed paper General Bank "banknotes". In a short time the bank

had issued 60,000,000 livres. Interest rates dropped to 4 1/2%.
If a lot of money is in circulation, interest rates often drop.
If a very little money is in circulation, interest rates often
remain high.

These notes issued by the General Bank were made "legal
tender" by the government of France. By government "decree" they
were now acceptable for all debts including taxes. This gave
them true value.

To expand the operation, in August 1717, the General Bank
absorbed the Louisiana Company, which was a combination of the
Crozet Company and the Canada Company formed in 1712. This new
creation was given trading rights over the tremendous land area
drained by the Mississippi, Ohio and Missouri Rivers in North
America plus trading rights in Canada.

In 1718 the new expanded Louisiana Company was additionally
given a "monopoly" on the trade over the entire region. This
alone was enough to make any company wealthy. The bank's name
was then changed to the "Royal Bank" to give it a better image.
The notes of the bank were guaranteed by the king - at least he
said he guaranteed them. This was a true "conglomerate".

In the meantime, a rival company had been formed in France
called the "Western Company". It was hostile to the Louisiana
Company and its Royal Bank. This new company absorbed the East
India, Oriental and China Companies, and changed its name to the
"French Indies Company". This rival company was given the monopoly of the mint and coin issue for nine years and also was given
the right to farm national revenues (collect taxes) under condition that they take over payment of the national debt. This was
the sweetest deal in the world. In essence, the government of
the King had abdicated and had turned the government's finances
over to two companies, the French East India Company and the
Louisiana Company. Make no mistake about it - these two companies were the biggest things in France, and probably in the world.

The next thing to happen almost surpasses belief. The two
companies merged! The price of the stock of this new company
went out of sight. Investors were ecstatic. The merchants and
farmers of France mortgaged their homes to buy stock.

Burst Bubble

Using past examples we know that in theory a usury bank does not need money to operate. A bank may open its doors without a cent. One can enter a bank, sign his IOU and exchange it for paper money. The paper money was created by the bank employees going into the back room and printing paper banknotes. One moment there is no money in existence, the next minute a bank employee comes out of the back room holding a wet paper banknote by the corner so that he won't get ink on his hands. Money has just been born! The borrower takes the banknote and goes up the street shopping. The backing for the "banknote" is the borrower's "IOU". The borrower may take the paper note he has just borrowed into existence and spend it.

Practically, people - especially merchants - don't trust usury-banks. They never have. There are very few people who would trust anyone who created money in the manner illustrated above. In the early 1700s, the only way a suspicious merchant could be persuaded to accept a bank's paper money was if he had the option to trade it for gold at anytime. This is the reason John Law's bank raised 4.2 million livres in gold by selling stock. He needed the gold to be able to cash the paper banknotes.

But what happened? New borrowers had come and borrowed 60 million livres worth of banknotes into existence - leaving their IOUs as collateral. Here we have 60 millions in brand new paper money in circulation and 4.2 millions in gold on reserve. A catastrophe was building. If everyone tried to cash in their paper money at one time, the bank would fold.

As if the "usury" problem were not enough, there were other complications. The Common Law states:

Woe unto them that join house to house, that lay field to field, till there be no place. Isa. 5:8

This is the command against monopoly. It is one of the oldest and most constantly-enforced Laws. As far back as Rome there were laws prohibiting private monopolies. The prohibition was given stimulus in Germany in 1512[8] when it was once more enforced. The reasons are obvious. The merchant who owns all the

---

8. Luther's Works, Vol. 45, Philadelphia, 1968, p. 241.

wheat for sale during a famine can force people to give everything they have for the wheat - or die. Whenever a group has a
monopoly, sooner or later there will be trouble, usually from an
unexpected direction. This great new business and banking combine in France was a monopoly pure and simple. It controlled a
large part of the commerce of the nation of France, and of the
world.

In addition to Law's monopoly, there was another monopoly.
The Church in France owned 1/3 of the land and 2/3's of the
capital. For centuries the devout had been dying and leaving
their estates to the Church:

**The priests....shall have no part nor inheritance with Is-
rael...the Lord is their inheritance. Deu. 18:1-2**

Instead of living on a portion of the offerings and using
the remainder to administer God's business, the priests had
turned the Catholic Church into a wealthy and powerful master
that owned much of the best land in the country. It was also an
exacting master and overseer to its employees, and a keen compet-
itor in business and politics. Many in France had good reason
not to like the Catholic Church.

There was a third monopoly. The crown and nobles owned
another 1/3 of the land. The king:

**shall not...greatly multiply to himself silver and gold.
Deu. 17:16-17**

Neither the king, nobles, nor church paid taxes - a gross
misuse of authority.

What floating supply of money there was was in the hands of
usury banks. These new kinds of banks had begun their operations in a big way. In 1703 there were 21 such bankers in Paris
alone. In 1721 - 51 and in 1775 - 66.[9]

In 1709-1710 France had a famine. The peasants and small
shopkeepers went deeply into debt to pay for imported food to

---

9. Pierre Vilar, A History Of Gold & Money, 1450 - 1920, Verso Editions NLB,
p. 271, London

keep from starving. By 1717 matters had become so bad that debts were discounted 25% by the Chamber of Justice.[10] This was the economic background of France. Monopoly laid on monopoly. First, the king and nobles with 1/3 of the land and their special privileges, next, the Catholic Church owning another 1/3 of the land and her special privileges. This was the economic base to which John Law added his empire. France was one vast monopoly.

John Law's monopoly was successful beyond anyone's imagination. People were getting rich! To get money to buy shares in Law's company, the merchants and farmers of France went to the usury banks and borrowed money into existence by the millions, leaving their IOUs and the deeds to their unmortgaged property for security.

On May 21, 1716, Law's plan to reduce the "gold backing" for paper notes was announced. This was the moment the competition was waiting for. The word was quickly spread that the Royal Bank was going to default and that if people wanted to save themselves, they had better cash in their bills for gold immediately. Long lines formed. The gold reserves used for backing the paper money were quickly paid out. When there was no gold left, the window slammed down.

The stock of the Royal Bank that had gone from 500 livres to over 18,000 plunged[11]. People who had mortgaged their farms to buy stock on margin were called to pay their loans. They couldn't. By the thousands Frenchmen bankrupted and the farms, estates, and businesses used for collateral were transferred to the bankers. The great Louisiana Company was broken up and turned over to gleeful creditors. Scores of wealthy usury-banks now owned the assets formerly held by one great company.

The nobles, the King, and Church had to move over. France was in the throes of developing a new master - the usury-bank... the master who would subdue all the rest and never leave France in peace again.

---

10. Vilar, p. 242

11. Ibid, p. 242.

Chapter 17

THE BANK OF ENGLAND

The creation of the Bank of England was the event which many economists point to as bringing "modern" banking to the West. This modern banking was nothing more than the old usury system brought to a virtually usury-free land. In a short time a large part of the economic and political life of Britain was controlled by this bank, and in a while longer, much of the world.

Officially, the Bank of England was founded by a Scotsman, William Paterson in 1694. The founder stepped down the following year and others took control. This has led to the belief that Paterson was no more than a "front man". No one will ever know the true story of the activities of the first years of this bank because the Bank of England says that the minutes have been "misplaced".

Certain facts are a matter of public record. King William borrowed money from Amsterdam bankers to capture the throne and in the process had become their servant. "The borrower is servant...." He then gave a group of bankers a charter to set up an interest-bank. Next, he gave this new bank his IOU for 1.2 million pounds. The new bank allowed the King to draw on it for 1.2 million and charged him 8% a year for the privilege. In eight years at 8%, the 1.2 million debt grew to 2.2 million.

Since the King didn't have 2.2 million pounds, he couldn't pay. He made more and more concessions to the bank. The King of Britain put Britain back on the usury hook and it has remained on the hook ever since.

King William could have used wooden Tallies to repay the 1.2 million loan. In fact, he could have used Tallies without taking a loan in the first place. It seems logical to assume that when someone pays hard money for something he could get free, it must be for a special reason. It is believed that this special reason was part of the original agreement made to the bankers back in

Amsterdam in exchange for a "hard money" loan. The agreement must have been not to use free Tallies once he became king. This may also be one of the reasons that the bank misplaced the minutes of its early meetings. One can speculate endlessly over this. In any event, in 1696, the Bank of England failed. The booms and busts had started all over again.

By 1719 the national debt had grown to Ŀ51,300,000. At 8%, the interest on this amounted to Ŀ4.1 million a year, a tidy sum. In fact, it was such a tidy sum that others besides the Bank of England tried to get it.

South Sea Bubble

In 1711 the South Sea Company was formed in England. It was granted a monopoly of all the British trade to South America and the Pacific Islands - a highly successful and profitable business.

In 1719 the directors looked around for ways to expand their operation and they spotted the Bank of England. The Bank of England was receiving over 4 million pounds a year for holding the British debt. It didn't take any special talent to "hold" the British debt and receive 4 million pounds a year for doing it, so the South Sea Company went to work to persuade the British government to turn the debt over to them and let them "hold" it.

They offered the government 3.5 million pounds. Not only that, but they said that they would let the government reduce the interest to only 1.5 million pounds a year instead of 4.1 million they had been paying to the Bank of England. The government debated the advisability of accepting the deal. The offer was raised to Ŀ7,567,000. The Bank of England could not match it. The government forthwith took its IOUs from the Bank of England and turned them over to the South Sea Company.*

This is the same as if today you offered the U.S. government a 75 billion dollar bonus if they would let you take over the nation's trillion dollar debt. You charge only 30 billion a year interest instead of the present 100 billion. The 75 billion bonus can come from 3 years' interest. This is really "something for nothing".

The South Sea Company was now a conglomerate just as the

---

* None of the textbooks are clear on this point, but the Bank Of England was probably reimbursed with stock in the new South Sea Company based on its market value.

Louisiana Company was in France. It had the income from the South American and Pacific Island trade plus Ł1,500,000 a year interest from the government's payment on its debt. The stock of the South Sea Company boomed. At the beginning of the year it was Ł128 10s. By June it had risen to Ł890. In July it had risen to Ł1,000.* To raise money the directors sold 5 million more shares at this inflated price. The stock was snapped up by eager buyers in a rush. In August the price peaked and started down. By November it had fallen to Ł135 a share. Thousands who had bought on margin while the stock was high were wiped out. Hundreds fled England to avoid debtors' prison.

The government investigated.** They found that favors had been purchased from the government with gifts. Implicated was John Aislabie, chancellor of the exchecquer; James Craggs, joint postmaster-general, the Earl of Sunderland, and Charles Stanhope, a commissioner of treasury. By Act of Parliament the estates of the accused were confiscated.

What was left of the South Sea Company continued on into the 19th century. The Bank of England - whose friends had disposed of the competition - took back the government IOUs and the interest it paid yearly on the debt. Britain was right back where she started.

Chapter 18

SPAIN'S PROBLEM

In the early 1600s private banks were everywhere. Most were interest-free banks. Cities of any size such as Amsterdam,

---

* If the stock of the Federal Reserve had been traded publicly since it was formed in 1913, instead of being privately held, it may have out-done the price of the South Sea Company stock.

** The English government's investigation shows that "it can be done". Our own Federal Reserve Bank refuses to be audited in spite of the repeated attempts of Congress. The government borrows from the Federal Reserve System of banks. "The borrower is servant to the lender." Therefore the government is servant to the Federal Reserve. A servant does not audit his master. A full scale "honest" investigation would be the "event of the century."

V - RETURN OF USURY TO THE WEST

Barcelona, Genoa, Hamburg and Venice set up "municipal banks". These municipal banks were versatile indeed. Most operated in the following manner:

1. Gold Bullion was received from merchants who were given credit on the bank books.

2. Clients were not allowed to overdraw accounts.

3. Surplus reserves were invested in public "tally" loans.

4. Bank deposits were easily transferred by deposit receipts. These receipts took the place of banknotes which appeared later.

Close watch was kept over private banks and money changers by both the church and civil authorities.[12] In other areas the fruits of usury were apparent. In Spain Charles V had squandered the ransom of the New World. Fantastic sums were spent on interest payments. The extent of this disaster has been played down by "establishment" historians for obvious reasons, but the disaster was no less a disaster.

	Ducats Borrowed	Ducats Repaid [13]
1520-1532	5,379,053	6,327,371
1533-1542	5,427,699	6,594,300
1543-1551	8,397,616	10,737,843
1552-1556	9,643,869	14,351,591

In the first year, 413 ducats were borrowed - in the last,

12. In 1604 certain money changers in Bruges were threatened with suppression because of malpractices. Money, Banking & Credit in Medieval Bruges, Raymond de Roover, Mass. 1948, p.351

13. Vilar, p. 148

1,929,000. Interest charges came to 17% in the first period and 49% in the last. The total borrowed was 29 million and the total repaid 38 million. External debts rose to 37,059,239 ducats - more than 2 million more than the total amount of gold and silver reaching Spain.

The Spanish King was "servant" to his lenders. He resorted to forced loans and high taxes to get money to pay them. Government agents of one sort or another were everywhere to ensure that duties and taxes were paid.

No scheme or plan to increase Spanish wealth turned out right. To increase trade the government subsidized building giant galleons. This ruined the small ship owners. Spanish wool was found to be profitable and sheep were allowed free grazing. This ruined agriculture. The population dropped as tight money conditions kept Spaniards from having children. Others migrated to get away from oppressive regulation and to make a living.

To fill the population vacuum, immigration was encouraged. The slaves were freed to borrow money into existence. The blood of the black slaves combined with that of the Morescoes and Maranos to darken the complexion of Portugal in a few short years and the country turned into a Samaritan nation.

By 1605 copper coins were heavily minted[14] to give the people some sort of money. By 1640 it took 400 pounds of copper coins to buy 100 pounds of cheese. Spain's usurers reduced the King and the people of the Iberian peninsula to a nation of beggars because of their usury contracts. They became sullen, oppressed, overregulated, misgoverned, and hypersensitive. Having rejected God's Laws that would have protected them, the race that manned the armies and fleets of the Conquistadors was no more - it had vanished.

Spain was later occupied by Napoleon. France, Germany and Italy were also occupied and governed by Napoleon. In 1808 Spain revolted against French rule. England's bankers, many of them descendents of Samaritan Maranos expelled earlier, came to Spain's assistance and allowed her to borrow money into existence at reasonable rates to buy munitions to fight the French. Spain was now obligated to German, French, Italian, and English bankers.

---

14. Vilar, p. 232

South American Revolutions

Spanish colonies in South America, long the victims of Spanish usury-banking practices, utilized the time of Napoleon's occupation of Spain to revolt. The Bank of England allowed both Spain and her revolting colonies to borrow from her at the same time.

Simon Bolivar traveled to London in June, 1810. He had been commissioned by the newly formed Junta of Caracas to seek military and economic aid for the new independence movement. He found the London bankers openhanded. On behalf of the new revolutionary government he was allowed to borrow money into existence by leaving an IOU and giving trade concessions as guarantees. He then returned to South America.

After years of conflict and the loss of countless lives, Bolivar delivered his people from the Spanish. A "liberation loan" at 5% interest doubles in 14.4 years. Bolivar's government now owed huge amounts to the London interest-bankers. The other two "liberators", Jose de San Martin of Argentina and Bernardo O'Higgins of Chile, followed Bolivar's example and borrowed heavily in England. South America was now saddled with the tyranny of London interest-banking.

London bankers now had a great deal at stake in their South American loans. The profits were enormous. At the same time there were threats of "reconquest" being made by Spain aided by Austria. This would have repudiated the tremendously profitable South American loans. To prevent such a thing from happening, Canning, the British Foreign Secretary, approached the American Minister in London, Richard Rush, with a proposition. The independence of the South American countries would be guaranteed by both nations. This resulted in the "Monroe Doctrine" being published in 1823. It had precious little to do with the love of South American nations and a great deal to do with the guaranteeing of British usury-loans.

South Americans have never in their history had enough money to repay their debts. Vain attempts to do so caused a flood of gold and silver to flow into England throughout the 1800s. It also helped the British to set up and maintain a much ballyhooed "gold standard", but it left South America drained. These poor people don't even own the products of their own land. Cuba's sugar is not owned by Cubans, Brazil's coffee is not owned by Brazilians, and relatively little of value in Mexico is owned by Mexicans.[15]

When South America was first settled, Spain did with the South American Indians as she had done with her Moresco and Marano population at home - she kept them to work the mines and plantations instead of displacing them. This resulted in the "Spanish problem" being brought to the New World. Not only that, but many of the Maranos expelled from Spain in 1492 came to the New World where they had almost a completely clear field to operate their money system. It made little difference what political subdivision they lived under since they operated as agents for the large Marano banking settlement in Amsterdam which later moved to London.

Since her "liberation" South America has followed the usury track straight and true. She did all the usual things in the usual manner right on schedule. When she was drained of money, her slaves were freed. This gave the government an excuse to borrow money into existence to pay the slave owners the cost of emancipation. The new money caused a burst of prosperity. As free paupers, the ex-slaves in turn borrowed money into existence to buy land. The banks then foreclosed the farms when the ex-slaves were unable to keep up payments. "Reformers" were in turn financed by the bankers, and they banded the landless peasants together and applied to London and Paris for additional loans once more to buy up land for economic reform. This caused another burst of economic prosperity.

The landowners who wish to keep what they have are looked upon as the real enemy. It is they who are reviled in the bankers' media. This is the group scheduled for liquidation to guarantee loans made to rival reform groups once they get into power. The money game has been going round and round in South America in the same manner for 300 years, and is the situation in South and Central America to the present day.*

---

15. Eustace Mullins, The Secrets of the Federal Reserve, P.O. Box 1105, Staunton, Virginia 24401. $10/copy.

* In the past the "sub-rosa" agreement reserved North America, including Mexico and Central America, to the New York banking interests who originated in Germany. South America was reserved to the Marano banking interests in London.

Conclusion

The curse of the usury-bankers sent Spain's armies over Europe chasing the end of the rainbow to pay the 11th peso with a pot of gold which was never found. They left their bones there. The land was drained of specie which reduced it to poverty and starvation.

Spreading to the New World at an early time, usury and the absence of the Law has reduced Spanish settlers to the same level as their Indian and black slaves. All became slaves together to the System.

South America, with the exception of a few isolated pockets, has become amalgamated into a Samaritan continent....a twisted, wrung-out husk of what it might have been. The continent undoubtedly will be "foreclosed" nation by nation, and in time will slide under the banner of Communism.

SECTION - VI
RUSSIA

Chapter 19

KHAZARIA

The Kingdom of Khazaria (c.100 A. D. - 1016 A. D.) occupied a territory larger than any single nation in Europe in the 600s A. D. It reached from the Black Sea through the Ukraine, encompassing much of Poland and what is now European Russia, Hungary, and Rumania. Racially they were Turko-Finn[1] or "Turks".

This nation achieved its importance because of its strategic location. Trade goods coming from central Russia and northern Europe destined for the market at Constantinople passed down the great Russian rivers. Long stretches of these rivers passed through the heart of the Khazar nation which exacted tolls and tribute from traders and travelers.

This ancient state was bordered on one side by the empire of Byzantium. On the other side was the equally powerful empire of Persia. It was the policy of the Christians of Persia to form strong alliances with the heathen rulers of Khazaria to thwart

1. British Encyclopedia, Vol. 15, Khazar, 1911 Edition.

their Christian brothers of Constantinople.

> **Thou shalt not hate thy brother in thy heart...Thou shalt not avenge, nor bear any grudge against the children of thy people. Lev. 19:17,18**

This alliance between Khazaria and Persia lasted from 200 to 350 A. D., at which time the Persian empire became so powerful that Khazaria became endangered. Switching sides, Khazaria took part in Constantinople's invasion of Persia in 363 A. D. Khazaria became Constantinople's buffer state to the north.

Unfortunately, its strategic location placed Khazaria in the middle of any invasion launched from the East. One of the first of these invasions was by Attila the Hun who scattered and for a time extinguished the independence of the nation. Khazaria became the kingdom of Attila's oldest son in 448. When Attila died, the Khazar kingdom reformed.

In 625 these people appear under the name "Khazars" in Byzantine annals.[2] To cement the alliance between Byzantium and Khazaria the King of the Khazars was offered an Imperial Christian princess.[3] In return for the princess and trade-treaties Khazaria furnished 40,000 men in a joint war against the Persians.

In 637 Christian Persia was struck down by the advancing power of Islam, and in 651 the Muslims began their subjugation of Khazaria with an 80-year war. In 737 the king and nobles were compelled to accept Islam. This state of affairs lasted until the Mohammedan flood ebbed. During this period, Christian Constantinople banished her Jewish inhabitants under instruction from her Christian priests.

> **Thou shall make no covenant with them. They shall not dwell in thy land, lest they make thee sin against me. Ex. 23:32-33**

These Jews fled northward to Khazaria where they were welcomed. The Khazars were also a mixed-breed race. They were of

2. British Encyclopedia, Khazars, 14th Ed.

3. Ez. 9:12

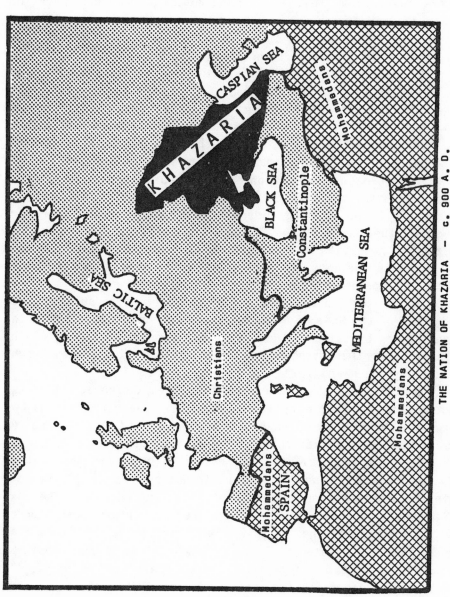

THE NATION OF KHAZARIA — c. 900 A. D.

(Symplified copy of the map of the 9th Century nation of Khazaria found in the Jewish Ency., Chazars.)

dusky Turkish/Tartar stock which included Mongol strains which came from the later Mongol invasion of their land.

The Mohammedans had been recent non-too-gentle conquerors. There was no love lost between Mohammedans and Khazarians. The newly arrived Jewish refugees from Constantinople brought with them a welcome choice from the Koran of Islam - the verbal "Traditions of the Elders" written in the Talmud.

King Bulan, the Khazarian ruler, chose this late arriving religion in place of the religion of the hated Mohammedans. He and 4,000 of his nobles became converts. The entire country followed suit in time. The language of the Khazars was adapted to the Hebrew alphabet (in much the same way that German is written with the Latin alphabet). The result was called Yiddish. There is no other connection between Hebrew and Yiddish other than the latter containing a number of Hebrew words.

In 775 Leo IV, a grandson of a Khazar/Jewish sovereign, ascended the throne of the mighty Christian Byzantine Empire and Byzantium was ruled by a Samaritan. During this period the King of Khazaria was honored in Constantinople as a potentate above even the Pope and other Christian kings of the West.

In 862 the quarreling Slavs of the north were subdued under the rule of the Russ of Sweden. These new conquerors named the land after themselves - "Russia". This was the beginning of the "threat from the north" as the combined Russ-Slav forces fought their way southward along the Russian rivers.

On the heels of this development, an explosion of Petchenig-Turks from the East swept into Khazaria. There was war on two fronts. The kingdom began to break up. In 884 Oleg, the Russian Prince of Kiev, passed through the Slavic tribes in the Dnieper basin who had been ruled by the Khazars with the cry "Pay nothing to the Khazars!" The day of tribute had ended. In 965 Sarket, Itel, and Semender surrendered to Swiatoslav of Kiev. The last flicker of independence was extinguished by a joint expedition of Russians and Byzantines in 1016. "Many members of the Charzarian royal family emigrated to Spain.... Some went to Hungary, but the great mass of the people remained in their native country."[4] This brought to an end the political state of Khazaria and forced its continuance as a religious state.

---

4. Jewish Encycl. Vol. IV, p. 5.

Khazaria's New Rulers

The nation of Khazaria was no more - the Khazar/Jewish converts remained. Most continued to live beside the great Russian rivers as they had done for hundreds of years. They formed tight, suspicious, autonomous groups who looked in upon themselves and excluded the world. They wanted to be left strictly alone - and that was the one thing their Christian, Mohammedan and Mongol conquerors would not do.

From 884-1016 the Russians conquered these porcupine-like enclaves, scattering Jewish refugees across Europe and into Spain. Then the Mongols stormed through in 1240, a cataclysmic event that pushed another wave of "Jews" into Europe.

This last wave of dark-skinned, Yiddish speaking alien invaders caused a reaction. Starting with England in 1290 the Jews were expelled from Europe and herded back to the East again to join their brothers in what was by now Poland. But there was no peace for these people without a country.

In time the Polish rulers were displaced by Russian overlords. Next came the Mohammedans once more, the Mongols, then the Hungarians, Austrians, Germans, and again the Russians. Most Khazarian settlements tended to remain generally where they had always been while the ebb and flow of war brought new masters and new national boundaries every few years.

In the 9th century a Sephardic Jewish scholar in Cordova, Spain, Hasdai Ibn Shaprut, heard of a Jewish national homeland in Khazaria. He wrote King Joseph to ask about it,[5] especially to learn to which of the tribes the monarch belonged. The answer came back:

> "We have found in the family registers of our fathers that Togarmah had ten sons, and the names of their offspring are as follows: Uigar, Dursu, Avars, Huns, Basilii, Tarniakh, Khazar, Zagora, Bulgars, Sabir. We are the son of Khazar, the seventh..."[6]

Webster's New World Dictionary defines Ashkenazim: "a German

5. Jewish Encyclopedia p. 265, short version.
6. Arthur Koestler, The Thirteenth Tribe, New York: Random House, 1976, p. 72.

Jew, earlier a German, after Ashkenaz, second son of Gomer...distinguished from the Sephardim." Jewish books are very careful to distinguish between Sephardic and Ashkenazic. Most individual Jews would like to claim descent from Spain for that is where the Khazarian royal family migrated in 1016.

The "Ashkenazic" Jews adopted the six sided "star of David" as their symbol. This differentiated them from the large settlement of Spanish and Portuguese Jews who called themselves "Sephardic" Jews. They had adopted for their insignia the "lion of David" with his foot on a ball.

Certain Christians and all Islamic conquerors of the Ashkenazics in eastern Europe tried to convert them to their respective religions. Being crude in their approach, the offer was often the simple choice of conversion or being sliced in two with a sword. This was a painful choice. Rabbis came to the rescue by resurrecting an ancient prayer which could be made in advance and would allow the Jews to repeat the Christian, Islamic, or any other oath, without actually doing so. It is called the "Kol Nidre Prayer" and from the earliest times down to the present is made each year on the "Day of Atonement". It goes as follows:

"ALL VOWS, OBLIGATIONS, OATHS, ANATHEMAS...WHICH WE MAY VOW, OR SWEAR, OR PLEDGE, OR WHEREBY WE MAY BE BOUND, FROM THIS DAY OF ATONEMENT UNTO THE NEXT...WE DO REPENT. MAY THEY BE DEEMED ABSOLVED, FORGIVEN, ANNULLED, AND VOID AND MADE OF NO EFFECT: THEY SHALL NOT BIND US NOR HAVE POWER OVER US. THE VOWS SHALL NOT BE RECKONED VOWS; THE OBLIGATIONS SHALL NOT BE OBLIGATORY; NOR THE OATHS BE OATHS."[7]

This "All Vows" prayer allowed the persecuted Jews to take any oath they felt necessary - with impunity. This was the thing which allowed the enclaves of Jews to remain together through the years without being destroyed. It has proved indispensable in their negotiations with unfriendly neighbors as we shall soon see.

Chmielnicki Massacres In Poland

Chmielnicki was an Eastern Orthodox Pole who fought with the Cossacks against Poland, which was Roman Catholic. In those days

---

7. Jewish Encyclopedia, Vol. VIII, p. 539.

Poland was the largest country in Europe. Her borders extended from near the Baltic almost to the Black Sea. While Islam was carving out a European empire and knocking on the doors of Vienna, the Christians, Eastern Orthodox, Roman Catholic, and Protestant, were butchering each other in war after war. Chmielnicki captured Kiev and indiscriminately massacred Jews and Roman Catholics whom he felt to be equally reprehensible.

This massacre triggered a chain reaction in eastern Europe in 1648-1649 which again sent thousands of Jews swarming into Western Europe. It was pressure from these new "Polish" arrivals which gave urgency to Ben Israel's 1655 petition to Oliver Cromwell for them to enter England.

The Nation of Russia existed to the east of the great country of Poland. Following the example of the other Christian nations, on December 2, 1742 all Jews were expelled from Russia by order of Tzarina Elizabeth Petrovna.

Russia Takes Over

Poland was partitioned (1772-1795) by Russia, Prussia, and Austria. In these divisions of Poland, Russia inherited all the Ashkenazic Jews which had previously been expelled from Russia, plus more than one million others.

The ruling Tzar of Russia at the time was Alexander I. At first he looked on the Jews as a people like any other people. At this time Alexander, in common with most other Russians, frankly did not know what a Jew was. In time he discovered that for ages they had lived in Kehillas, had autonomous rights, and had their own school systems called "heders". In spite of not having a separate country, they were in fact a separate nation requiring special treatment.

On Feb. 26, 1785, the inhabitants in the newly annexed Polish territory were given all the rights and privileges of other Russian subjects, without distinction of faith or nationality. Immediately the Russian rulers were inundated with petitions from the Polish Slavs requesting that they be protected from the Jews. This was notice that the Russians had another problem of which they were not previously aware. At the request of the Poles, all the old Polish restrictions against the Jews were gradually reinstated.

The Russians soon found that these Ashkenazic Jews had a

well-developed nation existing within the boundaries of Russia. While the Russian government was supreme politically, the Jews had their own government administered from their synagogues, their own religion, their own laws, and their own system of finance in which the forbidden practice of usury was the cornerstone. They also discovered that the Poles looked on the Jews as "a nation of bankers".

In dealing with their own kind, the Jews had a system of "building and loans" which made money available to any of their number who needed money. Sometimes these loans were made interest free. At other times the loans were made at rates between 9% and 12%, rates considered very high at the time. Jewish private schools were everywhere. Their "unofficial" governments had lobbies to influence first the Polish, and later the Russian government.

Alexander was advised by his Christian priests to kill or banish these heathen. Alexander flatly refused to kill them, and since no country wanted them, he couldn't banish them. A "Russification" program was undertaken. The Orthodox Jews put up a stonewall resistance to the Russians as they had earlier to the Poles.

In 1804 the "Russification" program was softened and new laws were enacted which provided for separate Jewish schools which were required to teach Russian. Even these new "softened" requirements were resisted.[8] The news of these disagreements between the Ashkenazic Polish Jews and the Russians reached the ears of Napoleon.

In 1806 on July 19th, at the Hotel de Ville in Paris an assembly of Jewish notables was held at the command of Emperor Napoleon. Napoleon wished to use the Jews for his own ends, but first he had to soften the harsh criticism of Jews by devout Christians. They were asked such questions as "Does the Jewish law permit the taking of usury from Jews? From Christians?" The answer was "No. Usury whether to Jews or Christians was forbidden by Jewish law."[9] This meeting was a prelude to bigger things next year.

Napoleon had in essence assured the Christians of Europe

<hr>

8. The Jews in America, Max Dumont, Simon & Schuster, New York 1978, p. 155.

9. Dumont, p. 75.

that the Ashkenazic Jews were a people just like any other people, and to the accompaniment of much publicity, he proceeded to give them rights and privileges not duplicated elsewhere until 160 years later. For instance, it had been assumed by Western Europeans that Jews would lie if given an opportunity and so a special Jewish Oath, "more Judaico" was administered. This oath was abolished in all countries under French control. Jews also could resume using Hebrew and Yiddish in their bookkeeping and also hold public office.

French agents in Russia made sure that the Jewish population there was made well aware that a "friend" and his army were on the way and that they could expect the same privileges as their kinsmen in The French Empire if they would join in with a revolt against the Tzar.

The idea of using Ashkenazic Jews for his own ends was well conceived and carried out with all the efficiency with which Napoleon's empire was noted - but it was a dud. The Russian Jews did as they always did when a new conqueror came - nothing! They could not care less about getting involved in a war where Christians were killing Christians. This betrayal and the Russian cold destroyed Napoleon. He had lifted the Christian Church's age old restrictions against the Jews for nothing, and now there was nothing to contain them, since the Christian Church had been virtually eliminated by the French Revolution's Terror. They were "out of the box". Their first major move was to expand their usury banking, a thing permitted by their religion.

Russia's Jewish Solution

To have an understanding of Russia's Jewish problem one must carefully study the map on the following page copied from a map in the Jewish Encyclopedia Vol. X, 1909, under "Russia". This area of Russia from near the Black Sea almost to the Baltic Sea constitutes the "Pale" - the modern name for the ancient nation of Khazaria.

According to the 1897 census there were 126,368,827 people living in Russia of whom 5,189,401 or 4.13% were Jews.[10] In the Pale the Jews made up only 11.46% of the total population. This

10. Jewish Encyclopedia Vol. X, 1909, Jews, p. 529.

THE PALE

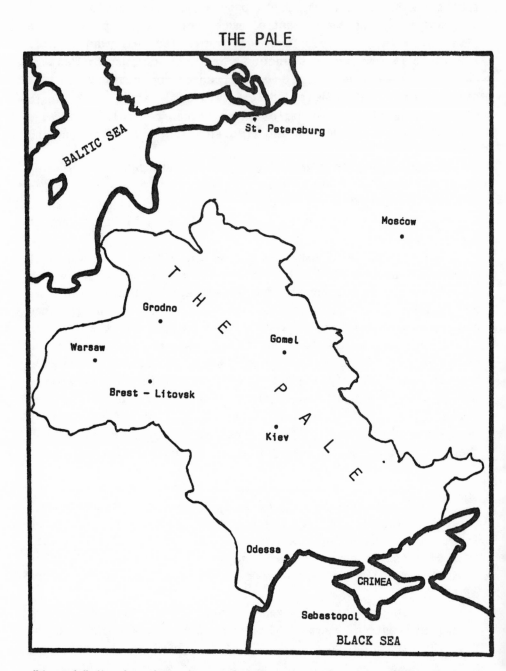

"The Pale" district of Russia occupied the same region as it did earlier when it was the independent nation of Khazaria. See earlier map of Khazaria p. 79. A map of The Pale may be found in the Jewish Encly. Vol X, 1909.

would at first glance seem to be a low population density by ordinary reckoning, but it is believed that the percentage had never been higher in the long history of Khazaria. The non-Jewish inhabitants of the land were descendants of the Slavic serfs of the ancient Khazarian overlords. Almost 94% of all Russian Jews lived in the Pale - only 6% outside.

Outside the Pale the Jews made up less than 1/2 of a percent of the population. This is the reason most Russians knew nothing about Jews. Most had never seen one.

On the map of "The Pale", you will notice the triangle made up of the three cities - Warsaw, Grodno, and Brest-Litovsk. In 1905 the heaviest concentration of Jews resided in this area. They made up about 20% of the population. The former Prime Minister of the Israeli state, Menachem (Wolfovitch) Begin, was born in Brest-Litovsk Aug. 16, 1913.

The area from Gomel in the center to Sebastapol in the south had the fewest, from 4%-5%. This low density was due to the Russian effort to resettle the Jews from this area. Most Ashkenazic Jews living in America came from this area. Cities such as Moscow and St. Petersburg had virtually no Jews at all.

Jews mate freely with their host countries. As a consequence the south Russian Jews tend to be dark complexioned from a preponderance of Turkish/Mongol blood, while the Polish Jews living in White Russia have fair complexions and eyes combined with a Slavic appearance. The Jews to the west of Warsaw often have a Nordic appearance. Many of these are indistinguishable from Westerners by appearance.

One of the "special laws" re-enacted at the request of the Poles prohibited foreign Jews from having right of residence or from buying land in the Pale. This restriction was passed to prevent the unbelievably wealthy Jewish Banking families residing in Western countries from buying up and monopolizing all the land in the Pale and excluding non-Jews from living there.

The Christian government of Russia had the greatest difficulty dealing with the closely knit bodies of Khazar Jews who reinforced their national identity with a different language and schools. The attempt to break up the groups living in cities failed. When banned from one city, like flocks of crows shooed from one forest, they regathered in the next. They formed new "kehilla" (local government) colonies in each city to which they were dispersed. Not only that, the Russians were amateurs in dealing with Khazarians, while the Khazarians were experts in dealing with Christians. Centuries of Christian restrictions had taught them to hate all Christian governments. As a consequence they were involved in every plot against the Tzar and his government. Every time an assassination took place or a bomb exploded, it was assumed that an Ashkenazic Jew was involved.[11]

The Russian solution to this turn of events was, as mentioned earlier, to force them out of the country. Millions left for America. The three waves of immigration to the U.S. are as follows:

1654 - 1840 Sephardic Jews - approximately 2,000.

1841 - 1880 German Ashkenazic.

1881 - 1920 Eastern European Ashkenazic.

The handful of early Sephardic immigrants to America came mostly from Portuguese and Spanish Jews who went first to Portuguese or Spanish colonies in South and Central America and then came to the United States.

The German wave was caused by German special taxes and quota laws enacted in the attempt to deal with the massive arrival of Polish Jews from the Chmielincki massacres in 1648, and then the German acquisition of Galatia from Poland in the late 1700s which brought with it a large complement of Jews. Rosenbloom also lists an additional factor, the failure of the liberal revolutions of 1830 and 1848.

Khazarian Economic Successes

Khazarian refugees fleeing the many invasions of their homeland formed colonies in virtually every city of the Western world. Their success in usury-banking gave them an immense advantage in all avenues of business.

Their Barons of usury-banking heaped riches upon riches. By 1730 more than 1/4 of all sugar plantations in Surinam were in

---

11. The National Geographic Magazine, May 1907, p. 310, Washington, D.C.

their hands. In the 1740s they began to control the Brazilian diamond trade. David de Pinto was the largest stockholder in the East India Company. In 1750 Tobias Boas was allowed by the states-general of Holland to share in a public loan for half of 1,000,000 gulden, and in another for half of 8,000,000. In 1793, Benjamin and Alexander Cohen participated in a 5,000,000 gulden Prussian loan. The Universal Jewish Encyclopedia p.432, calls them "the most outstanding Ashkenazim".

In the next century the foremost family banking house was easily that of the Rothschild family. By 1848 it is said of Nathan Rothschild that "while he lived the center of the finance of the world may said to have been his office in New Court,"[12] London. But control of unbelievably large amounts of money had been the Rothschild hallmark since the first of the century.

In the early 1800s Rothschild loans to the impoverished Austrian nobility totaled 24,521,000 gulden. The Austrian loan of 1815 was for 50,000,000 gulden. The French loan of 1816 totaled 350,000,000 francs. The Rothschilds had more money than most of the nations of Europe put together and nations were the only customers large enough to be worth their time and attention.

Partial List Of Rothschild Loans [13]

Year	Country	Amount	
1817	Prussia	1,500,000	gulden
1818	"	Ŀ5,000,000	
1819	Great Britain	Ŀ12,000,000	
1820	Austria	48,000,000	gulden
1820	Austria	20,000,000	"
1821	Austria	37,500,000	"
1821	Naples	16,000,000	ducats
1821	Sicily	4,500,000	"
1822	Prussia	Ŀ3,500,000	
1822	Russia	Ŀ3,500,000	
1822	Russia	Ŀ6,500,000	
1822	Naples	20,000,000	ducats
1823	Austria	Ŀ2,500,000	
1823	Austria	25,000,000	gulden
1823	France	23,000,000	francs
1824	Brazil	Ŀ3,500,000	
1824	Naples	Ŀ2,500,000	
1825	Duchy of Hesse	6,500,000	gulden

12. Jewish Encyclopedia, Vol X, 1909, p. 501.

13. J/E, Vol. X, 1909, p. 501.

1825	Brazil	£2,000,000
1829	Brazil	£800,000
1829	Brazil	25,000,000 gulden
1829	Hesse-Homburg	1,750,000 gulden
1829	Hohenzollern-Hech.	260,000 gulden
1830	Prussia	£4,500,000
1831	Belgium	50,000,000 francs
1831	Papal States	16,000,000 "
1832	Belgium	£2,000,000
1834	Austria	25,000,000 gulden
1834	Greece	66,000,000 francs
1834	Duchy of Hesse	6,500,000 gulden
1835	Britain	£15,000,000
1837	Duchy of Nassau	2,600,000 gulden
1839	Austria	30,000,000 "
1840	Duchy of Lucca	1,050,000 "
1840	Baden	5,000,000 "
1842	Austria	40,000,000 "
1843	Duchy of Lucca	1,120,000 "
1845	Papal States	2,160,000 francs
1845	Baden	14,000,000 gulden
1847	Irish Famine	£10,000,000
1847	France	250,000,000 francs
1847	Hanover	3,600,000 thaler
1848	Baden	2,500,000 gulden
1848	Bavaria	22,000,000 "
1848-51	Hesse (4-loans)	6,500,000 "

"In the year 1848 the Paris house was reckoned to be worth 600,000,000 francs as against 352,000,000 francs held by all the other Paris bankers."[14]

This quote indicates the importance of the Paris house of Rothschild alone, but the figures achieve true meaning when we remember that most of the remaining 352,000,000 was also held by other Ashkenazics. For all intents and purposes even at this early date, the entire finance of France was in the hands of the Paris Khazarian colony in exile. "The borrower is servant to the lender."

Interest At Work

So as not to forget the damage interest does in just a few years, look again at the table on the opposite page:

14. J/E, Vol. X, 1909, p. 496.

$1 at 7 1/2% Interest For 50 Years

$ 1	borrowed	
$ 1.44	owed in 5 years.	
$ 2.06	" " 10 "	
$ 2.95	15	
$ 4.23	20	
$ 6.08	25	
$ 8.73	30	
$12.53	35	
$17.99	40	
$25.82	45	
$37.08	50	

For each dollar borrowed, $37 must be repaid. Look at the nations that went into the "net"! The millions upon millions lent. Tens upon tens of millions had to be repaid for each million lent. By the 1840s the wealth of the Khazarian bankers was enough to stagger the mind.[*]

It is easy to see how that by the 1840s Europe was mostly mortgaged and servant to the Khazarian bankers. There was little else to be mortgaged that could enable debtors to borrow more money into existence. Consequently, it was time to "foreclose" mortgaged property from destitute borrowers, take possession, and sell it again to other debt-free borrowers.

Foreclosure

Karl Marx, son of a rabbi, was tapped to be the spokesman. He published the "Communist Manifesto" in 1848 to coincide with "The Revolution of 1848". The 1848 revolutions started in Sicily and almost instantly spread to Germany, France, Austria, Rumania, and the Papal States, exhibiting a remarkably high degree of coordination and planning.

The spark that ignited these revolutions initially sprang from old conflicts between poverty stricken workers and debt ridden owners: Czech, Hungarian, and Rumanian Slav nationalists vs. Western rulers; and political liberals vs. the old monarchists. Ashkenazics were active in every group in revolt with

[*] Just a single dollar lent in 1800 at 7 1/2% would by 1984 require a repayment of $255,044!

91

the established order.

These revolutions which swept across Europe were actively led and financed by thousands of Ashkenazic Jews who attempted to impose Ashkenazic solutions to Christian problems. They even furnished a few of the victims, which turned out to be a fortunate happening of which much was made later.

Most of the Christian problems had been brought about in the first place by the introduction of the Ashkenazic economic usury system in the West. The by-products were unemployment, lack of food and shelter which made necessary unemployment insurance, old age insurance, public education, etc. With more interest-created debts than money to pay, problems and solutions flourished.

When not active in the central leadership role as revolutionaries themselves, they supported and financed Western Slav nationalist groups. The Revolutions unsettled all the crowns of Europe, but only King Louis Philippe of France, the client of James Rothschild of Paris, was actually dethroned and his property seized. In Italy, the Pope fled for his life. The Russians moved their army into Rumania to put down the revolutions there.

Gradually order was restored. There was a frenzied attempt to disassociate European Ashkenazics from Karl Marx and communism by constant publicizing the fate of the few Ashkenazic victims. This bloody period, however, caused the entire Christian continent of Europe to become violently anti-communist. This in turn contributed to the migration.

Lastly, the failed communist revolution of 1848 caused such tight control and supervision of the European Khazarian colonies that the support of the large Ashkenazic bankers switched to activities back in the Pale.

The Russian Front

The new front became Russia. There was an outbreak of revolutionary activity resulting in bombings, assassinations and political agitation among the Jews and Slavs against the ruling Westerners. This wave of terror was met, as it had been earlier in Europe, by severe restrictions.

It culminated in the "Russian solution" of 1891-1892, with the expulsion of Jews from Moscow by order of Grand Duke Sergius, and from the interior of the country forcing Jews back into the

Pale. For all intents and purposes the Pale was an alien country in the midst of Russia, constantly patrolled by Russian armies and ruled by "friendly" appointees with the help of police.

Rather than return to the Pale most Ashkenazics living outside chose to emigrate from Russia entirely. This decision was encouraged by the Russian government. Thousands of shiploads of Khazarians set sail for America and elsewhere. The large Jewish migration took place between 1880 - 1920. They left, but they did not forget. The Askenazics formed colonies around their leaders in America and immediately turned their eyes back to their brothers in Russia.

Modern Finance

In 1905, Sergyei Nilus published a book in Russia called "The Protocols". The book purports to be the stolen plan of conquest made by the "300 elders" who rule the world. The Ashkenazics maintain that the book is a forgery.

This unwelcomed publicity resulted in a virtual blackout of information on Ashkenazic financial dealings. Things are now very secretive. While tables like that of the earlier Rothschild dealings in the 1800s were commonplace earlier as they boasted of their accomplishments, now a thundering silence accompanies most of their financial coups.

Certain things are common knowledge. The Ashkenazics monopolized usury banking in the Middle Ages since usury is forbidden to Christians. As early as the 1600s they had made servants of many of the rulers of Europe who were in their debt. By the first part of the 1800s they had a virtual monopoly of world finance so that entire nations who had adopted their usury system were their customers and servants. By the late 1800s they boasted of their princely bankers and their many titles. They backed their claims with proof.

The Rothschilds were one of the largest factors in the American real estate boom of the 1830s.[15] They were also one of the largest factors in financing the U.S. national debt of the 1860s.[16] Their operations in America have appeared low key since they have operated through agents under other names (see footnote

15. Robert Sobell, Panic On Wall Street, MacMillan, N.Y. , P. 42.

16. J/E, Vol. X, 1909, page 501.

page 95).

It is a well known fact that Paul Warburg of Germany came to America to set up the Federal Reserve System with the aid of a few associates. It is also a matter of general knowledge that the most important district of this Federal Reserve is the wealthiest; and that is the New York District.[17]

Exactly what is going on in the Federal Reserve is a dark secret. The banking organization is lender to the United States, is its master, and arrogantly flaunts the fact by refusing to allow itself to be audited by any "sovereign" state in the United States, or by the Federal Government.

Mullins' exhaustive research on the Federal Reserve sheds a great deal of light on the subject. On page 179 of his book "The Secrets Of The Federal Reserve", he uncovers the fact that as of July 26, 1983, the following banks owned 66% of the total outstanding shares of the F/R Bank of New York - the controlling district:

Ownership Of Shares Of The FR Bank Of N.Y.

Bankers Trust	6%
Bank of New York	2%
Chase Manhattan Bank	14%
Chemical Bank	8%
Citibank	15%
European Amer. Bk. & Tr.	2%
J. Henry Schroder Bk.	1/2%
Manufacturers Hanover	7%
Morgan Guaranty	9%
Nat. Bk of N.A.	2%

The above list seems innocuous enough. Opposite is another list which made the circuit a few years ago. This list was also given as being a list of the "true owners" of the Federal Reserve.

---

17. Eustace Mullins, The Secrets of the Federal Reserve, P.O. Box 1105, Staunton, Virginia 24401, p. 32.

VI - RUSSIA

Early List Of FR Bank Owners

1 - Rothschilds of London
2 - Lazard Brothers of Paris
3 - Israel Moses Seif of Italy
4 - Warburg Brothers of Hamburg, Germany
5 - Lehman Brothers of N.Y., USA
6 - Kuhn Loeb of N.Y., USA
7 - Chase Manhattan of N.Y., USA
8 - Goldman Sachs of N.Y., USA

This last list bears little resemblance to the first one. The chart* on the next page helps to bring the two lists into harmony by listing the New York banks that own a majority of the stock in the FR Bank of N. Y., and some of their connections.

National boundaries blur as we see that the actual owners of the FR are spread over Germany, England, and France, as well as the United States. All are parts of the whole.

A conclusion may be drawn from this. In spite of the lack of discussion on the subject, it is unrealistic to assume that the Ashkenazics and their agents are presently any less a world economic force than they were in earlier years.

Present Khazarian Population

The current Jewish world population is 14,396,000. The largest concentration of 5,860,000 reside in the US. The total increase in overall population is only +110 thousand over last year, less than 1% increase. Without converts they would soon cease to exist.

---

* The chart on the next page was compiled by Mullins and taken from p. 92 of his book "The Secrets of the Federal Reserve". The Rothschild name is not recognized in America since they operated through their agent - J. P. Morgan & Co. and others. Also printed in his book are several charts selected from a series of 75 such charts showing the connections of those who control the FR. They were presented in a study, by the House Committee on Banking, Currency, and Housing of the 94th Congress, 2nd session, August, 1976 "Federal Reserve Directors: A Study Of Corporate And Banking Influence." These charts have been in existence since 1976. The only reason their contents is not general information is because of the paper curtain thrown over the subject by the national media. An in-depth study of the FR showing the interlocking directorates of major American corporations, banks, and government, is outside the scope of this book. If you are interested in further study, please refer to the Mullins book mentioned in footnote #17.

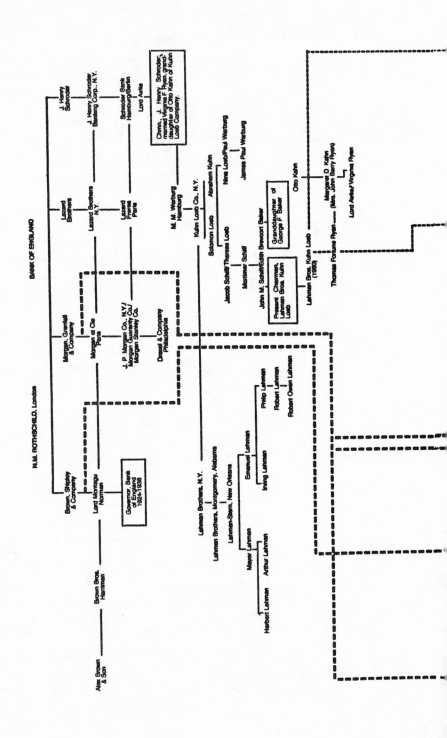

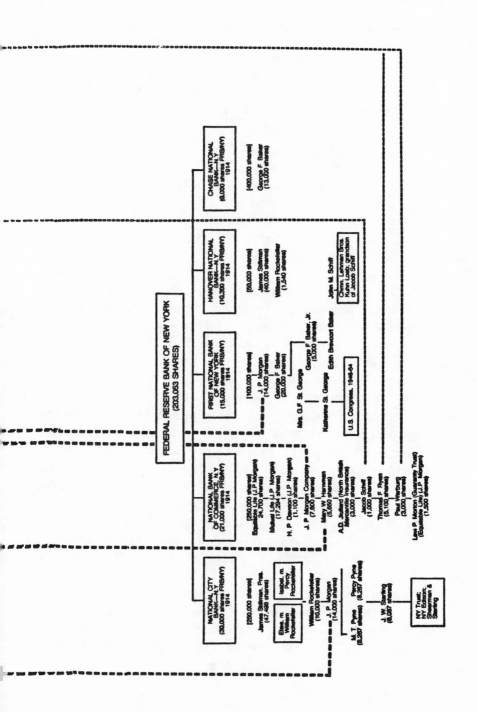

Location Of World Khazarian Population[18]

1,228,000	N. Y. City
1,998,000	Greater N. Y.
455,000	Los Angeles
295,000	Philadelphia
253,000	Chicago
225,000	Miami
272,000	Jerusalem
3,235,000	All of Palestine
2,660,000	USSR
650,000	France
410,000	Great Britain
305,000	Canada

Contention

For almost a thousand years there has been constant friction between Khazars - who call themselves Jews - and Christians. The starting point of contention is Law. The most abrasive subject is money. The Ashkenazics brought usury to the West. This gave them a tremendous advantage.

The Jewish Encyclopedia, subhead "England" p.162, notes that as early as 1168 before their expulsion from England the Jews' personal property was regarded as 1/4 that of the entire country.

Another quote from the same Jewish Encyclopedia, subhead "France" p.449, notes that in 1171, "The Jews...were then very numerous....many....come to sojourn in Paris; they had become enriched to the extent of owning nearly half of the city; they were engaged in usury; their patrons were often despoiled of their possession." In Spain it was charged that these people were the most powerful group monetarily and politically in the land.

This condition was and is true in other lands as well. As long as the widely scattered Khazarian colonies wield such power, there will be a never-ending series of charges of one sort or another brought against them. With their control of the media, however, they have learned to blunt and turn accusation against

18. Jewish Voice , p. 7, Jan. 1984

98

their enemies.

Among the first targets of their media were the Russian "pogroms". The Slavs of Russia and the rest of the world were alienated from the Russ of Russia by stories of Tzarist excesses. Right after WW II the Germans were accused of murdering 41 million people in death camps.

The first figure of 41 million deaths reported by their media was found to be untrue - so were the intervening 28 million, 12 million, and on down to 8 million, all of which totals were too fantastic to be believed. Now all totals have been quietly dropped except the one about 6 million Jews. There is a reason to keep this figure alive.

In 1933 only 580,000 Jews lived in pre-war Germany. Most of these migrated to other lands with large numbers coming to America. Still, the Germans are charged with killing 6 million. The evidence found in Western Germany does not support the charges, and so the search went to Eastern Europe to find evidence. The evidence that has thus far been discovered in the Eastern zone implicates the Soviets - not the Germans. It is the Poles who were the victims - not the Jews. The Katyn Forest massacre of Polish army officers was first blamed on the Germans but was found to have been a Soviet atrocity. Since then there has been a great reluctance by the Soviets to allow further investigations in their sector. Solzhenitsyn states in his books that the death camps in the Soviet sphere have from the beginning been the creation of the Soviet state and operated by Stalin and his successors.

To embarrass further the Jewish media, The Institute for Historical Review[19] offered to award $50,000 to anyone bringing proof, which would stand in a court of law, that "gas chambers for the purpose of killing human beings existed at or in Auschwitz Concentration Camp during World War II". The offer remained open from April to December 1982. During that period not one serious attempt was made to collect the money. With hundreds of thousands of first-hand witnesses who claimed to have been actual inmates of the camps and who now live in every city of the world drawing reparations and hardship checks from Germany it would seem that it wouldn't be difficult to gather the necessary proof

19. The Institute for Historical Review, P.O. Box 1306, Torrance, Calif. 90505

- if such proof exists.

There may be another explanation for the perpetual "holocaust" theme. The book, "West German Reparations", discloses that between the years 1946 - 1978, the Germans were forced to pay the Israeli nation many billions of dollars. This is in addition to reparations which are paid to each camp inmate. If the Israelis were deprived of this enormous flow of tribute money, there is reason to believe that their country would be in serious difficulty. In other words, their media has been placed in a position where it MUST harp on the "holocaust" theme if the Israeli nation is to continue to receive its payments from Germany. The German government, which owes its existence to Germany's conquerors, does not permit open discussion of the so-called holocaust subject in Germany. Publicly expressed doubt lands the doubter in prison. An open discussion would tend to implicate the Soviets in the overall subject of "death camps" and result in tribute termination, as well as indignant demands for its return.

It is easy to see that it is far cheaper to continue the 40 year-old weekly TV charge of "holocaust" against the Christians of Germany than return the money. The "reruns" cost only a few million a year. The return would result in billions. It's good business! Incidentally, the Institute for Historical Research was firebombed and burned to the ground in July 1984. Where money is involved - tempers grow hot.

*   *   *   *   *

Every nation and region of the West has endured these kinds of attacks at one time or another - the Germans are only the most recent victims. This will doubtless ensure that the centuries-old friction will continue.

Interbreeding

There is also another point which is receiving increasing attention. As early as the 9th century there was contact between the Sephardic Jews of Spain and Ashkenazic Jews of Khazaria. Later the royal family of Khazaria fled to Spain. The overwhelming majority of the Jewish population in the rest of Europe is composed of Ashkenazic refugees from the many invasions of the ancient nation of Khazaria, their original homeland. A Jew today is a composite of many races. Their Talmud places restrictions on inter-FAITH marriages, but none on inter-RACIAL marriage. That is why there are black Jews, Chinese Jews, Slavic Jews, South American mixed-race Jews, and blue-eyed blond-haired Jews. The Christian religion is the only religion that prohibits both inter-faith and inter-racial marriage.[20]

Unlike the Jews, Westerners who are of "Israel", "Isaacsons" - "Saxons", are all of the same race and look alike regardless of which country they live.... Their opposition to racial intermarriage with strangers (zûwr) is felt by the Jews to be a source of danger [21] to them because their extremely low birthrate has forced them actively to seek converts among the progeny of mixed marriages. If mixed-marriages were stopped, the Jews would soon become few in number.

Who Rules The USSR

There is debate as to whether or not the Russian Ashkenazic Jews still wield the same power they held at the end of the Russian Revolution.[22] Some say that the Russian Slavs have recouped much of the power. The fact is that the Jews are practically the only ones allowed to travel to and from the USSR. The recent visible head of the government, Andropov, was a Jew, and the Slavic "samaritan" version of the Christian religion - the one practiced for almost 1000 years - is suppressed. These events would be unlikely if Russia were ruled by Slavs.

In any event the argument appears irrelevant since "The

---

20. Deu 23:2

21. "Studies show that at least 40 percent of Jews marry outside the faith. In Western cities, the rate may be as high as 60% . . . some leaders...now see this trend as having the potential to enlarge their community. Studies show that 7 out of 10 children in mixed marriages are raised as Jews. . . Under ancient law, the child of a Jewish mother and non-Jewish father is a member of the faith, but the child of a Jewish father and a gentile mother is not. Increasingly, non-Jews who marry Jews are converting to the faith." U.S. News & World Report p. 44, Apr. 4, 1983.

22. Max I. Dimont in "The Jews In America", p. 151 states that early in this century the Jews split ideologically. The Religious ones such as Weizman, Ben-Gurian, and Jabotinsky became "Zionists" and the non-religious ones such as Trotsky, Litvinov, and Kaganovich became "Communists".

Note: The Law was placed in the heart of Israel. The Law against racial interbreeding is universally known. The absence of outrage at the sight of interracial couples is taken to be one of the identifying marks of a "Marano" (See page 55).

borrower is servant to the lender" and the Gosbank of the USSR has borrowed heavily from the banks of Europe. According to law this has made the entire country of the USSR servant to them. These European banks were re-established at the end of WW II under the watchful eye and control of the banks of our Federal Reserve. Our Federal Reserve was initially established by agents of these very same European banks. Thus, the banks of the Federal Reserve indirectly control the Gosbank which in turn controls the USSR. The System - the Babylonian system of lending 10 for 11 - rules them all.

Chapter 20

RUSSIA & THE COMMUNE

The nation of Russia developed long after Khazaria and must be studied apart from Khazaria since it has only been in recent centuries that the two nations came into prolonged and abrasive contact.

The Russ

For hundreds of years the Russ of Scandinavia and their kinsmen traded and conquered on the rivers of Russia. They would sail the rivers from the Baltic in the northwest until they reached a point in the interior of Russia where they would beach their dragon ships. Placing them on wheels they would have oxen drag them a relatively short distance to another Russian river flowing in the opposite direction. Launching their ships again they sailed two thousand miles until they reached the Black Sea. It saved the long dangerous trip down the Atlantic, around Spain, and through the Mediterranean.

Many trading posts were founded the length of the route. These Russ conquered the native Slavs instead of killing them or driving them away, and thus was born the nation of Russia, a combination of Russ master and Slav worker. Cemeteries in Moscow show a progressive broadening of skulls as racial interbreeding progressed down through the centuries[23]. At the end, there was only the Tzar and a thin veneer of Nordic Russ aristocracy left. This was swamped in the bloody wave of the Russian Revolution.

It has been estimated that 20-30 million Westerners were

---

23. Lothrop Stoddard, The Rising Tide Of Color, Noontide Press, P. O. Box 1248, Torrance, California 90505.

exterminated by the Slavs and Ashkenazics during and after the takeover. These deaths were accounted for by blaming them on the Germans in World War II. At the end of World War II additional Nordic settlements were banished from Russia. Millions more were herded into Gulags to die. There still remain a few of our people in Russia and great numbers of mixed-breeds. Since the land was no longer "the land of the Russ", "Russia", the name was changed to "Union of Soviet Socialist Republics".

The old religion was the Christian Eastern Orthodox with the Tzar as ruler and head of the Church. As is always the case, the Christian message passed from the Tzar and his priests through the "Slav filter" and came out "Samaritan". There was little resemblance between the Christian religion practiced at the Tzar's court and that practiced in the distant Slav villages. The Samaritan religion of the villages was a composite of old Slavic beliefs in elves, fairies, and magic in a "Christian" wrapper.

Russia is a land of few natural boundaries. There was

Note: The word "Slav" is Latin for "slave". The Romans captured these people for slaves and gave them their name. Later, the Vikings and Russ enslaved them to sell to the Saracens. Still later the Teutonic knights captured them to sell to ready Islamic buyers who prized them because they made excellent slave warriors. Islamic raiders also preyed on them. The Mongols overran their land and ruled it with the help of Tatars and Khazars for centuries - and incidentally gave many of the Slavs a distinctly oriental look. In spite of their warlike qualities, and their obvious genius in many fields, their quarreling, moodiness, drunkenness, and general lack of self restraint has prevented the Slavs from being able to form a Slav country unaided. Wherever one finds a Slav country, a close examination will uncover another race at the head of the government. For protection they have always placed themselves under an overlord. Poland was no exception. The Polish aristocracy contained large numbers of Westerners who were encouraged to migrate to that country. The traditional overlord of Russia has been the "Russ" of Sweden. The Russ became the Russian aristocracy. They were a different race from the Slavs they ruled.

Unlike European Westerners, American Westerners have almost no experience with Slavs. Their coloring can be deceptive, often being identical to that of the Westerner. Their usual mark of identification is the shape of their skulls which around the hat band can be almost completely round. This compares to the Western skull type which is longer from front to back. Some, like Khrushchev have very long arms in proportion to their legs, no visible waist, and almost no visible neck.

Their own legends say that all Slavs descend from three brothers - Chech, Liakh (Pole), and Rus. Practically, there are three different branches of Slavs. The Southern (Greek, Bulgarian, Yugoslav, etc.), Central (Czechoslovakian, etc), and Northern - (Pole, Great Russian, etc.). Their original homeland is unknown, but is presumed by many to be the Pripet Marshes. All different branches are the result of mixing with other races. The "northern blondness" combined with round skull type is presumed to have resulted from mixture with Westerners; the "slant eyes" of many come from the Mongols; the "dark skin" of others - from the Turks. The Poles are split from other Slavs by religion. They are Roman Catholic. The others are Eastern Orthodox. There has never been any love lost between the two.

nothing to stop the Mongols when they swept in from the East. The Mongols had only 4,000 of their own people and so they conscripted Turks and Khazars into their forces. The Tartars and Khazars ruled the land of Russ and collected taxes in the name of the "Golden Horde". Over the centuries these invaders were pushed back. This long subjection is the reason the Soviet Slavs hate the Turks to this day, as well as distrusting the Tartars living within their borders. It is also the reason for the high feeling of the Slavs against the Khazars. The Khazarian Jews tread a very cautious path among the people they once ruled harshly in their own name and later in the name of the Mongols.

The political state which developed while pushing out the Tartars resulted from the knowledge that Russia's only wall of defense is the people themselves. As land was regained, the Tzar would grant that land to one of his nobles. The noble must be able to get enough "serfs", or serving people, to occupy the land, work it, and defend it...thus the desperate need for Slav workers. If ever an estate stopped serving the needs of the Tzar, that estate would revert back to him. The noble owned his land in the sense that he could will it to an heir, but he was bound to give service. If a woman were an heir, she must take a husband to serve the ruler.

The Tzar taxed the land to raise money for defense. The nobles in turn taxed the serfs. Frequent crop failures often forced the peasants to go into debt for taxes, rent, seed, and even food to live on. These debts continued to mount. In time these debts became so heavy that many of the peasants sold themselves into slavery to cancel their debts and get themselves off the tax rolls. Slaves lived better than free men.

At other times the peasants fled the estates seeking to escape the burden of debt forced upon them. They would flee to the new estates on the ever-expanding Russian frontier. This caused conflict between the old and new nobility because this flight of serfs from the old areas concentrated debt on those remaining. If nobles and peasants on the estates had difficulties paying their taxes and debts before the flight of some of their number, they had an impossible job with them gone. After a time the Russ nobles passed a law which prohibited the Slav serfs from leaving the land and getting off the tax rolls. The courts authorized the return of runaways to prevent the entire political and economic system from breaking down. This is the identical thing that had happened earlier in Rome.

By the beginning of the 1600s the larger part of the peasantry were slaves or near slaves. It was in this way the nation of Russia sought to ensure that its taxes would be paid, that there would be sufficient workers, and that there would be sufficient fighting men if and when the need arose. It is important to remember that the state needed defense money whether or not the landholding noble was having difficulty keeping workers. The noble had to pay taxes even if his peasants were gone.

Periodically there were tax revolts against the Tzar. The most noted was that of Pugachev in 1773 when 30,000 Slavs revolted to show their discontent - a prelude to what was to happen 146 years later. Just before our Revolutionary War in America about 40% of the peasants belonged to the Tzar. Almost 80% of the population lived in bondage. This gives an indication of the racial breakdown of the nation.

The great blow to serfdom was the defeat suffered by Russia in the Crimean War of 1854-1856. The system of "Tzar-nobles-serfs" all combined for the defense of "little mother Russia" broke down. Theoretically the nobles were to raise their regiments, arm and clothe them, and lead them into battle. The Russian regiments facing the allies in the Crimea were of this kind. They were personal property of their officers. When a Russian regiment was shot to pieces in service of the Tzar, the commanding noble was economically ruined, if he survived. He had no one left to work his estates and consequently could not pay the taxes. His lands could be taken from him. Many other nobles were so deeply in debt in the effort to pay taxes that they could only raise regiments but not arm or clothe them. Other nobles, fearing that their regiments would be shot up and that they would suffer financial loss, dawdled en route to the battlefields. The only system that Russia had ever known was outdated.

Five years later the serfs were freed. The great reforms of 1861 allocated them land. It was not a gift. The Tzars took their jobs very conscientiously as head of the Christian Church in Russia. As a natural consequence the "Year of Jubilee" Law was invoked. This Christian Law orders that all debts be paid or forgiven every 7 years and that land be returned to its true owners every 50th year. While debts were not forgiven, the serfs were given 49 years to pay for their land so that when the 50th year arrived the land would be free from debt. The plan was to have the peasants owning their own land by 1910. The state collected the payments, which in turn paid the former land owners who in turn could pay their own debts.

The obligation for the payments was placed upon the entire peasant population of an estate commune. This method of working off debt had been customary for the past several hundred years. The commune itself rather than the individual peasants was given the land to manage and to allocate among its members. The hopes and expectations of the Slavic peasants knew no bounds.

The System Brings On Revolution

Commodity prices peaked world wide in 1864. What were reasonable prices for land in 1864 became unreasonably high prices as land and commodity prices collapsed into the great worldwide depression which did not bottom until 1896. The deeper the depression went, the lower the price received for farm produce. The less the income, the more the peasants fell behind in payment for their land. The great hopes of 1861 faded into sullen belligerency in 1896.

Not all Russian peasants were in bad condition by any means. By 1905 Lenin estimated that 10,500,000 peasants had small holdings that were relatively prosperous. Over a million had prosperous farms averaging 40 acres each. This is not much by American standards, but by Russian standards it was head and shoulders above the bare subsistence level endured by most Russian peasants. These advances, however, were not sufficient to satisfy the great masses when confronted with increased taxes stemming from the unsuccessful Russo-Japanese War[24] of 1904-1905. The peasants and communes, finding it impossible to pay interest, current taxes, land payments and rents, still had to find enough to feed their families. They revolted when the cost of the war was added. This was the "Revolt of 1905".

The land situation in Russia at this time was as follows: The Tzar, who was the government, was the most extensive landowner as is the case in all nations. The Church was next larg-

24. The News Of The New World, January 1984, p. 23, P.O. Box 830, Honeydew 2040. S.A. $12/yr. refers to Jacob H. Schiff, of the Wall St. Bank of Kuhn Loeb & Co. by saying, "Schiff personally had taken a close interest in promoting the revolutionary movement in Tzarist Russia from the days of the Russo-Japanese war which he financed for Japan."

est. As in other lands, the devout through the generations had willed their lands to the Church. Unlike the marshes, woods, and steppes which comprised most of the Tzar's land, Church land was mostly prime acreage. The remainder of the land was owned half by nobles and half by peasants. "The Great Emancipation of 1861" with the plan for land ownership free of debt by 1910 set the stage for the Bolshevik Revolution in 1918. What started as a generous idealistic gesture turned out to be a nightmare as land and commodity prices tumbled lower and lower. There was no way most peasants were going to get their land.

The Tzar, who was the government, owed exorbitant loans to the European Khazarian bankers.[25] There was abundant collateral but there was no way to foreclose. While it is true that "the borrower is servant to the lender", the problem of the creditors foreclosing can be difficult, especially when the debtor has an army and the creditor has none. The Tzar, the Church, and the nobility certainly were not going to give up easily their possessions to satisfy their Ashkenazic creditors. They would fight first.

Road To Revolution

The Commune developed naturally through the years as taxes were levied on lands. The holders of the lands divided the responsibility among the workers in the form of "production quotas". This system of ownership was common in ancient Rome and is natural to Russia and her many different races. For generations they have been conditioned to think in collective terms.

Russia has always been a complex land with over 25 different races, each selfishly clamoring for its own wants. As noted earlier, this conglomerate was in the beginning ruled by descendants of the Nordic Russ who reinforced their blood line by marriages with other Westerners. The large minorities such as the Poles, Cossacks, Georgians and Khazarian Jews were rebellious at times.

The Poles were always trying to break away and re-establish Poland, the one-time giant of eastern Europe. They could not

---

25. Lionel Nathan de Rothschild raised Ł 16,000,000 for England to fight Russia in 1854, and for 20 years he was also the agent of the Russian government. Lending to both sides is considered proper insurance to the survival of the System and the lender. Whichever country wins is the right one. Since the "borrower is slave," the lender to both sides will survive perpetually while the borrowing nation's chance of winning a war is seldom much more than 50/50.

care less who ruled Russia after their own independence was established.

The Cossacks were of the same race as the Russ but were broken into 11 different groups and were too fragmented to be a viable political force. Georgia was talking about breaking away and re-establishing her own country.

Then there was the land of Khazaria. Her Ashkenazic Jews were scattered throughout the Pale and colonies abroad but were still united by language and religion. This group had the choice of being taken over and ruled by yet another conqueror or taking over the rule themselves. A choice of being ruler or being ruled is no choice at all. The Jews went for the top post. This left the perpetually rebellious and contentious masses of Slavs to split their loyalty between Khazarian revolutionists, who were their ancient rulers, and their more recent rulers, the Russ, led by the Tzar.

The fragmentation of the Russian Empire appeared to be just a matter of time. The Russo-Japanese War had been a fiasco for Russia. Tzar Nicholas II had no choice. To have an excuse to borrow money quickly into existence to avert revolution at home required the mobilization of his army. He knew that his Christian cousin, the German Kaiser, had warned him that a Russian mobilization would be looked upon as an act of war. Still, he had to have an excuse to borrow money into existence to help curtail the suffering of his country and deflect the blame for the land distribution failure, the unemployment, and the bankruptcy from himself, and at the same time keep his own creditors at bay. In 1914 he gave the order for mobilization. Germany immediately declared war. New money was rapidly borrowed into existence to pay for the mobilization. For a moment, Russia breathed a sigh of relief as money again flowed and debts were paid.

Reality quickly replaced the euphoria caused by the flow of this new money. Russia was faced by the German army, the finest army in the world. The Russian army facing them was big, but not nearly big enough to deal with the Germans. In desperation Russian Slavic peasants were mobilized, marched to railroads, loaded into cattle cars by the hundreds of thousands and shipped to the front. There they were pointed in the direction of the enemy and given orders to advance. Many of them had no guns but

were ordered to advance anyway. If possible, they were to pick
up a weapon from a dead comrade. Food and supply services were
often primitive, and in many cases, non-existent. Medical attention was scarce. These Russian levies sometimes found themselves
in the awkward position of winning a battle while starving. More
men were lost to minor wounds and sickness than to direct enemy
action.

The day arrived when the armies suffered a reverse. Large
numbers of disillusioned peasant soldiers deserted, killed their
Nordic-Russ officers who were also their landlords, and started
home. They were followed by others. The Russian fronts col-
apsed. On March 15, 1917, Tzar Nicholas' train was stopped, and
he was told that his government was ended.

Chapter 21

THE BIRTH OF THE USSR

Russia had fallen. It was time to take over from the Slav
"liberals" who had been helped to start the work and finish the
job of foreclosing. The financiers made their next move. The
new borrower would soon have vast collateral to mortgage. To
guarantee that the loans to this new government would not mis-
carry, the lenders sent their own people.

"....Trotsky arrived from the United States followed by
over 300 Jews from the East End of New York and joined up
with the Bolshevik Party." (The Surrender of an Empire,
Nesta H. Webster, Boswell Printing, 10 Essex Street,
London, W.C. 2, 1931, p.73).

"Individual revolutionary leaders of Jewish origin - such
as Trotsky, Zinoniev, Kamanev, and Sverlov - played a
conspicuous part in the revolution of November, 1917
which enabled the Bolshevists to take possession of the
state apparatus." (Univ. Jew. Ency. Vol. IX, p. 668).

"The White Armies which opposed the Bolshevik government
linked Jews and Bolsheviks as common enemies." (Univ.

Jew. Ency., Vol. I, p. 336).

The London Times correspondent, Robert Wilton, reported:
"out of 556 important functionaries of the Bolshevik
State...there were in 1918-1919, 17 Russian, 2 Ukrain-
ians, 11 Armenians, 35 Letts, 15 Germans, 1 Hungarian, 10
Georgians, 3 Poles, 3 Finns, 1 Karaim, 457 Jews," (The
Mystical Body of Christ in the Modern World, Brown &
Nolan, Ltd., Waterford Dublin, Belfast, Cork, London,
1939, 1947 3rd Edition, Forward, Rev. Denis Fahey).

U.S. Document No. 62 of the 66th Congress Vol. III, gives
slightly different figures. It states that of 388 members of the communist government meeting in Petrograd,
Russia in 1918 - 16 were Russian, 1 an American Negro,
and 371 Jews. Of these 371 no less than 265 were believed to have been Ashkenazic Jews from America.

"Mr. Bakhmetiev, the late Russian Imperial Ambassador to
the United States, tells us that the Bolsheviks, after
victory, transferred 600 million rubles in gold between
the years 1918 and 1922, to Kuhn, Loeb, and Company," a
New York firm (A. Goulevitch: Czarism and Revolution,
p.225).

The foreclosure was successful. The new borrowers turned
over old mortgaged property to the banks and pledged newly confiscated property to raise new money. The American and British governments at the command of their financial masters sent
armies to the USSR to keep watch over mortgaged properties marked
for foreclosure. Once sufficient guarantees were received that
the revolutionists would not welsh on old contracts, the American
and British armies were called home.

The Khazarian minorities were exultant as can be attested by
the newspaper stories of that period. They had pulled off a
masterful stroke. In the land which had closely regulated them
for centuries, they had taken over the banking system in toto,
caused the Russ-Nordic nobility to be exiled or killed, had
Christianity banned, and had their courts outlaw "Anti-Semitism"
as a safety measure. They had become "the most recent" master of

the Slav. After 901 years, the Khazarian kingdom had been born again and now stretched over eastern Europe and northern Asia.

Regicide is a necessary part of usury. If the Tzar or any of his family came back into power, loans to the New York and London banks could be repudiated. As an unfortunate business necessity a former business client, the Tzar and his family, were shot.

The Tzar had also been head of the Christian Church in Russia. His execution took care of who owned the vast holdings of Church lands. They were confiscated for use as collateral by the state. There was no one now left alive who could put in a legitimate counter-claim.

Just Business

The bankers of England and France proceeded to foreclose the German, Austrian, and Turkish empires conquered in World War I.

Paul Warburg, founder of the American Federal Reserve System, was one of the American peace delegates at Versailles. At this conference he met his brother, Max, head of the German Secret Service and also a peace delegate from Germany. It was under Max's watchful eye that a sealed German train transported the communist revolutionary, Nicolai Lenin, from Switzerland across Germany to Russia while the war was going on. It was a regular family reunion. The Warburg family banks had financed the Kaiser. The Kaiser had been also financed by the Schroder Bank of Hamburg/Berlin. F. C. Tiarks, a partner of J. Henry Schroder, was a director of the Bank of England. Schroder financed England during the war. Schroder also had branches in the United States.[26]

Benjamin Freedman disclosed[27] that he was one of 117 Zionist delegates headed by Bernard Baruch at the peace conference whose job it was to claim Palestine from Britain in return for bringing America into the war on Britain's side. It also turned out that a large number of the leaders of the communist revolts that had brought Germany to her knees - and forced her to sue for peace -

---

26. Mullins, p. 92.

27. Speech, Tape No 71, Kingdom Cassette Service, Box 830, Honey Dew 2040, S. A., $10/yr.

were Ashkanazics. Germany was completely flabbergasted at this overwhelming Khazarian political presence in her politics.

It wasn't all one sided by any means. The story of Sir Ernest Joseph Cassel (1842-1921) also came out. This financier left Germany for England where he set up business. He founded the National Bank of Turkey which had helped finance Turkey's war against England. He also consolidated Vickers-Armstrong, the British munitions manufacturer. Vickers had completed the fortifications of the Dardanelles for the Turkish Government in July 1914. The next year British soldiers, also armed by Vickers, suffered a bloodbath of almost 100,000 casualties attacking these same Vickers-built Turkish fortifications.

Each new country created by the victors became a new borrower and was required to borrow fresh new money into existence from its conqueror to pay tribute. This helped bring about a spate of prosperity after the war.

Slavic Poland was re-created after having disappeared for almost a century and a half. They were allowed to borrow money into existence to buy arms. In 1920 they went off in full cry after their ancient enemies, the Khazarians, now called Bolsheviks. If the Poles smashed the Reds, the newly negotiated loans with the New York and London banks would be endangered.

The Poles were within 40 kilometers of Moscow and enjoying amazing success when Khazarian led trade unions in England and France went on strike to prevent further supplies reaching the Polish armies. The Poles, a flicker away from victory, were forced to retire for lack of supplies.

These loans to the USSR continued safe and profitable until Adolph Hitler again went after the Bolsheviks in World War II. The bankers had to bring America into the war to prevent again the conquest of Russia and the repudiation of the loans.

Khazaria has come a long way. Managing to survive after all these years is perhaps their most impressive feat. Furthermore, their movement into European banking by small colonies of usury bankers has been crowned by unbelievable success. Finally their successful move to America and the harnessing of its power has made them the premiere force of the entire world.

Consolidation

With the rise of the Bolsheviks all Russ-Nordic land reforms immediately ceased. The land the Tzar had distributed to the Slav peasants was seized. The peasants who resisted were shot.

Except for a few small independent farms which produce most of the food in the Soviet Union, the country has in many ways gone back to the serf system of the 1600s. There is still very little freedom of expression or travel. There can't be - and still have "the few" rule "the many". The Soviet "Commune System" is the same as it has always been. It is the only thing the land has known for hundreds of years. In spite of its drawbacks it is something everyone understands.

The present government has taken the place of the Tzar and his court. Political propagandists have taken the place of "Christian" priests. Powerful "commissars" have replaced the large land owning nobles and often live in their old palaces. Low profile private enterprise multi-millionaires proliferate as before the revolution.[28] All the while the great mass of the Slav peasants in many cases are working the same land their fathers tilled 300 years ago. Tractors, electric lights, and airplanes are the main difference, and this is just in the field of technics. The "production quotas" are the same.

The Noose

The men who formed the present government of the USSR were the representatives of those who for centuries had ruled the kings, presidents, and governments of the West through the power of the purse. While not wise they were highly educated and shrewd. They well knew how the prohibition of usury and debt in the Christian West in earlier years had hurt them and benefited Westerners. The lesson was not forgotten.

This land of the Russ that they had first ruled as Khazaria, and again as the Tartar-Khazarian tax collectors of the Mongols, had for the third time been returned to their rule. Now, in the role of ruler, they naturally set up an economic system most advantageous to themselves. For their new state, they reinstituted the "tally system".

The new Soviet government was given the power to issue

28. USSR, The Corrupt Society, Simon & Schuster, N. Konstantin M. Simis, 1982.

rubles in any amount, at any time they chose, and tax them out of existence again, leaving no debt as a bad aftertaste.

What use would it be for the USSR to copy the Tzarist system and the United States system of borrowing from and owing the Rothschild banks? Russia had been conquered. It had been foreclosed. What was needed now was a simple workable system that would not cause trouble later on. Today, Western governments are deeply in debt to the international bankers. Each day that goes by this debt grows larger and larger. If the Soviets do nothing but encourage the West to borrow increasing amounts of money for defense and giveaways, in time this load of debt will inevitably grow to the point that it will strangle the West. They will be unable to raise and equip armies to defend themselves because of this debt.

All the while, the government of the Soviets owes nothing. When they need a dam, a merchant fleet, or a manufacturing plant, they simply issue rubles to pay for the expenditure and then tax them out of existence again. The internal debt of the Soviet government is - nothing!

For The Slav

In the Soviet Union freedom from debt is one more government monopoly. For the Slavs the economic life is the same. They are in debt for refrigerators, cars, furniture, and are servants to their usury banks.

The banking system which owns this debt is now the "Gosbank", the Soviet copy of a Western central banking system. It issues interest-free money for government expenditures, but at the same time, its method of lending 10 rubles for 11 to private citizens is exactly the same as in pre-revolution Russia. Its effect on the people is also the same.

The Gosbank is debt free within the USSR. It, however, owes the banks of Europe tens of billions of dollars.

Since the Gosbank is borrower from the banks of Europe, according to God's Law they are "servants".

The borrower is slave to the lender. Prov. 22:7

As servants, they can only do what they are ordered to do. The ones doing the lending reside in New York and London. The Gosbank receives its orders from the lenders who are now headquartered in New York and London.

This is the reason the Soviet Union suffers no reverses. The Slavs of the USSR have become the "Slav horse" which is used by the international banks to foreclose debt-ridden borrowers the world over who can no longer produce interest to pay on their loans.

The Ashkenazics

Christians point to the fact that Israel's ex-leader, Begin, is an Ashkenazic Jew, as is Gus Hall, the secretary of the Communist Party USA, Karl Marx, the so-called "spokesman" of communism, as well as the illustrious Rothschild family. Everywhere one looks one finds Ashkenazic Jews in government, in business, on TV, everywhere. Christians then point to Genesis 10:1-4 to explain this phenomenon:

"Now these are the generations of the sons of Noah; Shem Ham, and Japeth...The sons of Japeth; Gomer...and the sons of Gomer; ASHKENAZ."

ASHKENAZ IS THE SON OF GOMER. In Ezekiel 38:4-16 God says;

"...I will bring thee forth, and all thine army...Gomer and all his bands...the house of Togarmah...In that day when my people of Israel dwelleth safely...thou shalt come from thy place out of the north parts...and thou shalt come up against my people of Israel.."

The descendants of Khazar, the 7th son of Togarmah, along with the Ashkenazic part of Gomer, came down from the north and first prepared the way with their financiers and merchants. Now they have massively invaded, occupied, and rule the kings and lands of Christian Israel in the West as well as the lands promised to Christian Israel in the Holy Land. Christians read the scriptures and tremble. The thing that God warned would happen in the last days has come to pass. ASHKENAZ, the son of GOMER is here!

Note: There is much confusion over the ownership of the land of old Israel in the Near East. God made a covenant with Abram (Gen. 15:18-21), to give his seed the land "from the river of Egypt (Nile) unto the great river, the river Euphrates." The only seed born to Abram while he had that name was Ishmael (Gen. 16). The present descendants of Ishmael living in that area base their claim on this promise.

Abram's name was then changed to Abraham (Gen. 17:5) and he fathered Isaac, who fathered Jacob, whose name was changed to "Israel" (Gen. 32:28). The children of Israel were then given Canaanland, a small portion of that larger land grant, but only on a conditional promise, i. e. they had to obey God's Laws, Statutes and Judgments, or they would lose the land. The promise of the larger area to the Ishmaelites was unconditional and so could not be lost.

The Israelites disobeyed, lost their claim to Canaanland, and were driven out, first to Assyria and then to Babylon. Although a tiny remnant returned under Nehemiah to rebuild Jerusalem, they never again occupied all of Canaanland. Finally, all Israelites were driven out of even that small area of Palestine by persecution a few years after Jesus' death and resurrection. A thousand years later the united effort of the entire West during the Crusades was unable to secure this land for much more than a few generations. The feeble ownership effort by the British between WW I and WW II was easily broken.

The Khazars, who call themselves Jews because of their religion, now claim this land from the Ishmaelites. This was prophesied in Ezekiel 36:2 "Thus saith the Lord God; Because the enemy hath said against you, Aha, even the ancient high places are ours in possession." That "enemy" is given a name in verse 5, "Idumea," meaning Edom. Edom means "red", so reds would take possession of "the ancient high places" in the old land of Israel while Israel would multiply in other lands to fulfill numbers "as the stars of heaven, and as the sand which is upon the sea shore." (Gen. 22:17). The Khazarian claim is not by covenant but by force. It was prophesied. All that is presently happening is working out precisely as written.

SECTION - VII
USURY COMES TO AMERICA

Chapter 22

CAPTAIN JOHN SMITH

John Smith was born on a farm in England. Seeking adventure he journeyed to Vienna and joined a company of cavalry fighting the Turks. His natural talents as a soldier were early recognized and he was promoted to captain of a company of 250 men. At that time the Christian armies were fighting the Mohammedan armies at the very gates of Vienna in the heart of Europe.

The champion fighter of all the Turkish armies challenged the champion of the Christian armies to single combat. Smith was chosen to represent the Christians.

Meeting on level ground, the two champions spurred their horses at each other, Smith's lance passed through the head of his Saracen opponent. Quickly severing the Turk's head, he rode from the battlefield with the grisly trophy held high on the point of his lance.

The next day another challenge was made by the second best Saracen champion. Smith met the new challenger on the same ground. Spears were broken on the first pass. Smith then drew his pistol and fired, breaking the rein arm of the Turk which caused his horse to lurch, throwing him from the saddle. Smith quickly dispatched him, and for a second time carried the head of his opponent from the battlefield.

The third day yet another challenge was made by the third best of the Saracen warriors. This time it was a close thing. Spears were broken. Smith's battle ax was knocked from his hand. As the Saracen champion raised his ax to finish him off, Smith quickly drew his dagger and thrust it under the Saracen's raised arm where the armor joined, killing him instantly. For the third time he rode from the field with the head of his foe. The three best warriors of the entire Muslim army had been vanquished by a single Christian champion in three successive days. Captain John Smith was the hero of the Christian armies. The king presented him with a coat-of-arms appropriately emblazoned with three Saracen heads.

Soon after there was a terrific battle between the opposing armies. In the meleè Smith was knocked unconscious and fell under a pile of bodies. He was later found by Saracen looters, made a prisoner, and taken to Constantinople and sold as a slave. A Turk bought him and took him to the far side of the Black Sea, a long way from the war in Austria. The master was brutal. Smith took a wooden pole close to hand and smashed in his skull. Making his way northward to Russia, iron slave collar and all, he was passed from one friendly hand to another until he had made his escape back to his regiment where he was given a hero's welcome.

Deciding that he needed a rest after the rigors of fighting and slavery, he asked for, and received, his discharge. He was awarded a large bag of gold for his services.

His ship to England was attacked by pirates. The vigorous defense of the ship's crew and passengers enabled the ship's captain to capture several of the pirate ships. These captured ships brought a fine price when sold in Italy.

Leaving his ship, he continued his journey by foot. He walked the length of Italy, across southern France, and through Spain into North Africa. Arriving in England after having seen much of the known world, he heard about some sort of adventure getting underway having to do with a settlement in far off Virginia. Quickly bored with the quiet English countryside, he joined the venture.[1]

---

[1]. Captain John Smith, The True Travels & Adventures of Captain John Smith, Edited by Alex J. Philip, Geo. Routledge & Sons., Ltd. N.Y., E.P. Dutton & Company.

Settlement At Jamestown

Shares for the new Virginia Company sold for ₤12.10s. On November 20, 1606, the crown instructed the newly appointed Virginia government to 1) preach the Christian religion, 2) see that land descended as it did in England, and 3) ensure that there would be trial by jury.[2]

In 1607 three ships, Susan Constant, Godspeed, and Discovery, reached Jamestown Island, Virginia. After a period of indecisive leadership, Captain John Smith took command. This was a shock for both the colonists and the Indians.

Smith was accustomed to the rough and tumble of military life, giving orders and being obeyed. He recognized that to survive the colony would have to whip itself into shape in the limited time that remained before winter. Like it or not, everyone worked. Tender hands quickly blistered applying ax and shovel to fort and shelter. Lips that cursed in protest found a pitcher of cold water poured down their sleeve. One pitcher for each curse. The Bible forbade cursing. Lying was cured with the whip. This hard-bitten leader who had killed scores in defense of his Christian faith would not allow a light trespass of its laws. Religious services were held morning and evening.

The new leader quickly came to grips with the Indian problem. The English government had expected to utilize native labor to work gold and silver mines in the Spanish manner. To prepare them for this task, the Queen (Head of the Anglican Church) instructed her colonists to make samaritans of the natives instead of driving them out. As a consequence, the colonists handled the Indians with "kid gloves". The result was that the colonists were cowed by the ferocious natives and afraid to take any actions to stop their constant depredations. They brazenly entered Jamestown anytime they chose, bullied the settlers, and stole whatever they liked.

Smith, the new governor, witnessed an Indian openly walking into the fort and stealing a valuable possession belonging to the beleaguered colony. He drew his sword and cut down the offender. Stealing stopped. From that time on the Indians held Smith in

---

2. C. Campbell, History Of Colony & Ancient Dominion of Virginia, 1860.

awe.

John Smith traveled extensively in Indian country trading with them. His observations built in him a strong dislike of what he saw. He wrote:[3]

> "the Turkies, and other Beasts and Fowle, will exceedingly increase if we beat the Salvages out of the Country, for all times of the yeere they never spare Male or Female, old nor young, eggs nor birds, fat nor leane, in season nor out of season with them all is one."

Each Indian village had its wooden idols. At times there were tribal dances. Standing in a circle the braves would dance and repeat names of children. When all had agreed on one name, that child was fetched and thrown into the flames.[4] No Indian family was safe. In order to pacify their gods, even the chiefs had to give up their children if their names were selected.

The treatment of prisoners, especially whites, filled the settlers with horror which in time developed into a deep hatred. Many times prisoners would be captured when wounded and nursed back to health. They would be well fed so that they would be strong. In this way they could endure torture a long time.

At a chosen time the prisoners were led to the center of the village and bound to a stake. The Indian women and children were brought forward and allowed to work on them. They were masters of the art. They would remove the flesh from the prisoner's face and head, his private parts, and his intestines. All this was done with amazing deftness. A tortured prisoner was a horror indeed to behold. With careful attention the Indians could keep such a tortured prisoner alive for three days. If "rescued", such prisoners always begged for death - not to be "released". This introduction to the American Indian encouraged our ancestors to obey the Biblical injunction with a will:[*]

---

3. Capt. John Smith, The General Historie, Richmond, 1819.

4. ". . . thou shalt not let any of thy seed pass through the fire to Molech. . ." Lev 18:21.

* The American Declaration of Independence states: "He (the King) ... has endeavored to bring on the inhabitants of our frontiers, the merciless Indian Savages, whose known rule of warfare, is an undistinguished destruction of all ages, sexes and conditions."

"......I will send my fear before thee...I will not drive them out from before thee in one year; lest the land become desolate...By little and little I will drive them out from before thee, until thou be increased and inherit the land...They shall not dwell in thy land, lest they make thee sin against me." Ex. 23:27-33

This Law was the blueprint for the conquest of America and was followed almost in its entirety. The results can be compared with the Spanish rivals in South America where this Law of dealing with "strangers" (Heb: zûwr) was held in contempt. The United States today is the world's leader while the Samaritans of South America with more natural resources are each year slipping farther into the darkness of superstition and backwardness.

Smith also observed that the Indians seldom smiled. They still don't. Accepting the Christian religion easily, it became a Samaritan Christianity. They shed it as easily as they received it. Good neighbors for years, they were the first to try to kill you when they took to the warpath. In the early 1900s whites were dying at the hands of the Indians in exactly the same way their ancestors did in Virginia in 1607. Only with the advent of usury and the need to convert every debt-free human into a borrower came the concept of the "Noble Savage" weeping tears over beer cans thrown on the ground.

This picture of the Indian is a creation of Madison Avenue. It does not exist any more than the false picture of the Indian killing only what he needs. Game is scarce on their reservations because it is totally harvested and as a result - exterminated.

This ignoring conservation of wildlife is also a trait of others who do not have the "law in their hearts". American conservation organizations are even now protesting that groups of Vietnamese and other oriental immigrants are going through areas of the American west taking birds, eggs, fish both large and small, and all game that moves. They reap a great one-time harvest and leave a wasteland behind them.

Today these sullen, hard-eyed, unsmiling people have been released from their reservations and they have come to towns and cities where they prey on Christians and each other. As a consequence, the jails of the American west are filled with them:

...those which ye let remain of them shall be pricks in your eyes, and thorns in your sides, and shall vex you in the land wherein ye dwell...I shall do to you as I thought to do unto them. Num. 33:56

After John Smith returned to England, the colony almost died from starvation. This phase ended in 1613. In 1615 my ancestor, Bartholomew Hoskins, a boy of 15, reached Jamestown. His brother was Protestant chaplain to the Catholic king of England, a situation which landed him in the Tower. His family thought the king might seek revenge on the lad and so he was sent to Virginia for safety.

Chapter 23

VIRGINIA TOBACCO NOTES

1618 The price of merchandise was fixed. Governor Argall decreed that "all goods be marked up 25% and tobacco be sold for 3s per pound." Penalty for offenders - 3 years servitude.

1624 Indian Massacre. The colonists were told by the King's preachers that the Indians had become samaritans and that they had changed. As a consequence they were again allowed the free run of the plantations. In a simultaneous uprising these "friends" almost wiped out the colony. The saving grace was word received from one Indian - only one, of all the "so-called" friends - that an attack was imminent. Except for that warning, Virginia would have ceased to exist. As it was the casualties were heavy and certain of the preachers were first to be skinned alive.

In spite of the loss of many settlers it appeared that the Virginia Colony was going to be successful and profitable. To reap the lion's share of the profits the Crown took the colony from the private stockholders and made it a Royal Province. All royal grants of land from this date provide that the Crown receive 1 shilling for each 50 acres of land. This followed the classic government practice of "mining someone else's pocket". Virginians were required to pay these rents ("quit rents") due the King on their land in coin. They had virtually no way of obtaining a supply of this valuable commodity since their main money crop was tobacco. Distress was widespread.

1630 Statutes were passed in Virginia vigorously punishing immoral association of races - Christian and red infidels or black proselytes. (Ezra 9:11-12)

1632 Tobacco warehouses and inspectors were established. These were initially put into operation to control the quality of the product. The large quantities of poor tobacco sent to England was bringing down the value of the good product.[5]

A wise royal governor came up with a solution to Virginia's lack of money: since tobacco had been a valuable staple of the Colony since the earliest days, and was used by everyone to pay debts, the governor officially declared it to be Legal Tender. It was a relatively complicated variation of the ancient "tally" system.

A law was passed requiring all tobacco to be presented to the government warehouses established by the colony. There the hogshead container was inspected and weighed. Poor tobacco was burned. This meant the loss of the whole 800 pound lot. Good tobacco was accepted and stored in the warehouse.

A "Tobacco Note" was then issued which could be exchanged for a hogshead of prime tobacco at the location printed on the note. This Tobacco Note was "money". It was an article created by Virginia government and it was accepted in payment for all kinds of debts in the colony including TAXES.

Not only were these notes acceptable in Virginia, when discounted to pay for transportation costs, they were accepted in New York, Philadelphia, and Charleston. English tobacco buyers coming to America did not bother to visit every plantation to buy tobacco. They simply bought up "Tobacco Notes". When they had enough for their purposes, they went to the warehouse where the tobacco was stored and claimed their tobacco.

5. Dr. William Z. Ripley, The Financial History of Virginia 1609 - 1776, Columbia, N.Y. 1893.

It was a neat, workable system that served the colony with great success for more than 150 years.

Spanish Silver & Paper Money

Since there were few English coins in circulation in Virginia the colonists encouraged the importation and circulation of Spanish coins along with the native Tobacco Notes. The Spanish coins were valued for their intrinsic worth and were accepted in private trade and for private debts. They were also accepted by English merchants in payment for debts. Since, however, they were not "legal tender" (acceptable for taxes) in England one never knew whether or not they would be accepted by government agents in payment of taxes.

As far as Britain was concerned, the colonies were the place for the younger sons, speculators, and political and religious misfits. The Crown valued them for the revenues and trade they produced. There were certain things the colonies were not allowed to do, but other than that, whatever worked was all right. When Virginia needed money, she invented Tobacco Notes. It was workable...a sort of colonial "tally".

The Northeast solved its money problems in a different way. In 1690 Schenectady was destroyed by the French and Indians in a night attack. Something had to be done right then for defense, and there was no money. The General Court ordered an issue of paper bills.[6] This money was backed by nothing but the promise to pay in silver. It was the first paper money authorized in the English colonies. Seven thousand pounds were issued. Since taxes could not be paid with them, they promptly dropped 50% in value. The reason the wooden tally in England was valuable was because they could be used in payment of taxes. Massachusetts liked to issue these pieces of paper, but did not like to receive them herself, if she could help it.

Later these paper notes became legal tender, but New England issued them faster than she taxed them out of circulation so they were continuously depreciating as their numbers increased. By 1720 Massachusetts had issued 200,000 pounds which had depreciated to 1/3 their value. Rhode Island's paper money declined 26 to 1, and South Carolina's 8 to 1. Pennsylvania issued over 250 different paper notes. This section of America never mas-

6. George F. Holmes, History of the U.S., Univ. Pub. Co. N.Y. 1840.

tered the art of price stabilization through taxing unwanted paper money out of circulation.

American/British Balance Of Trade

To understand the first economic cycle in America, we must return to Britain to review a little background history.

The Bank of Scotland was established in 1695. In short order it spread its tentacles across Scotland. Thousands of Scottish prisoners of war from the wars of 1715 and 1745 were sent to America as indentured servants for 7 years.[7] Soon after the wars came the flood tide of Scottish refugees. These refugees had been dispossessed of everything they owned by the new usury system adopted by the Scottish Banks. Their homes, cattle, businesses, land, everything went in default to the owners of the new interest-banks. The merchants who remained in Scotland sank deeply into debt. The farmers who remained moved to squalid tenements in the cities. It was a replay of the Roman scenario.

Virginia planters had been accustomed to order goods from their Scottish and English agents. They would settle the books when their tobacco was shipped. This had been the custom for 100 years. The British merchants were now in debt to the new interest-banks. When a Virginia planter placed an order for farm implements and clothing with a merchant in Britain, that merchant now had to borrow money to fill the order. Unable to absorb the cost himself, he passed the cost along to his customer by adding 5% or 7% to the bill.

Five or 7% doesn't sound like much, but over a period of years see the result on the next page. Starting in the year 1705 the trade balance between Britain and America for the prior five years is even. The pluses (+) mean in favor of the American Colonies; minus (-) means in favor of Britain.

---

7. ". . if thy brother. . . be sold unto thee and serve six years; then in the seventh year thou shalt let him go free. . .'Deu 15:12. This Law did not apply to blacks since they could not "blush", were not descended from Abraham, Isaac, and Jacob, and were not believed to have received the "law in their hearts." They were regarded and treated as aliens and "zûwr" strangers instead of "brothers".

Balance Of Trade With England
(Five Year Periods)

1705	Even Trade Balance
1710	+ £ 200,000
1715	Even Trade Balance
1720	+ £ 400,000
1725	+ £ 100,000
1730	+ £ 400,000
1735	+ £ 300,000
1740	- £ 100,000
1745	+ £ 200,000
1750	- £1,300,000
1755	- £2,500,000
1760	- £6,200,000
1765	- £3,800,000
1770	- £9,000,000
1775	- £4,800,000 [8]

You can see in the 5 year period ending in 1740 the balance of trade started to run heavily against the Colonies. This was the period when the interest-banking system of Britain began to get its roots down and affect the trade of the nation. The American Colonies had no experience in dealing with usury. The Church of England ministers in America were representatives of the British King who was head of the Church of England. The King himself was deeply in debt to the money lenders and was their servant. It was no wonder his ministers did nothing to protect their flocks. They did not dare to preach against the usury system for fear of offending their master and high priest, the King. There was no one to warn the people any more than there had been anyone to warn the English and Scottish people back in Britain 100 years earlier. The imposition of usury into the British-American trade put a drastic drain on the colonists and made the Revolutionary War inevitable.

1705 Massachusetts passed laws forbidding marriage between blacks and whites. These laws were reinforced in 1786.

1717 Maryland passed a law forbidding racial intermarriage.

1764 Good times. The Seven Years War (French & Indian War in the Colonies) brought a flash of prosperity as war always does.

8. Historical Statistics of the U.S., Colonial & Pre-Federal Statistics, U.S. Govt. Printing Office, Washington 1970, p. 1176.

When borrowing for the war stopped, hard times dropped over England like a blanket. Ben Franklin landed in England fresh from the War Phase "good times" in America and proceeded to lecture England of that fact. When asked for the reason for these good times, he replied:

"That is simple. It is only because in the colonies we issue our own money. It is called "Colonial Scrip" and we issue it in the proper proportions to the demands of trade and industry."[9]

All this sounded very nice, but it was not exactly the truth. He forgot to mention that while New England printed "Colonial Scrip" by the ton, they had no intention of taxing it out of circulation again.

America and Britain were being flooded with their paper scrip. Confronted with this torrent of paper money which grew worth less in value each day, the British merchants appealed to the British government.

The British government was servant to the Bank of England. The Bank was also tired of this American Colonial Scrip. It infringed on their monopoly.

The bankers instructed Parliament to pass a law against allowing Colonial Scrip to be used as legal tender. This law was to take effect after September 1, 1764. To make matters worse for the colonists they "prohibited extension." This meant that when the notes were due to expire * they were not allowed to continue circulation as had been the practice in the past when notes "came due". This effectively put an end to America's competition with the Bank of England.

---

9. David Astle, The Babylonian Woe, Monetary Science Publishing, P.O. Box 86, Wickliffe, Ohio 44092, p.120.

* In this period paper notes had a due date. On due date they were supposed to be automatically withdrawn from circulation and burned. Their place was to be taken by gold and silver coin that was supposed to have miraculously appeared from somewhere. Since the valuable coins did not appear from "somewhere" - the paper notes were of necessity continued in circulation past due date. It was either that or the colonies would have no money. To prohibit "extension" was to force the colonies to burn their paper money on due date and leave them owing debts and no money with which to pay them. Instant foreclosure and instant depression would be the result.

1764 To get back some of the money Britain had spent on the French and Indian War in America, a Stamp Act was passed. This was one of the most irritating taxes ever passed. On top of depriving the colonists of much of their money, the tax was instituted at the very time when there was almost no money to pay them. Every legal page in a court case was taxed 3d. Each common law action 3d, each pleading in a Chancery suit 6d, admiralty court and other 1s, bills of lading, bonds, contracts, and newspapers were taxed, advertisements 2s, a pack of playing cards 1s, a pair of dice 10s. This exceptionally high tax gives an indication of the general feeling against gambling. Certificates given to students for their college degrees were taxed b2. Double stamps were required if the document were in a foreign language.[10] Predictably, destruction of stamps and intimidation of agents was general.

1765 "Ordinary Rates" (tavern room and board rates) were again published - being unchanged year to year. Public watermills were regulated. Pendleton went surety for a friend in defiance of Biblical Law prohibiting it - and lost when his friend defaulted. In England business was in dire straits. Thousands were unemployed. The Colony of Virginia was near anarchy. Archibald Ritchie, a merchant of Tappahannock, Virginia, said that he would sail his ships with British stamps on his merchandise. Four hundred "Sons of Liberty" met in two long lines on the main street across from Ritchie's house. A committee visited him. Ritchie agreed not to use the stamps again. A wise decision. To cool tempers the Stamp Act was repealed.[11]

10. John David Mays, Edmund Pendleton, Vol. I, (1721-1803), Harvard Press, Cambridge, Mass. 1952, p.160.

11. Mays, page 171.

VII - USURY COMES TO AMERICA

Chapter 24

THE ROBINSON DEBACLE

On May 11, 1766 John Robinson died. John Robinson was a
congenial man; he liked people and people liked him. The one
thing that he could not stand was for his friends to be in
trouble, and they were in trouble - most of them. Virginia had
just gone through the French and Indian War and everyone was
heavily in debt to England. John Robinson was Treasurer of
Virginia and had access to the Ł100,000 which was in the treasury, a good portion of which was past "due date." To relieve the
suffering of his fellow Virginians he lent them the "past due"
Ł 100,000 in the treasury at only 5% interest. (This was not
illegal at the time - unwise, but not illegal.) John Robinson,
in trying to do his friends a favor, really did them in. A debt
of Ł100,000 at 5% interest grows into a debt of Ł200,000 in 14-
1/2 years.

When the officials of the state audited the Treasury of the
State of Virginia, they found it empty! All they had to show was
a box full of IOUs. They discussed the matter and decided that
the money must be collected plus the 5% interest. Officials were
sent out to collect. After the first Ł100,000 was collected,
there was no more money in circulation in the colony. Plantations were thrown on the market for what they would bring, which
was almost nothing. When there is no money in circulation,
"things" have little value. This was the generation that was
wiped out. This was a time of misery and destitution in Virginia.

When someone tells me that their family has always owned
their land going back into the early 1700s, I check John Robinson's "good deed list". If their ancestor was on that list,
there is good reason to doubt that he held onto his land. Few
did. If his name was NOT on that list, there is a good chance
that that person is telling the truth.

As a matter of general interest I have listed a dozen or so
of the names. They were selected from several hundred names for
no other reason than some of their present day descendants may
find it interesting.

A FEW OF THE DEBTORS TO THE ROBINSON ESTATE IN 1766 [12]

Name	Amount Owed
Byrd, William Esqr.	Ł 14,921 . 19 . 3
Buckner, Saml. Estate	Ł 31 . 7 . 14
Carter, Charles Jr.	Ł 3,834 . 16 . 2
Christian, Francis	Ł 15 . 0 . 0
Digges, Dudley	Ł 65 . 0 . 0
Fitzhugh, Henry	Ł 1,239 . 19 . 7-1/2
Henry, Patrick Jr.	Ł 11 . 6 . 8
Lee, Henry	Ł 30 . 12 . 6
Lee, Richard Henry	Ł 12 . 0 . 0
Lewis, Fielding	Ł 54 . 3 . 3
Mercer, John	Ł 2,713 . 14 . 0
Pollard, William	Ł 315 . 0 . 0
Pendleton, Edmund	Ł 1,020 . 12 . 7
Randolph, Peyton	Ł 10 . 11 . 8
Randolph, John	Ł 996 . 19 . 4
Richards, John	Ł 554 . 3 . 0
Ruffin, John	Ł 92 . 16 . 0

Apologists for the interest system maintain that the inflation in the American Revolution allowed everyone to pay their
debts. This is another untruth which needs to be set at rest.
In 1792, twenty-six years after the death of John Robinson and
almost a decade after the war, there were still more than two
hundred names of debtors to the Robinson Estate. Here are a few
of them and the amounts then owed. It gives an idea of how a
family once in the net gets out only with the greatest difficulty.

12. Mays p. 358

A FEW OF THE DEBTORS TO THE ROBINSON ESTATE IN 1792[13]

Name	Amount Owed
Armistead, John	₺ 13 . 0 . 10
Chamberlayne, Thomas	₺ 1,520 . 12 . 1
Dandridge, N. W.	₺ 19 . 11 . 7
Roan, John	₺ 598 . 12 . 7
Strother, William	₺ 35 . 0 . 0
Taliaferro, Walker	₺ 494 . 1 . 0
Todd, Richard	₺ 97 . 18 . 0
Wormly, Ralph	₺ 832 . 3 . 4

These debts are substantial debts - enough to debilitate a family from any useful endeavor for generations. Much of Virginia remained enslaved to interest long after the war which was fought to free them from this slavery. The "free" people were the Bible-believing, God-fearing people who believed in "owe no man anything but love" and refused to take or pay interest. Most of Virginia fell into this class. While many prominent Virginians borrowed from Robinson, most didn't.

1769 Money was so short in Virginia that lotteries were resorted to to sell Robinson Estate holdings. Even the tickets had to be sold on credit since there was almost no money - paper or specie. The Virginia Gazette was crowded with announcements by debtors in distress. John Mercer quit his law practice to collect ₺10,000 owed him. He collected almost none of it.

1770 Religious revival spread over America. Since the Bible forbids Strangers and Christians living together, Virginia again passed Anti-Slave Trade laws. The King of England prohibited Virginians from passing such laws in instructions to his Governor in Virginia. [14] The King desperately needed

13. Mays p. 370

14. Beverly B. Munford, Virginia's Attitude Toward Slavery and Secession, Richmond, 1909, p. 17.

his share of the slave trade profits to pay his own debts and accumulated interest.

1771 Six Baptists were in jail at Caroline Court House at one time. Some of them had been jailed and whipped by supporters of the Church of England for preaching in their homes.[15]

1772 Virginia again petitioned England to prevent the importation of slaves. The King, desperate for money, wanted the trade continued. The petition was refused.

1773 There was much counterfeit paper money because of the desperate need. The death penalty was passed to attempt to control illegal printing.[16]

1774 A trade boycott against Britain was in full force. Merchants in Glasgow, Scotland, with more than Ŀ1 million in loans outstanding in America, complained that they faced utter ruin from the American boycott of their goods.

1775 There was dire poverty in Virginia. There were floods and poor tobacco crops. Even food was scarce. On August 1, George Washington offered to raise 1,000 men to march to the relief of Boston. "Enforcement Committees" operated as vigilante groups to enforce measures taken against English sympathizers. Price ceilings were posted - and woe to the man who did not follow them. People signed the "Association" or were branded an enemy. The American/British balance of payments was Ŀ4.8 million in favor of Britain since 1770. A $7 Continental Note was authorized. It was to be redeemable by $7 in Spanish milled dollars. It was first circulated in August 1776.

Thomas Jefferson wrote "All 'men' are created equal". The ruling classes of America were educated men who were conversant

---

15. Pendleton, p. 263.

16. Munford, p. 18.

with Latin, Greek, and Hebrew. They were well aware of the Hebrew translation of the word "man" (adam) - he who "blushes red". For this reason they limited slavery (indenture) to 7 years for their own kind (Heb: Gêr) who could "blush red" as required by Biblical law. At the same time these same men owned black slaves (Heb: zûwr) and held them in perpetual slavery because they could not "blush red". According to the law of their God, one was "equal" - the other was not.

> and strangers ("zûwr" - racial aliens) shall stand and feed your flocks, and the sons of the alien shall be your plowmen and your vine dressers. Isa. 61:5

The word "adam" was not extended to include "everyone" until the ignorant French revolutionaries translated the American Declaration of Independence from English to French and mis-translated "men" so as to include "everyone". This was something the originator of the phrase and the owner of more than a hundred "zûwr" slaves did not intend.

Note: Knowledgeable classical students of the 1700s were aware that the ancient Egyptians colored the "man" figures in their tombs red so that there would be no doubt as to their adamic descent. This was their "blush red" proof. It was also a custom of the ancient Mycenaeans and others.

SECTION - VIII

VIII WAR CYCLES PEACE CYCLES

Chapter 25

CYCLES OF WAR & PEACE

As has been illustrated earlier, when Seth in Babylonia borrowed 10 talents and had to pay back 11 talents when there were only 10 in circulation he became destitute. When Tom, the Englishman, had to pay back 2,000 pounds when there were only 1,000 in circulation, he also became destitute, and in Virginia the people who took John Robinson's generous loan of 10 pounds and had to pay back 11 when there wasn't that much money in circulation also had an impossible task. They, too, became destitute. A destitute person is a dangerous person who is likely to feel that he has nothing to lose. He is far more dangerous than a person who is wealthy and content. The stage is set for desperate and extreme measures, and these measures follow a definite and measured Historical War Phase and a measured Peace Phase. Watch the following dates closely:

1764 - Prices were high, times were good.

1775 - A time of ruin, low prices, and destitution.

1814 - High prices, boom years.

1843 - Low prices. A period of absolute doom and depression.

1864 - If you were in the North, these were great times, boom times, high prices. Money flowed freely.

1896 - Destitution, terrible times.

1920 - We are now getting close to the present! High prices, good times. We all know about 1929, but the period of destitution was later.

1933 - Destitution, awful times.

1980- Prices exploded to the top.... It seemed as if everyone owned a $17,000 Mercedes automobile and a cottage at the beach! Good times! And, in my opinion, the end of one phase and the beginning of another.

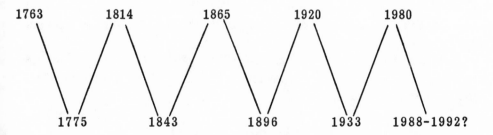

Chapter 26

THE FIFTY YEAR WAR AND PEACE CYCLE

The dates just outlined encompass what may be called the over-all "Fifty-Year Economic Cycle." This cycle is divided into two parts. The War Phase which occupies the first part in turn is followed by the Peace Phase which completes the Cycle. In order not to be misleading, I wish to emphasize that every year there is a war going on somewhere, and this is how it has been since the beginning of time. Among highly developed nations which use the "Interest System", however, major confrontations usually occur only while commodity prices are rising - with occasional spill-over wars at the top.

This WAR PHASE is followed by a PEACE PHASE in which "brush-fire" wars are constantly going on, but major confrontations seldom occur. Let us look a little more closely at this interest-created WAR and PEACE Cycle.

The First Peace Phase 1763 - 1775

The period 1763-1775 was the first time the American colonies had to cope with an interest-induced economic cycle. Without interest there would have been no reason for war. As it was, the effects on the country were drastic. Emotions welled up giving birth to a Revolutionary War, independence, a Constitution, loans through France and the Netherlands to America, and the American equivalent of the British Banking System which had caused the war in the first place.

Since each of the subsequent "Peace Phases" is very similar to the first one, more time and detail will be given it than those that come later.

The Continental Disaster

The first issue of Continental notes in 1776 was followed by others. By 1780 there was a flood of Continentals. To complicate a bad situation, the British counterfeited these notes and passed them everywhere. The story of "not worth a continental" is well known.

The concept of "Continental tallies" was historically sound, but to be of lasting value, it is necessary that the quantity of money be regulated by taxation. Surplus bills must be taxed out of circulation. This was the key thing missing. The colonies were so fragmented that there could be no effective general taxation.

The Continental Congress depended on the individual states to manage taxation. In practice, if one state taxed continentals heavily, it caused a shortage of money in that state. A shortage of money caused prices to drop. Lower prices attracted speculators from a nearby untaxed colony which had lots of surplus money. These buyers would come with bushel baskets of money to buy commodities, driving prices back up again. For this reason the individual colonies were reluctant to tax the continentals. It would give the neighboring colonies an advantage. Money piled up everywhere.

Just because this issue of continental money did not work, did not mean that it was not a good idea. It was a great idea; but to work, it was necessary to have effective taxation and a ban on interest. These two things the new country did not have.

Chapter 27

ASSIGNAT DISASTER - FRANCE

On the heels of the Continental Disaster came the Assignat Disaster. From the time of John Law's Mississippi Bubble in 1716 until 1789, the French went from one monetary patchwork expediency to another in the attempt to hold the mightiest country in Europe together. The usury bankers were solidly in the seat and were determined to gain control of the lands of the king, church, and nobles. The country went deeper and deeper in debt. France borrowed money for its wars, the peasants borrowed money for their crops and farms, and the aristocracy borrowed money to work their estates. Everyone borrowed to keep the wolf away.

In the last few years before the revolution, the debt inflation went its predictable way. Rents were up 25% while wages were off 25%. The very bad harvests of 1788 drove prices sky high. Eleven million Frenchmen were reduced to poverty and were desperate. The bankers could make little money lending to the same old debt-ridden and hostile aristocracy.

What was needed were new debt-free borrowers who had collateral. Since such borrowers did not exist they were created. This was done as it will always be done as long as a single usury system exists - by financing the revolutionists. In this way an entirely new class of debt-free borrowers was brought into existence.

These "created borrowers" brought about "The Terror" to deal with the large land owners who had mortgaged their estates to the lenders. They encouraged their followers to hunt propertied men with axes, to hack their limbs off, gut them, smear blood on their cheeks, and parade through the streets holding pieces of their victim's carcass and intestines over their heads.[1] Such things could not have occurred with the Templars as France's bankers. The Templars did not charge interest and borrowers could not owe more money than was in existence. It was forbidden.

The revolutionary government at last confiscated land owned by the church, king, and aristocracy. These lands amounted to two-thirds of the nation. These lands were first used as backing for an issue of notes in December 1789. By November 1791 the "assignats" (the name of the notes) had dropped in value -18%. By August 1792 they were off -43% more. In August 1793 a law was passed preventing citizens from accepting the assignats at a discount. This "Forced Circulation" was backed by the death penalty. In 1794 the "Maximum" price ceiling was repealed and prices went wild. In 1797 obligatory acceptance was abolished. The country declared a two-thirds bankruptcy of the national debt. Nothing was done to help the private debtors.

Napoleon was financed by the same bankers who had financed the earlier government and he was placed at the head of government to bring order out of chaos. The bankers now owned much of the confiscated land. France now had a new monied aristocracy in addition to the military aristocracy created by Napoleon.

What went wrong with the assignat issue? While the American

---

1. Otto J. Scott, "Robespierre", Times Books, N.Y., 1979

"Continental-tally" issue was strictly paper, the French "Assig-nat-tally" issue was paper backed by land. This should have given it value. It didn't. The immediate cause of the failure of both the Assignats and the Continentals was the same. In America the states wouldn't tax Continentals out of circulation, and in France they couldn't. The French still had their anti-quated system of taxation dating back to the time of the Roman Empire - "contract taxation." The French were the best tax dodgers in Europe. Next to the Italians, they still are. The issues of Assignats continued until paper money lost all value. It would have been the same if they had issued diamonds. Too many diamonds would have flooded the market and caused their price to collapse.

Again it must be noted that because of interest, the debts were always much larger than the supply of money. Taxation or the lack of it will help determine the success or failure of an issue of tallies - paper, land, wood, or gold, but any monetary system will fail in the long run as long as there is more debt than money to pay the debt.

War Phase Heroes

War Phases have their heroes: Napoleon Bonaparte, George Washington, Tom Jefferson, and Andy Jackson in the first cycle ending in 1814. Peace Phases have few heroes - just good busi-ness, bad commodity prices, booming stock markets, high unemploy-ment - and they end with crashes and misery. The only thing that could raise the blood pressure a bit during the 1815-1843 Peace Phase was the fuss between President Andrew Jackson and Biddle of the Second Bank of the United States over who was to rule the country; not whether or not the "system of interest" was to rule. If Jackson won, the "system" existed under the direction of the politicians. If Biddle won, the "system" existed under the direction of the bankers. This was a battle of personalities only; it was agreed that the "system" was to remain whoever won.

1816 The 2nd Bank of the U.S. came into existence. The Federal Government again issued a 20-year charter to a private group of investors who formed the "2nd Bank of the United States." This bank was everything the 1st Bank wasn't. It was a mammoth operation. It acted as the government's fiscal

Note: Thomas Jefferson inherited land and debts before the Revolutionary War. To pay the debts he sold land. The outbreak of war prevented payment. By war's end his Continental money was worthless. Because of a law that he helped pass he still owed the debts. By 1810, interest had caused many of the debts to double. The "Sage of Monticello" was overwhelmed in debt and almost everything he posses-sed was foreclosed at his death.

agent. It issued notes and dealt in bills of exchange.

Having the ability to return state-bank "paper notes" to the issuing bank for redemption in gold coin, it assumed the position of absolute economic master over American banks. Any bank it wished to curtail was doomed. It gathered its paper notes and presented them for gold. Any bank it wished to favor it was lenient to. The president of the bank did not exaggerate when he boasted that the bank had power of life or death over state banks.[2] It used this power to gain still more power for its investors, and did it at the expense of other sections of the country - as we shall soon see.

1816 March 22. Feeling apprehension over the actions of the newly created interest-banks, Mathew Carey wrote the following to the directors of the 2nd Bank of the U.S.:

"...The plan adopted (by the banks) was to make money scarce by a sudden and violent curtailment of discounts...they are literally masters...of the destinies of those of their debtors not in tolerably independent circumstances. They may at pleasure reduce some to bankruptcy...and may by undue accommodations enable others to make great fortunes out of the distresses of the public...When money is plenty...they entice men to use their capital. When money is scarce, they withdraw it, and become absolute masters of their fellow citizens."[3]

1817 The American Colonization Society was formed in Washington, D.C.[4] Its purpose - to finance the return of blacks to

2. Herbert V. Prochnow, The Federal Reserve System, Harper & Row, New York, 1960, p.7).

3. Mathew Carey, Essays on Banking, pp. 27-34, 41-45.

4. This old and respected organization is still in existence. Its address is The American Colonization Society, Inc.", P.O. Box 8340, "New Fairfield, CN 06810", Mr. Andrew B. McAllister, Pres.

Note: In 1800, Rhode Island passed a law forbidding ministers the right to marry whites and blacks. In 1815 New Hampshire passed laws prohibiting anyone except whites from serving in the militia. New England's stand against zuwr strangers along with the work of the American Colonization Society came under attack from the zuwr money interests.

Africa. Its founder - Rev. Robert Finey, a Presbyterian minister. The reason - Israel was to separate themselves from strangers lest they learn their ways. The group immediately came under attack from the "liberals" of the usury-banking interests who wanted the slaves freed and kept in America so that they could borrow money into existence.

1819 The 2nd Bank issued all of its supply of specie to any and all of its cronies and friends who wished to convert paper notes into gold, and faced bankruptcy. In a frantic effort to get liquid, it called on the bank's debtors to pay these loans immediately. The interest plus principal equaled more than the floating supply of money. Most debtors could not pay. They went bankrupt by the thousands. America plunged into the Crash of 1819. Many of the western towns built in the boom of 1816-1818 were abandoned in the Panic of 1819.[5]

1831 February 2 - Senator Thomas Hart Benton of Missouri offered a Resolution against rechartering the bank.

"I am informed that the notes of the banks south of the Potomac and Ohio, even those of the lower Mississippi, are generally refused at the United States' Branch Bank in St. Louis, and in consequence, are expelled from circulation in Missouri and Illinois, and in the neighboring districts. This exclusion of the southern notes from the northwest quarter of the Union, is injurious to both parties, as our travelers and emigrants chiefly come from the South, and the whole of our trade goes there to find a cash market. The exclusion . . . is general, and extends to the banks in Virginia, the two Carolinas, Georgia, Alabama, Mississippi, and Louisiana . . . it fastens a vampire on the bosom of the state, to snatch away its gold and silver . . . These states, without rice, without cotton, without tobacco, without sugar and with less flour and provisions to export, are saturated with gold and silver, while the southern and western states, with all the real sources of wealth, are in a state of the utmost destitution. For this . . . the Bank

5. Murray N. Rothbard, America's Great Depression, D. Van Nostrand Co., Princeton, N.J., 1963, Ch. II, Note 25.

of the United States stands forth preeminently culpable . . . . a statement in the National Intelligencer of this morning . . . exults on the quantity of gold and silver in the vaults of the United States' Bank. It declares that institution to be 'overburdened' with gold and silver; and well may it be so overburdened, since it has lifted the load entirely from the South and West.

". . . the Bank needs . . . friends in Congress and in the presidential chair. Its fate, its very existence, may often depend upon the friendship of the President and Congress; and in such cases, it is not in human nature to avoid using the immense means in the hands-of the Bank to influence the elections of these officers . . . of usury at the rate of forty-six percent. . . . What an interest in keeping those away who might suffer (the bank harm).

"If these banks are beneficial institutions, why not several? . . . If malignant, why create one?

". . . Eternal drawing out, and no bring back, is a process which no people, no country, can endure . . . So will any people be exhausted of their wealth, no matter how great that wealth may be, whose miserable destiny shall subject them to a system . . . which is forever levying, and never refunding."[6]

1832 February 2. Representative Augustin Clayton of Georgia commented:

"The amount of gold and silver coin and bullion sent from western and southern branches of the parent bank since its establishment in 1817 . . . is supposed to be fifteen or twenty millions, and, with bank interest on bank debts, constitutes a system of the most intolerable oppression of the South and West."[7]

6. Register of Debates, 1831, VII, 46 FF.
7. Sobell, p. 39.

In spite of the opposition of the 2nd Bank, President Jackson won a stunning victory over Henry Clay in the presidential contest of 1832. This kept the office of president free from bank control until Fillmore's election 1849.

After Jackson was elected, he discovered that the 2nd Bank had almost doubled its loans from $42 million in January 1831 to $70 million in May 1832 in an effort to bring numerous new borrowers under its control. "The borrower is servant..." The bank was careful to warn its debtors of the ruin which might overtake them if Jackson were reelected. In addition, Jackson discovered that some of the largest sums were lent on very unusual terms to owners of newspapers. These papers, of course, took Clay's side in the election. This infuriated Jackson. He determined to weaken the bank by removing public moneys from the 2nd Bank and depositing them in state banks. The 2nd Bank in an attempt to turn the people against Jackson by creating "hard times", called on debtors to pay their loans. A panic ensued. The public turned their hostility against the bank instead of against Jackson. The bank became alarmed by this turn of events. They relented and extended the loans.

1835 There was a crop failure. The farmers who had borrowed to buy their farms and to pay interest on their mortgages went to the wall. Jackson made matters worse. He took money out of circulation by paying the national debt down to zero, and didn't spend new money back into circulation.

1836 The charter of the 2nd Bank expired. The worst of all things happened - a second crop failure. It was all over for the farmer. Progressively lower prices for commodities combined with two years of crop failure did it.

Meanwhile, in Texas the Mexicans stormed the Alamo and exterminated its defenders. At the Battle of Goliad Col. Fanning surrendered with 520 men. All but six were massacred. Americans' opinions about Mexican "strangers" began to harden.

The Crash Of 1837

The Crash of 1837 was the inevitable result of the peak in commodity prices in 1814. Of course, there was the temporary panic of 1819 engineered by the 2nd Bank of the U.S. calling in loans, but after that was over America went right back to borrowing $10 and agreeing to repay $11. Total debts soared. America was on a land buying spree. The amount of land changing hands was astounding as it is at every peak in land prices.

$$1834 - 4.6 \text{ million acres}$$
$$1835 - 12.6 \text{ million acres}$$
$$1836 - 20.0 \text{ million acres}$$

The total acreage traded was up +425% in three years! Lots in Bangor, Maine which were $300 in 1831 brought almost $1,000 in 1836. The London Rothschilds are said to have been the biggest factor.[8]

Many states repudiated their debts.[9] The farmers walked away from their neat, well-tended farms and let them grow up in brush. Those farms the bank owners didn't want were thrown on the auction block for what they could get for them. This started the land crash. Early in 1837, 9/10ths of the eastern factories were closed.[10] Phillip Hone wrote: "No man can calculate to escape ruin, but he who owes no money. Happy is he who has little and is free from debt."[11]

The following gives an idea of what happened to stocks:

Issue	1837 High	November 25, 1841
United States Bank	122	4
Vicksburg Bank	89	5
Kentucky Bank	92	56
North American Trust	95	3
Farmers Trust	113	30

8. Sobel, p. 42.

9. George L. Leffler, The Stockmarket, Ronald Press, N.Y., 1957, p. 93.

10. Sobel, p. 72.

11. Sobel, p. 67.

American Trust	120	0
Illinois State Bank	80	35
Morris Canal	75	0
Patterson R.R.	75	53
Long Island R.R. [12]	60	52

In May, all banks suspended converting their bank notes into gold. Six hundred banks broke down. New interest-banks were forming so rapidly that the decrease really doesn't show up on the history chart on page 179.

To help debtors who were being abused and imprisoned, Congress copied the old Roman Bankruptcy Law and called it the Federal Bankruptcy Law. This wiped out $450 million of debts that were "non-collectible". After taking everything the debtors had, it allowed them to start borrowing money into existence again. The new "borrowing" was more valuable than the old "worthless debt".

In contrast to the rest of the country, the government itself was in fine shape. It owed no money and was servant to no one. When it needed money, it simply printed and spent it into circulation. Between 1838 and 1843 seven issues of treasury notes totaling $47,002,900 were printed.[13]

1840 President Tyler vetoed another attempt to establish a national bank.

While chaos had enveloped the mainstream of commerce, in the backwaters life was still relatively tranquil. Samuel E. Mayo of Virginia recalled that for generations "it was considered fashionable not to race horses for money, but they were kept and run just to keep up the stock . . . no betting was allowed on races."[14] The same went for borrowing money, and the prohibition against gambling and usury was still obeyed in large areas of the country. As a consequence of this obedience they were protected from the miseries afflicting the usury-banking regions of the rest of the country.

---

12. Pratt. Work Of Wall Street, p. 13.

13. Sobel, p. 70.

14. Ironworker, Winter, 1980, Lynchburg, Va., p. 8.

1841 Oct. 11th. The 2nd Bank of the United States failed. The long list of foreign stockholders was made public.

1842 The "New Abolitionists," the spiritual descendants of the French Revolutionists, were bankrolled to replace the Plantation Owners as the nation's rulers. They became venomous in their attack on the South. The original Abolitionist movement, the "American Colonization Society," was based on the Biblical Law of Separation. It was formed by Virginians in Washington in 1817. Gaining members and finances they began buying up slaves and sending them back to Africa as colonists. The first shipload left on the "Elizabeth" in 1819. To aid in the eventual repatriation of all blacks from America, Charles Mercer and John Floyd of Virginia led the effort to have a bill passed to have armed cruisers stationed off Africa and America to disrupt the slave trade to America.[15]

Needing new borrowers and spurred by this American example, Britain in 1833 abolished slavery and borrowed $20,000,000 into existence to compensate their owners. No provision was made to return the blacks to Africa. To have done so would have defeated the purpose of their emancipation.

The New Abolitionists from the Northeast were sponsored by, and were agents of, the banking interests. They made no bones about what they wanted. They didn't want the black slaves sent back to Africa. They wanted them freed with no compensation to their owners and they wanted them kept here in the United States. Three million new potential borrowers added to the population at one time! The potential profits staggered the imagination.

The main obstacle to the spread of the interest banking system was the debt-free southern plantation system that sent debt-free anti "central bank" legislators to Washington. The self-sufficient plantation was made possible by the originally unwanted slave. If the slaves were freed with no compensation,

---

15. Mnford, p. 36.

it would destroy the plantation system, the debt-free owners, and the southern opposition all at the same time. To give compensation would be to leave the former slave owners debt-free and independent, and in their same old powerful position. It would allow them to continue their opposition to the N. E. banks.

In a usury system a freed slave is free only to borrow money into existence - not to leave. Later on in the chapter on "African Colonization", we will examine what happens to blacks who rebel and try to return to their African homeland on their own in defiance of the bankers' politicians.

Chapter - 28

BOTTOMSIDE TRANSITION YEAR

1842 For the first time since 1814 commodity prices stopped going down. They didn't go up much, but they did stop going down. This was the Bottomside Transition Year that brought to a close the first Economic Cycle since the country had been founded. The "War Phase" of the second Economic Cycle was ushered in.

1844 Old debtors and new speculators started borrowing again. The money supply was up +14%. This was good. The next year the money supply was up only +6%. This was hardly enough to pay interest. Things got tight again. The United States started looking for something that would stimulate economic activity. Mexico warned the U.S. not to annex Texas. The U.S. annexed Texas. This was the stimulation needed.

1846 War with Mexico. The Mexicans ambushed an American detachment, killed eleven, wounded five, and captured the rest. The U.S. had been attacked! She declared war eighteen days later. The initial preparations for war sent the money supply up +9%. The next year it was up a hearty +16%. Times were looking good in the United States.

1848 Peace! The Treaty of Guadalupe Hidalgo was signed. It

brought an end to the brief good times. The money supply
was up only +4%. The following year it wasn't up any at
all, but gold had been discovered in California and that
made the difference. The gold rush was about to start.

1849 The usury banks at last elected their man President of the
United States, Millard Fillmore of New York. This little-
noticed event marks the year the office of president passed
into control of the banks and was used to advance their
causes. It has remained in their hands ever since. The
Congress was soon to follow.

1851 The gold flood from California started reaching the East.
The money supply was up +19%. This was even better than the
Mexican War. Octagonal $50 gold slugs minted by Moffat and
Company of California circulated throughout the country.
Every man without a job talked about going west to mine
gold. Many did. This newly minted gold for a time short-
circuited the bankers' "Usury Contracts" by creating the
11th dollar with which interest could be paid. These were
"gold-tallies". Thousands of debtors paid their debts and
got off the hook. For the first time they "owned" their own
farms.
        Others looked for still greener pastures. A group of
"filibusters" were lent money by the banks and sailed from
New Orleans to try to take Cuba away from debt-ridden Spain.

1853 The money supply was up +11%. The gold flood seemed never
to end. William Walker invaded the debtor nation of Mexico
and set up the short-lived "Republic of Lower California".

1854 The Crimean War started. This resulted in war contracts
going out in Russia, England, France, and Turkey. All the
world benefited as this new flood of money was borrowed into
existence.

English and French rulers found themselves in a ticklish
position. For hundreds of years they had furnished Crusaders to

fight the Saracens. Now they were making treaties [16] with these very same Saracen heathen who were long-standing enemies of their own countries to fight against the Christian nation of Russia. Most Western history books of that period carry long explanations why the Christian rulers of France and Britain felt compelled to ally themselves with the infidel.

The thousands of British, French, and Russian wounded lying together on the Battlefield of the Alma could only smile wanly at each other and repeat the one word that all understood - "Christian". There were very few Mohammedans killed on the allied side in the campaign - just Christians. The queen city of Christendom, Constantinople, and 15,000,000 Greek Samaritans were allowed to remain in Turkish hands. The purpose of the war was to help the economy, and the banks, not to free people or their cities, and certainly not to ruin a potential borrower - Turkey.

1855 Time was running out. The gold flood slowed. There were no wars, no new money being borrowed into existence. Interest payments caused the money in circulation to contract -2%.

1856 The money supply was up a trifling +2%. Hard times had arrived. Pump-priming money flowed from the banking centers of the Northeast to a terrorist in Kansas. On the night of May 24, this man, his four sons, and three others butchered five southern sympathizers at Dutch Henry's Crossing at Pottawatomie Creek. The men they killed were family men. They were taken unarmed from their homes at night one at a time, had their arms hacked off and were gutted. The case never came to trial. His name - John Brown. The terror of the French Revolution was spreading to American revolutionists. Tempers began to flare. John Brown was earning his pay. Brown professed to be a "Christian". The closest thing we have today to compare with his theology are those certain Judeo/Christians who are "saved by grace" to do anything they want to do.

---

16. Judges 2:2, Exodus 23:31-33, Exodus 34:12-16. This constant dealing with non-Christians has taught our people their ways. President John F. Kennedy is reported to have required his staff to read Machiavelli's "The Prince", the book that teaches lying and deception as a standard political practice.

1857 Unemployment was rampant. Municipalities couldn't collect taxes to pay on their indebtedness. Defaults were beginning, most of which were in the North. Something had to be done to relieve the unbearable economic situation. Chicago and Philadelphia defaulted; so did Jefferson, Ohio. In Philadelphia 10,000 workers met and demanded work; a public works program was set up. The Bank of Pennsylvania failed. Girard bank suspended specie payments. Cedar County, Iowa and Jefferson, Ohio defaulted their bonds. The Ohio Insurance Company went broke. Four thousand nine hundred and twenty businesses failed - a record!

1858 Knox, Indiana defaulted; so did Rome, New York; Union, Ohio; Crawford County, Pennsylvania; and Johnson County, Iowa. John Brown, the Kansas killer, was brought east. He was financed by men in the very areas being "squeezed" in the Northeast. Sent to Virginia, he murdered four more men, setting passions aflame. The newspapers belonging to the banking interests of the Northeast called him a martyr. The relatives of the men he murdered were living in an area which had little debt. They did most of what little banking business they did with England as their ancestors had for the previous 150 years. They said he was a murderer. An unknown backwoodsman was tapped to be the spokesman of the monied interests. He started making warlike noises. His name was Abraham Lincoln, an American "Robespierre".

1859 Davis, Indiana defaulted its bonds; so did Lawrence County, Pennsylvania and Janesville, Wisconsin. The money supply was up +7%. Still, 3,913 businesses failed.

1860 Kansas had a terrible drought and famine. This was compounded by raiders financed from the Northeast. New London, Connecticut, defaulted; so did Hancock, Ohio; Bissell and Jeffersonville, Indiana; Beloit, Wisconsin; Butler County, Pennsylvania. Municipal debt had grown ten times from 1840 to 1860, and the payments were becoming unbearable; as always, because of interest there was far more money owed than was in existence. 3,675 businesses failed.

Here are some more facts many history books filter out:

The richest man and largest slave owner in Jefferson County, Virginia, was a black. He owned 91 slaves. Another black, Charles Rogers, owned 47, and Marie Meteger, also black, owned 58. Solomon Humphries of Macon, Georgia was the town's leading grocer, and John Jones was proprietor of one of Charleston's leading hotels. Both were blacks. Thomy Lafon of New Orleans was a prominent philanthropist; the city erected a bust in his honor in a public building. He, too, was black.[17]

The assessed valuation of all United States property at this time was 12 billion - one-half in 11 southern states with only 8 million whites.[18] These 8 million whites exported 57% of the total exports of the nation. The South was wealthy, had a debt-free citizenry and really did not know that the usury centers of the Northeast were being devastated by a usury induced depression.

1860 The straw that broke the camel's back occurred when the money supply declined 1% putting pressure on debtors all over the Northeast. These poor people were enmeshed in the net of debt which was drawing tighter and tighter. They were finding it impossible to pay two thousand dollars of debt with only one thousand dollars in circulation, as countless generations before have found. Nevertheless, they had to get interest payments somehow or lose everything they had.

Nov. 6, Abraham Lincoln was elected President. Fearing the threats of Lincoln, South Carolina seceded on December 20th.

---

17. W. E. Debnam, Weep No More My Lady, Graphic Press, Raleigh, N.C., 1950, p. 41.

18. Debnam, p. 39.

SECTION - IX
THE WAR BETWEEN THE STATES

Chapter 29

HOW IT STARTED

Early 1861, a whole flock of northern municipalities defaulted on their bonds: Schuyler, Illinois; Genoa, New York; Sterling, New York; Waterloo, Wisconsin; Rochester, Wisconsin; Marshall County, Iowa; Pittsburgh, Pennsylvania; Milwaukee, Wisconsin. Before the year ended, 6,993 businesses had failed.

William Henry Seward, Secretary of State, suggested a diversionary foreign war to reunite the country[1]. It was a good idea, but Lincoln had other plans.

---

1. Lincoln, Works, IV, pp. 316-318.

March 15 - Assurances were given the Confederate Government that Fort Sumter would be evacuated within a few days.[2]

March 28 - In spite of these assurances, Mr. Lincoln completed plans for fitting out an expedition to invade Charleston Harbor.[3]

April 5 - Transports and vessels of war with troops, munitions, and military supplies sailed from northern ports bound southward.

April 6 - More ships set sail from northern ports to join the fleet.

April 7 - Still more ships sail from port to join forces. The newspapers picked up these warlike events and fully exposed them in Washington and elsewhere.[4] The southern peace delegation read these reports, became alarmed and confronted the Lincoln government with the charge of "deception". The Lincoln government "pooh-poohed" the whole matter and referred to the imminent evacuation in a note which said, "Faith as to Sumter fully kept. Wait and see." Unfortunately for Mr. Lincoln's reputation, this message was in writing.

At the very same time the war fleet was on high seas the Lincoln government continued to maintain that Fort Sumter would be peacefully handed over to South Carolina and there would be no war.[5]

April 10 - A message was sent from the South Carolina Peace Delegation in Washington to General Beauregard at Charleston. "The Tribune of today declares the main object of the

2. Jefferson Davis, The Rise And Fall Of The Confederate Government, Appleton and Co., N. Y., 1881, p. 278.

3. W. A. Harris, The Record of Fort Sumter, Columbia, S. C., 1862.

4. Davis, p. 280.

5. Davis, p. 270

expedition to be the relief of Sumter, and that a force will be landed which will overcome all opposition."[6] This was how South Carolina learned that a United States invasion fleet was shortly due to storm Charleston.

April 12 - The fleet arrived but was kept out of Charleston Harbor by a terrible storm which upset the time schedule. The South Carolinians were now reduced to one of two choices: to allow the fleet and fort to combine forces and subdue the greatest commercial harbor in the South, or to reduce the fort before the storm died down and the fleet could enter. A choice of this kind is no choice at all. Naturally, they bombarded the fort and received the stigma of firing the first shot. Lincoln had won - the war was on. Contracts went out; bank profits boomed as the money supply jumped to +11% versus -1% the horrible warless year before.

1862 - Bank profits skyrocketed as the money supply jumped another +25% - happy days were here again! For the first time since 1854 money was freely flowing. It allowed the poor farmer to keep his farm; it allowed the hard-pressed businessman to pay the mortgage and keep his business; and it allowed people to pay their taxes which kept cities from defaulting their bonds. This made the holders of those bonds happy indeed. The bloody war which cost hundreds of thousands of lives did have a silver lining.

1863 - There were only 495 business failures. Lincoln has been blamed for the war. Of course he gave orders, but the "Usury System" had created hundreds of others who were capable of doing the same thing. There was Seward who suggested a diversionary war. This would have accomplished the same thing economically that a civil war did. It was he who suggested the closing of southern ports to all trade except northern trade.

These men were created by a system which demanded that money be borrowed into existence, whatever the cost, to relieve the suffering of the nation. Of course, for the sake of history the

---

6. Davis, p. 279.

reasons must be changed to be acceptable to future generations. It sounds better to fight to preserve the Union and to free the slaves, than to fight to increase the money supply +25% giving debtors another chance to pay a $2,000 debt while only $1,000 is in circulation. The real reason - the thing that breaks strong men, turns women into workworn hags and early widows, and starves children - the Wolf of Interest - is never mentioned. The interest-bankers who run the system selected Lincoln, a willing tool, and told him what to do. He broke almost every rule in the book. He started a war by himself without the approval of Congress. He jailed 38,000 of his own countrymen as political prisoners to silence their opposition. He suspended the Writ of Habeas-Corpus and he suspended newspapers that dared oppose him.

His countrymen repaid him with draft riots in New York, massive desertions from his armies and a rebellious underground "Copperhead" movement which was present in every northern state. There was scarcely a northern state that didn't have its own armed battles between "pro" and "anti" Lincoln factions.

Lincoln surrounded himself with a galaxy of men of doubtful reputation...each his own selection. Sumner in his cabinet - the brutal, cold-hearted extremist; Grant - the hard-drinking general who issued orders to burn every citizen's house and dwelling within 10 miles of any train derailment in northern Virginia. This was the same Grant who refused to issue orders to protect Virginia civilians behind his lines.

Thieving and rapacious soldiers could enter any private dwelling at will, take anything, and do anything they liked to the occupants. Seldom was there disciplinary action. On occasion, officers of the lower ranks did what they could to protect civilians, but this was the exception. It did not extend to those in higher authority. Mr. Lincoln knew of this condition. General Custer hanged Confederate cavalrymen until the hanging of his own men in reprisal put a stop to it. He received no reprimand. Sheridan burned the Valley of Virginia - **after Confederate troops had left.** Nothing was said about this either.

From the beginning of the War Northern and Southern POWs were exchanged as a humanitarian act to prevent the rigors of POW camps. This practice was ordered stopped. A delegation of hungry and sick northern officers at Belle Isle Prison near Richmond were released on their word-of-honor so that they could go to Washington to beg Lincoln to reinstate prisoner exchanges. At this very time Lincoln's own sons were safely holding down desk jobs in Washington far from the dangers of the front lines. Lincoln refused these men's petition.

Lincoln was apprised of the fact that captured Southern soldiers were placed in the most exposed POW camps with little shelter, almost no blankets and clothing to cope with the frigid weather, had little food, and that blacks were placed over them for guards.[7]

These blacks were encouraged to do what they liked to the prisoners. Lincoln knew this. He was also aware of what Sherman was doing in the deep South. Sherman was not only not removed from his command - he continued to receive honors from Lincoln. The argument cannot be made that he did not know what was going on. He stayed in my great-grandfather's house at Kelly's Ford. With his own eyes he saw the crimes of his soldiers to the very place he was staying and had others pointed out to him. He said nothing and turned away.

This is the Lincoln "the System" has portrayed as a soft-hearted, sensitive, lonely man who tried to prevent the blood bath that inundated America. The Law states: "Can two walk together, except they be agreed?" Amos 3:3. His apologists say that he would have made things different had he lived. Perhaps.[8] Perhaps our merciful God spared his children "The rest of the Lincoln story".

Chapter 30

1864 - TOPSIDE TRANSITION
YEAR - WAR PHASE ENDS

In 1864 the Wholesale commodity price index peaked. This marked the end of the War Cycle and the beginning of the Peace Cycle. The War Between the States staggered on a few months longer and died at Appomattox. The northern survivors talked

---

7 ". . .thou mayest not set a stranger over thee who is not thy brother." Deuteronomy 17:15

8. "By their fruits ye shall know them". Matthew 7:20

about their part in "saving the Union", the southern survivors about the sacrifices they had made for "States' Rights" and "Southern Independence". Almost a million men were dead in their graves.

Gold And The Gould Syndrome

My great-grandfather, Dr. William Hoskins, late surgeon of the 59th Virginia Infantry, accompanied by his cousin, Dr. Christopher Nunn, was on his way home from Appomattox. They rode through devastated and still smouldering Richmond early in the morning and on into King William County on their way home to King and Queen which is just on the other side, when they heard a woman screaming.

Drawing their pistols they rode into the yard of an old plantation house where they discovered two Union stragglers abusing the female inhabitants.

Shots were exchanged. The stragglers lay dead.

Not having eaten for two days they searched the knapsacks of the dead marauders for food and in the process discovered two $20 gold pieces. My grandfather took one and Dr. Nunn took the other.

The story has been handed down in the family that these two coins were almost the only money there was in King and Queen County for the next ten or fifteen years. This was part of the story which was hard to understand. Why should two $20 gold pieces be so valuable?

Could it be that a $20 gold piece was worth more than $20? In an attempt to solve this puzzle I wrote the Congressional Library and half a dozen other agencies of the U.S. Government. The answers returned were always the same and said to the effect that the price of gold since 1792 was $20.67 until President Roosevelt had it changed to $35 an ounce in 1934, and called in the gold. This was the Government of the United States talking and so I dropped the subject.

One day I was studying a book[9] when I ran across something which clarified matters. This is what I found:

---

9. Francis Eames, The New York Stock Exchange, p. 120.

Highest And Lowest Prices Of Gold

Year	High	Low
1862	$134	-
1863	173 1/2	$151 1/2
1864	287	151 1/2
1865	233 3/4	128 5/8
1866	167 3/4	125
1867	145 5/8	232
1868	150	133 1/4

It seems that while our "government authorities" were technically correct in saying that the price of gold had remained the same for over 100 years, they were speaking of the "official" price of gold. The "market price" was another thing altogether.

During the War Between the States the flood of paper money in the North and the tremendous increase in prices made people flee paper into gold. Then, too, there was real reason to believe that the esprit of Southern Chivalry might overthrow the brave but uninspired masses fielded by the Three Sisters - Philadelphia, New York, and Boston. If this were to happen, Union paper money might become worthless.

It can be seen from the above table that the two gold coins picked up at the close of the war were far more valuable than their face value would indicate. They were more valuable when you consider that there was virtually no other money in King and Queen - paper or specie.

These two coins went from one person to another, and were used as collateral until 1879 when the market value of paper and gold money were both $20.67.

From that time we hear no more of the coins. I still have my grandfather's pistol, a .44 Starr, the same make as carried by Gen. Robert E. Lee.

Jay Gould

In the last century there was no law against "corners". A "corner" was created when a group of men - on purpose or by accident - trapped another group in an unfavorable position that could cost them dearly or even wipe them out.

IX - THE WAR BETWEEN THE STATES

Jay Gould, a well known speculator of his day, was the most ambitious and came nearer success than almost any speculator in gold before or since. He wanted to do something that men have dreamed of doing for hundreds of years. He wanted to "corner" the men who owned gold....something that had never been done before.

In 1869 a normal day's gold trading activity was in the neighborhood of $50 million with the commercial interests taking only $5 to $6 million. The other was just speculative activity with the participants buying on 90% - 95% margin as is the case today.

In this type of situation there may be $5 million worth of actual gold but speculators sell much more gold than that at what they consider high prices with the intention of buying back when it declines in price. Thus, with only $5 million in actual gold changing hands on a given day, $50 million may be sold and promised to be delivered.

This works well as long as gold declines. If gold is sold at $287 and bought at $100, it yields a $187 profit - the same as if one had bought at $100 and sold at $287. On a 10% margin this results in 645% profit one way and 1070% the other. Heady stuff! But, if gold rises in price after a trader has sold it short - then we have another story, a dangerous story for those on the wrong side. This is especially true if they are unable to buy the promised gold for delivery!

The Corner Closes

This is precisely what happened. Jay Gould, his partner Jim Fisk, and their cohorts saw that the gold decline was slowing and they quietly began buying the metal. Gold stopped its descent and started rising. It did not take a lot of buying to put gold in short supply. If $2 million worth of gold were bought, this would leave only $3 million for all the others to buy.

Five years after gold had reached its peak of $287, it had declined to $100 and was technically oversold. People had begun to forget about the dream of $1,000 and $2,000 an ounce which had created such a frenzy a few years earlier.

When the short sellers realized that big buyers were running up the price, they panicked and added to the upside pressure as they themselves tried to buy back gold at any price. The Corner was being closed.

Stories were planted in friendly newspapers telling of the great profits that had been made in gold in the past and the great profits which were currently being made. New speculators wanting to get in on the action flocked to buy. Gold surged to new highs for the move and the trapped shorts continued to bid against each other in their desperation to buy back gold for delivery. So many buyers - so little gold. The day of reckoning was rapidly drawing nearer.

If delivery day arrived and the sellers of that tremendous amount of gold did not actually have the gold, then Mr. Jay Gould could demand $1,000 an ounce, $2,000 an ounce, or even $10,000 an ounce - and get it. He owned almost the only gold for sale and could demand whatever he chose to demand. The law was on his side.

President Grant's Move

A glimmer of hope broke through for the shorts. The rumor was that President Grant was going to allow the sale of government gold to break the corner so that many prominent people could avoid bankruptcy. The price dropped to $120.

Jay Gould went to see President Grant, a visit well covered by the press. He asked President Grant not to sell government gold. Grant puffed on his cigar, grunted, but did not say what he was going to do. Gould left Grant's office and let the press believe that he and Grant had "a deal" and that government gold was not going to be sold. In fact, Gould did not trust Grant, believing him to be a weak sort who believed the last person who talked to him was right. There were only a few men with the Gould Syndicate and there were a lot of men trapped in the "Corner" who would be paying trips to the President. Gould determined to get out of the action when the opportunity arose.

The news hit the front pages that Gould and Grant had an understanding and that gold was not going to be sold by the government. The short sellers again panicked and the price of gold rose to $169 an ounce. Jay Gould sold his gold to the frantic buyers. He didn't tell his partners. The price dropped. Jim Fisk lost heavily and was ruined, as were many others in the Gould Syndicate. Gold started down again and kept on going down until 1879 when it finally reached $20.67 - even par with paper money. It was a long and eventful trip from the $287 high in 1864 to the $20.67 low in 1879.

In 1865 General Robert E. Lee borrowed a suit to take office as president of a small Virginia college, later to be known as Washington & Lee. His home, Arlington, had been confiscated and used as a cemetery. The wealth of the South was gone. Planters, unable to keep up the plantation houses, moved into smaller over-seers' cottages. Deserted mansions crumbling into ruins dotted the countryside. Untended fields grew up in trees. As a conse-quence, practically every stand of old trees in Virginia today is 120 years old.

Poor and beaten, the South was still debt-free and proud. An impoverished debt-free people may regain both their wealth and power. Her elected representatives in Washington opposed every move made by the Northeast monied interests.

1866 With the war over the money supply dropped -13%. One thou-sand six hundred and forty eight banks closed. Economic chaos spread.

1867 In a panic to get the economy moving again the radicals passed the "Reconstruction Acts" in the attempt to make debtor/servants out of free people. It was nothing personal about these acts - the drastic times demanded drastic solu-tions. Southern whites were denied the right to vote and blacks were given the vote to implement new economic poli-cies. Federal troops were moved in to enforce the laws. The new black legislatures in the South were carefully instructed by northern usury-bankers how to vote hundreds of millions of dollars into existence to pay for all sorts of extravagances, and make the whites go into debt to pay for them. This was the first time in modern history that a Christian people had been persuaded to put their own blood brothers under the rule of "zûwr" strangers.

"...and their nobles shall be of themselves, and their governor shall proceed from the midst of them." Jeremiah 30:21

IX - THE WAR BETWEEN THE STATES

> "...thou mayest not set a stranger over thee who is not thy brother."   **Deuteronomy 17:15.**

The Babylonian "system" makes one do strange things.

Extortion, lawlessness, rape, and brutality descended on the South. A group of veterans approached General Lee with a request for him to lead an underground resistance organization. Feeling himself too old, he recommended General Nathan Bedford Forrest, the "one-man army of Tennessee". General Forrest accepted. He called the new organization the Ku Klux Klan. Almost every Christian gentleman in the South belonged to it. Its symbol - the red cross of the Templar crusader knights. This underground organization was the only police the South had. The weapon of the KKK was "counter-terror". There was no hiding place for the the tyrants. Brutal blacks, sadistic police, venal corrupt judges and legislators were treated like Gideon treated the "zûwr" strangers in the Bible. A thrust of a knife; a pistol shot in the night. Blacks and renegades refused to hold office. These offices were in time filled by Christians. It made little difference, however, to the usury-bankers that their minions had been killed or driven away. They had served their purpose. The South was saddled with a back-breaking debt.

This exercise in black terror cost the South more money than four years of warfare had. It was not until the early 1960s that Virginia paid her last Reconstruction debts.

Greenbacks & Silver

During the War Between the States Lincoln came in conflict with the banking interests who had put him into office. Lincoln wanted to raise money quickly for military expenditures. The agreement between the banks and government was to have the government borrow from them. This was all right with Mr. Lincoln, except the banks were not content with the usual interest; they wanted extremely high interest rates since there was a war. This posed a problem. Lincoln didn't want to pursue an unpopular war or to have to explain to the voters why he was paying exorbitant interest to the banks.

The bankers had elected him and felt that they owned him, and they simply refused to modify their demands. Lincoln, in a rush to get things done, did one of the two things that may have cost him his life. He instructed his government to print and issue "greenback" tallies to pay for wartime purchases.

These "greenbacks" did not go through the banking system. They were printed and issued directly by the government. They were interest-free paper tallies. The operators of the usury system were furious. They felt betrayed. European newspapers carried news items about this "revolutionary" development. Millions of "greenbacks" were printed by the government and spent into existence, and not a dime in interest was paid to the banks. In a legal counter attack to protect themselves, the bankers had Congress legislate that the greenbacks were not legal tender for taxes. This meant that they could not be taxed out of circulation, could not be used for interest on the nation's debt or for import or export duties. In this way they were able to drive their value down to 30% of par. Still, this was a dangerous precedent for the entire concept of "interest-banking". People had begun to demand that the government replace all interest bearing debt to the banks with interest-free greenbacks. It would save tens of millions in interest each year and could free the nation from the usury net.

Lincoln was killed. Immediately, the banking system demanded that the offending "greenbacks" be "retired". As the supply of greenbacks dwindled, it forced debtors to borrow interest-bearing replacement money into existence from the banks. A money shortage developed causing a panic in the stock market. Ten thousand businesses failed. To get some money into the hands of the people the "Act of 1873" was passed allowing anyone who had silver to present it to a government mint and have it minted into "trade dollars".

These silver trade dollars were given "legal tender" status - taxes could be paid with them. Everyone who had any silver at all immediately brought it in to be minted. Almost overnight silver dollars appeared everywhere. Leather pocketbooks for men came into vogue to handle the increased weight of the money. At the same time this was going on, Germany went off the silver standard and on the gold standard. This created additional surplus silver which flooded America and helped cause the silver price to decline. For a time debtors had money to pay their debts. The banks, again confronted with something which threatened to ruin their monopoly, brought their forces to bear to have this act repealed in time to save mortgages from being paid.

1874 – 1876   The Greenback Party

"The Greenback Party" became a force in American politics. This party was made up of debtors who wanted the repeal of the "Redemption Act" that was taking greenbacks out of existence and leaving the country without money. This movement was successful. The law to repeal the Redemption Act passed in 1875, but since the borrowing government was servant to the lender banks, the law was simply ignored. They continued to retire greenbacks out of existence. The depression grew deeper and deeper and didn't reach bottom until the beginning of the War Phase in 1896 - 32 long years after commodities had peaked in 1864.

Islam In Europe

Islam made a great impression on the rulers of Europe by its rapid conquests of Egypt, North Africa, Sicily, Spain and its invasion of France in the heartland of the West, so narrowly turned back at Tours. Following this effort a new invasion of Europe was commenced by the Turks in the East. Their first great success was the capture of the greatest Christian city in the world, Constantinople, and the massacre of its defenders.

This invasion was tremendously successful as it progressed northward up the Danube Valley. It reached the walls of Vienna, spreading a wide path of death and destruction in its path. It was in fighting this invasion that Captain John Smith made his reputation.

Almost 100 years later the issue was still in balance. It wasn't until 1683 that the Polish cavalry lifted the seige. This marked the high tide of Moslem conquests in Europe. Millions of Slav Samaritans, however, had passed under Islamic rule. These captives belonged to the Eastern Orthodox Church. All the free nations of Europe - Christian and Samaritan - aided in the defense of Vienna in order to halt the march of the dread Muslims. It was the head of the Eastern Orthodox Church, the Nordic Czars of Russia, who led the series of Slav/Turkish wars. They were inconceivably brutal. The Turks considered the wars to be a continuation of the Crusades. They started small, but ended up involving most of Europe and the Middle East.

IX - THE WAR BETWEEN THE STATES

1812 - 1833 The Greek War Of Independence

In April 1821, Archbishop Germanos raised the standard of the Cross as a signal for a general rising of the Slavs of Greece.* This beginning of the war was marked by the advance of peasants marching against the Turks armed with clubs, scythes and slings. These Greeks assaulted Turkish strong points and put their defenders to the sword. The war was marked by massacres of Turks by Greeks, and Greeks by Turks. Everywhere was repeated the same scenes of butchery. In September the citadel of Tribolitsa was taken by storm. The Greek general rode in triumph through the streets carpeted with Turkish dead. At the end of the parade 2,000 prisoners of all ages and sexes were slaughtered. The whole tone of the war was one of mutual extermination.

1824 This Greek revolt, financed by western banks, showed surprising strength and resilience. The newly purchased armaments "had their effect" and the Turkish sultan reluctantly despaired of suppressing the insurrection himself. He summoned to his aid Mehemet Ali, Pasha of Egypt. These allied Islamic peoples proceeded to exterminate Slav resistance throughout Greece.

1827 In February, the Greek Government borrowed more money from European banks. Soon thereafter the Albanian Turkish garrison surrendered to the Greeks on terms. They too were massacred as they were marched away under escort. Despite these setbacks to the Islamic cause, the combined forces of Turkey and Egypt were turning Greece into a vast cemetery. Pacification was in sight.

A reconquest of Greece by the Turks would have defaulted the loans made to the Greek revolutionaries by Western banks. To halt this approaching economic debacle, British and French warships were sent into the harbor of Navarino to attack the Turks.

---

* The usury system of ancient Greece swept the land clear of its native adamic (blush red) population - the ones who had built the temples and left their statues. Those who could fled and those who couldn't ceased to have children. The vacuum was filled by Slavs from southern Russia. These immigrants were ruled first by Byzantine and later by Mohammedan conquerors.

Victory in the resulting battle combined with a successful Russian land campaign insured Greek independence and the safety of their loans to Western banks.

1854 - The Crimean War

The Turks were the only ones left in this part of the world not deeply in debt to the Western banks. When the next disagreements started between the Russians and Turks, England and France switched and aligned themselves on the side of the Islamic Turks. This allowed them to extend loans to a new customer. This war was a revelation to the Western soldiers who did the actual fighting. Their new allies, the Turks, were long on promises of aid, but when the fighting erupted they were nowhere to be seen. Westerners were left to fight the Slavs. It was as fatal to leave the Christian wounded in the hands of "friendly" infidel allies as it was the Russian Slav enemy. British soldiers wrote home outraged that on the battlefield of Alma the savage Slavic foe combed the battlefield searching out wounded Britons to kill. Officers complained that British medics were often attacked and killed by the wounded Russian soldiers they were trying to aid.[10] These reports of Slav treatment of Westerners who had fallen into their power were confirmed many times over during the World Wars I and II. At Stalingrad a quarter of a million German soldiers were surrendered to the Slavs. Only eight thousand came home after the war. After World War II many millions of Westerners living in Slavic lands in the east were uprooted and sent treking westward to their own people. Millions died of mistreatment, starvation, and exposure en route. Gomer's press in the West will not discuss the atrocity.

The War of 1877 - 1878 between Russia and Turkey was triggered by the continued oppression of the Slavic subjects of the Sultan. Turkey had promised to grant better treatment to their captive Slav populations after the Crimean War, but the following years brought no changes. In 1875 an insurrection broke out in Heicegovina and Monte Negro, to be followed by Serbia openly taking up arms against Turkey. Russia, the long time ally of the rebels by reason of race and religion, joined in. Russian Slav volunteers flocked in great numbers to join the Serbian Slavs.

---

10. Henry Tyrrell, The History Of The War With Russia, London Printing and Publishing Co., Ltd., London and New York.

IX - THE WAR BETWEEN THE STATES

This culminated in Slavic Rumania declaring her independence. Bulgaria, another Slavic land, also became independent. The Mohammedan world was fast losing their booty of conquered Slavic peoples and lands.

The two main lessons to be learned from the Slav-Saracen confrontations are:

1. Confrontations between these two are absolutely ruthless. They are the actions of those who do not have "the Law" in their hearts.

2. The Saracens will make treaties with or against either the Slav or the Christian West as it suits their needs, in spite of the enmity which runs deep against both.

1881 Bankers used European armies to force Turkey to pay them the revenues from government salt and tobacco monopolies, taxes on fishing and spirits, and raw silk production. They even took the annual tribute paid by Bulgaria to Turkey. The bankers, in effect, ruled Turkey for the next 25 years.[11]

1896 - Bottomside Transition Year

1896 The commodity prices bottomed out. The War Phase started. William Jennings Bryan attempted to ease the shortage of money by advocating "free coinage of silver". Anyone with a mine could take their silver to a bank and exchange it for "legal tender". Free coinage and cheap money was the issue. Mark Hanna, William McKinley's campaign manager, easily collected $4 million from banks and corporations to stop the "free coinage" issue. If debtors could obtain "legal tender" to pay their debts, the banks could not foreclose. McKinley won.

---

11. Wall Street Journal, p. 1, Jan 12, 1984

1892 France sent a battleship to aid the French owned national bank in Santo Domingo to foreclose debtors.

1898 The U.S. minister in Spain knew that Spain would give up Cuba; might even cede it to the U.S. His knowledge was ignored. The U.S. warship Maine mysteriously blew up in Havana, Cuba. American politicians disclaimed desire for new territory. Money was immediately borrowed into existence to expand the armed services. MI money supply is up +13%. As they said at the time - "it was a splendid little war!"

1899 Money supply up +17%. The British did their part by invading South Africa and starting the Boer War.

1904 Santo Domingo threatened default of $32 million. President Theodore Roosevelt sent in troops, took over 55% of that country's customs revenues for repayment of debts. He sent troops into Nicaragua and Haiti for the same reasons.

Wars began to break out all over the world. The Russo-Japanese War, the Philippine Insurrection; the War Cycle was in full stride as borrowed money again flowed and debtors were able to pay their debts and borrow still more money into existence to buy fantastic bargains before the prices again rose. Actually, if a person could have borrowed enough money, he could have become rich! Those who were verging on bankruptcy and unable to pay any more on their mortgages were saved by the fresh flow of money from the war borrowing.

This era outdid itself with a war of all wars - World War I. An entire world at war - money being borrowed at a fantastic rate, public and private!

Increase In M1 Money Supply

1915 - + 7%
1916 - +19%
1917 - +19%
1918 - +10%

1919 - +16%
1920 - +12%

This enabled the world to pay on their older debts while adding new ones. A splendidly profitable age, except for the widows in black and the shattered survivors who could not seem to understand why. . .

Chapter 31

1920 - Topside Transition Year

The year of incredible price rises. Good times, boom times! Land and commodities trading at record levels. As always, the time arrives when almost all available property is mortgaged and there is no way people can borrow new money into existence to support high prices. Prices then decline.

In 1920 prices peaked and started down. Farmers were caught in the commodity decline and began to suffer. The stock market bottomed out and started up. This always comes as a shock to those who look for everything to go up together and come down together. When prices are rising, companies use up most of their profits buying raw materials which are ever increasing in price, and paying labor which is ever increasing in its demands.

When prices start down, companies which are not weighted down by debt can buy raw materials at ever lower prices, hire labor more cheaply, and make a profit in selling the finished product almost every time - if they are fortunate. Of course, this, too, has an end to it: prices can only go so low and then another set of problems arise.

The wholesale price index also peaked out and rapidly started down. Nineteen-twenty was a year which was far more important than the much talked about 1929.

1921   The stock market started rising. Unemployment reached 22%. A number of corporations which were heavily in debt went under and the M2 money supply dropped -10%. Real estate got sticky and in places like Florida it plunged.

There was another milestone passed in 1921. The total number of banks which had been growing year after year peaked at 31,076. This event is of such importance that it has been delayed until now. The article in the next chapter is from PORT-FOLIOS INVESTMENT ADVISORY Newsletter No. 84 and is printed with permission.

SECTION X

THE WORLD TODAY

Chapter 32

BANK WARS

In the "1920s Turkey Shoot", over 16,000 banks folded or were merged out of existence.

This story began more than 200 years ago. In 1780 the United States had two interest banks. Prior to this time it had none. The people didn't believe in interest since it was forbidden by their Christian religion. By 1800 perhaps 20 of these banks had come into existence.

It was during this 20-year period that events occurred which shaped the history of the country. These events caused the War Between the States, the rapid settling of the West by bankrupt easterners, and World War II. These two decades made inevitable everything that has followed since.

1780 The forcible ejection of the British and their banking activities left a vacuum in America. Immediately a rush was underway to fill that vacuum. Alexander Hamilton presented three arguments for a central bank. He wanted to do to the brand new United States what the Bank of England had done to

England, and he wanted it done by himself and his backers who were reputed to be the Rothschilds and the Bank of England.

1781 The private Bank of Pennsylvania* in Philadelphia was replaced by the Bank of North America. It was later absorbed into the Pennsylvania Company for Insurance in 1923. Cornwallis surrendered the British Army at Yorktown, Virginia. Events moved fast.

1784 Bank of New York founded - a Hamilton creation. Oldest existing commercial bank in the country. The Massachusetts Bank also formed. Virginia settled her counties of Ohio, Indiana, Illinois, Michigan and Wisconsin, and spun them off as states. Virginia, an unwilling slave state, also saw that a law was passed prohibiting slavery in these new states.

1786 First major economic depression brought on by these new banks lending 10 and demanding 11 in payment. Banks foreclosed debtors forcing them into poverty and debtors' prison. The state of Massachusetts had heavy debt and levied heavy taxes on its citizens to pay interest on this debt. This was exactly the same thing England had been doing. It ruined many of her own farmers.

Led by Captain Daniel Shay, 2,000 of these desperate men seized Worcester, Massachusetts and other towns. This uprising threatened the establishment of interest-banking in North America. The Governor of Massachusetts quickly took the field against the "rebels". "Shay's Rebellion" was suppressed on February 27, 1787. The Interest System won its first victory.

1787 The Constitution was fittingly put together in Philadelphia, the home of the Bank of North America. Next, New York City, the home of the Bank of New York, was proclaimed the temporary capitol of the country.

1789 Washington was elected President. In a move toward conciliation he appointed Alexander Hamilton Secretary of the

---

* As in the case of Holland and England earlier, many of the new nation's rulers were in the usurers' pockets. Among those who were permitted to get in on the original subscription to this bank were Benjamin Franklin, Thomas Jefferson, Alexander Hamilton, James Monroe, John Jay, John Paul Jones, and Commodore John Barry. Robert Morris, superintendent of finance for the Continental Congress, was a leading force. The bank opened with capital assets of $335,000 on January 1, 1782. In four years it had assets of $2,000,000 - a 600% growth. This bank grew until it had 68 branches in its own trade area. In 1836 it included the Bank of St. Thomas in the Virgin Islands. In 1935 it took over the National Bank of the Danish W. Indies, an international network based in London. In its possession is the oldest check drawn on a bank in America dated March 18, 1782.

Treasury. This put the fox in the hen house and it doomed Washington's beloved Virginia to be devastated by a war of assimilation 71 years later.

1791 First Bank of the United States was chartered. This was a private bank to which all the government's money was entrusted. Its charter was for 20 years and was also Hamilton's creation. Rep. James Madison of Virginia on February 2 opposed the bank because he said that it would;

1. Banish precious metals through inflation of the money supply, and

2. Result in runs on banks and bank failures.

When its successor the "Second Bank of the U.S." went bankrupt 50 odd years later it was discovered that 64% of the bank's 25,000 shares were owned by foreigners - mostly British. Friends of the Bank of England had been active in America. Madison had been right.

1792 History books say that Hamilton's influence shortened the panic that calling $11 in loans when there were only $10 in existence had caused. History also says that the victors write the history books.

1794 Heavy taxes needed to pay interest on state debts caused farmers to revolt in western Pennsylvania. George Washington did what his economic advisor told him to do - he crushed the rebellion. Creditors called the uprising "The Whiskey Rebellion" as a "put-down". It was a tragic time for the farmers of America. Another victory for interest-banking.

1824 The Boston Revolt. In Boston, Massachusetts a number of small private banks had been hurriedly thrown together and were eager to "sock it to the public!" In addition to lending $10 for $11, they issued paper money. They also threatened the big banks by underbidding them for business.

The big banks retaliated by having laws passed requiring gold to be given to anyone presenting a paper bank note to an issuing bank. The big banks were too big for retaliation. This effectively brought banking rebels to "heel", and they have continued to be obedient ever since. Today, the present policing organization keeping surveillance over the smaller banks is called "The Federal Reserve System". It is a power unto itself, refusing to allow itself to be audited since its official creation in 1913.

The Boston Revolt was actually a civil war within the new banking system. It was the third and last revolt against the big interest-banks in the Northeast. Shay's Rebellion, The Whiskey Rebellion, and the Boston Revolt - two attempts with force and one financial - all three defeated. This was how the Northeast was secured.

Conquest Of The North, Central & South

For the next 61 years the energies of the new banking system were directed into the north-central part of the country, into the former Virginia counties of Ohio, Indiana, Illinois, Michigan and Wisconsin. After this was accomplished, the stone wall to interest expansion presented by the plantation system of the mother state Virginia and the rest of the South was broken by armed force in 1861. The "arrogant Southerners" were brought to heel in the same manner as their brother farmers in Massachusetts and Pennsylvania earlier.

The Boom In Banks

1812 By the time the War of 1812 ended there were more than 250 banks in existence. In addition, there was one notable subtraction which was a first:

Note: Big banks always encourage small banks to develop a following of borrowers. When as many people have mortgaged their property as are likely to, the big banks pass regulations which are impossible for the little banks to comply with. In 1824 it was "gold backing", in the 1920s it was "reserves". When the small banks are not able to comply, they close or are bought out. Their assets (mortgages) are taken over by the big banks. The small bank has been used as a "finder".

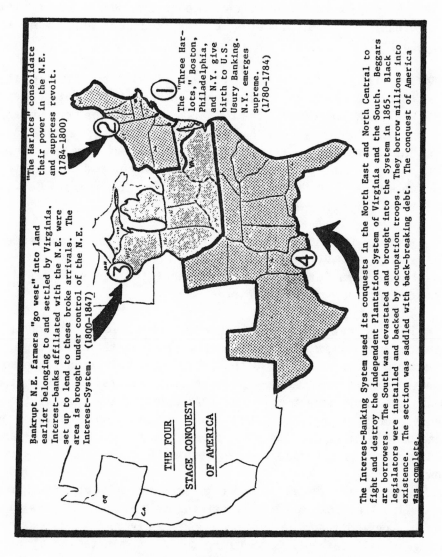

The "Three Har-
lots," Boston,
Philadelphia,
and N.Y. give
birth to U.S.
Usury Banking.
N.Y. emerges
supreme.
(1780-1784)

"The Harlots" consolidate
their power in the N.E.
and suppress revolt.
(1784-1800)

Bankrupt N.E. farmers "go west" into land
earlier belonging to and settled by Virginia.
Interest-banks affiliated with the N.E. were
set up to lend to these broke arrivals. The
area is brought under control of the N.E.
Interest-System. (1800-1847)

THE FOUR
STAGE CONQUEST
OF AMERICA

The Interest-Banking System used its conquests in the North East and North Central to
fight and destroy the independent Plantation System of Virginia and the South. Beggars
are borrowers. The South was devastated and brought into the System in 1865. Black
legislators were installed and backed by occupation troops. They borrow millions into
existence. The section was saddled with back-breaking debt. The conquest of America
was complete.

THE 4-STAGE CONQUEST OF AMERICA

1809 The Farmers Exchange Bank of Gloucester, Rhode Island went broke. This was the first of the thousands which were to follow.

1834 You will note on the chart on page 179 that by this date the total number of banks had grown to 506. The fight between President Jackson of the U.S. and Biddle of the Second Bank of the U.S. has been omitted because the issue was not "interest-bank" vs. "interest free bank," but merely who was going to control the country. Jackson won and delayed the complete bank takeover of the country for years. He was tough. Biddle's bank bankrupted in 1841.

1837 "Crisis of 1837". In May of this year all banks suspended specie payment. Six hundred banks broke down. New interest banks were forming so rapidly that the decrease really doesn't show up on the history chart.

For the next 84 years - through depressions and booms - interest-banks grew like cancer cells. Even in the awful depression which bottomed in 1896 the total number of banks increased almost yearly. Businessmen, farmers, and workers, caught in the meshes of the interest-contract, bankrupted by the tens of thousands pouring riches into the coffers of banks holding the contracts. This was the time when starvation stalked the land - and banking tycoons and their cronies were building mansions in every town.

Look at the dates on the big mansions in your town. You will find that most were built between 1880 - 1910. It was also in this period that the farmers began to give up the impossible struggle with interest compounding debt, and started to move to the cities, as happened in the identical same manner in Rome 2,000 years ago. The hills that used to be farmed in New England and the South have gone into pasture and bush.

The Roman Parallel

At the peak of her might Rome invaded the land of old Persia. She levied a fine of 20 million. If the Persian cities did not pay, Rome would raze them as she had Corinth. Persia had no money. Roman bankers generously lent 20 million. In a few short years principal plus interest made the debt grow to 40 million. Interest payments to Rome annually were from 2 to 4 million. This compared with the annual tribute of only 1.5 million to the Imperial Roman government. The bankers were raking off more than the state.

Money is power. The borrower is servant to the lender. This 2 - 4 million annual interest payment represented a lot of power to the banking class of Rome. A dictator came to power in Rome and declared 2,000 of these wealthy Roman banker/knights "traitors" and confiscated their wealth (loans). This was done in the name of the state. The dictator ran the state. Now he owned the loans - and the interest. For a time he became a super banker!

This is the type of power play which was missed by the masses in Rome. It was again missed by the masses during the "1920s Turkey Shoot" in America.

The Birth Of The Giant Bank

1913 In America the business of "guaranteed profits" whetted the appetites of greedy people all over the nation to get into banking. The number of banks grew to 27,285. Instead of stamping out these new banks, the Northeast giants encouraged their growth in spite of the fact that when a pie is cut too many ways, no one gets a big slice. There were too many banks and most of them were not making as much money as they could have if there were fewer banks. To reclaim their advantage when the time was ripe, the big banks instructed the politicians to create a central regulatory commission run by the same big banks.

The Federal Reserve was created. This new creation acted much in the same manner as the Roman dictator had earlier. A lot of regulations governing banks were issued. The act bringing the Federal Reserve System into existence was co-authored by Senator Carter Glass (whose house is three blocks from where this article is being written).

1921 Seven years later the ballooning total of banks peaked at 31,076 and the big banks snapped the trap shut on the small

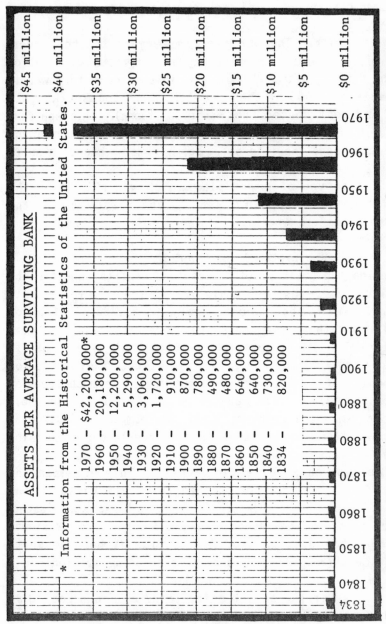

ASSETS PER AVERAGE SURVIVING BANK

Information from the Historical Statistics of the United States.

1970	$42,200,000*
1960	20,180,000
1950	12,200,000
1940	5,290,000
1930	3,060,000
1920	1,720,000
1910	910,000
1900	870,000
1890	780,000
1880	490,000
1870	480,000
1860	640,000
1850	640,000
1840	730,000
1834	820,000

* Information from the Historical Statistics of the United States.

ASSETS PER SURVIVING BANK

The tremendous number of banks being formed in the 1800's kept assets per bank low. It was not until 1921 when wholesale bank failures started that the "good times" came. While banks were folding from 1920 to 1930 the assets per survivor rose 83%. In the catastrophic 1930 depression the banks lost a total of 55% of their number. The assets per surviving bank rose another 71% by 1940. It was a profitable time - for the surviving banks.

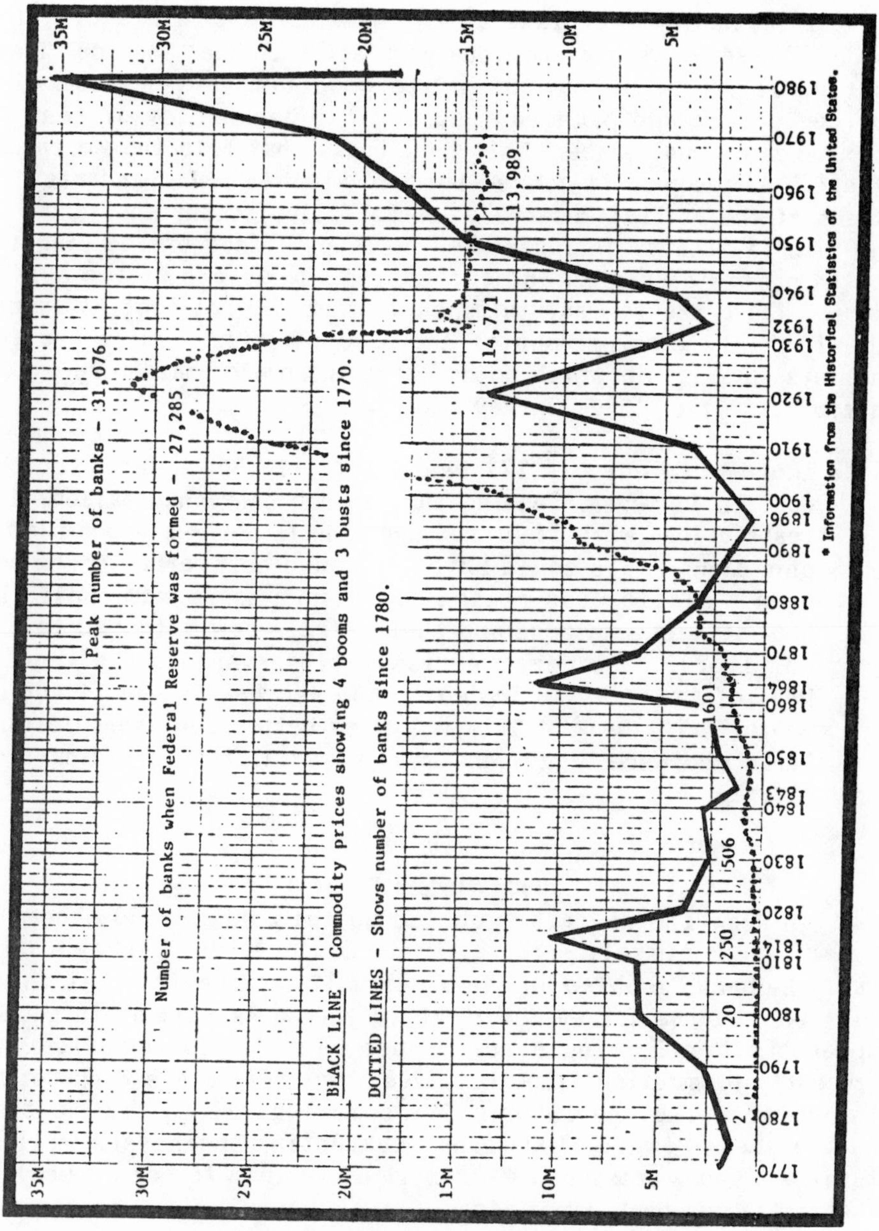
Peak number of banks - 31,076
Number of banks when Federal Reserve was formed - 27,285
BLACK LINE - Commodity prices showing 4 booms and 3 busts since 1770.
DOTTED LINES - Shows number of banks since 1780.
14,771
13,989
1601
506
250
20
2
35M
30M
25M
20M
15M
10M
5M
1770
1780
1790
1800
1810
1814
1820
1830
1840
1843
1850
1860
1864
1870
1880
1890
1896
1900
1910
1920
1930
1932
1940
1950
1960
1970
1980
* Information from the Historical Statistics of the United States.

NUMBER OF BANKS SINCE 1780

banks. Bank failures, "shotgun" mergers and consolidation of assets began under the watchful eye of the Federal Reserve.

In assuming its place as the new banking "dictator", the Federal Reserve issued numerous regulations. The "Topside" Transition Year of 1920 put an end to good times when commodity prices peaked and plunged, causing the bankruptcy of tens of thousands of businesses. This hurt banks that held the worthless loans. As planned it caused them to violate rules and regulations of the Federal Reserve. Banks failed by the thousands.

These massive failures had the happy effect of reducing the total number of banks, and increasing the assets of the survivors. There are few surviving banks that did not profit tremendously by the closing down of their competition. There are few hamlets in Virginia which do not contain an old boarded up bank - a trophy of the "1920s Turkey Shoot".

1933 There were only 14,771 banks left; 16,305 had bitten the dust in 11 years. Feeling that enough banks had failed, the restrictions were lightened and bank failures stopped almost on a dime. This could have been done earlier if there had been a single good reason to do so. As it was, half the competition was gone and their assets now belonged to the survivors. The borrower is still servant to the lender. Half of America was in debt - and servant to the 14,000 or so surviving banks. This was much better for the surviving banks who were bigger and more powerful than anything seen before.

1980s Turkey Shoot

In Rome the dictator gobbled up the bankers and became a super banker himself - for a time. In the "1920s Turkey Shoot" half the banks gobbled up the other half. I predict that there will be a "1980s Turkey Shoot" where the banks will again gobble up each other leaving a few "super banks". Commodities are presently plummeting like the 1920s. Businesses are bankrupting in numbers like the 1920s. It seems logical to assume that certain banks owning IOUs from bankrupting businesses will in turn come under pressure. This will cause them to become prey to their stronger bank competitors.

In the "1920s Turkey Shoot", 55% of the banks hit the dust. If 55% of existing banks bite the dust again it will leave approximately 6,300 banks. This precedent can again be found in Rome where the dictator came back the second time and took over the assets of 2,000 more banker/knights.

Perhaps the Cycle Theory will come into play. It took 73 years from a low of 715 banks in 1847 to the all-time high of 31,076 in 1920. If the 73-year retracement principle holds true there may be only 715 super banks left 73 years from 1920 - or in 1993. Each will represent an average of 43 or more other banks whose assets it will have taken over. Its slice of the interest-pie will be bigger than anything we can imagine since there will be fewer banks to share.

Bank Trust Departments

In the 1920s most of the information in this book was common knowledge among informed people. Since that time an iron curtain of silence has descended on the West. The way this censorship is managed is most interesting.

Almost 45% of the total stock of corporations in the United States is held in trust at bank trust departments. The banks don't own these stocks. They don't keep the income from these stocks. But the banks vote these stocks.

Without having to have a single dollar of their own money at risk, the banks of the United States vote the stock that they hold in trust for others.   The traditional "rule of thumb" says that if an individual votes as much as 10% of a company's stock at a stockholders meeting, he is usually considered to have control, or near control, of that company.   The trust departments of America vote 4 times this amount. A full 30% of all the stock in the country is voted from the trust departments of the banks of New York.

It is true that some trusts reserve voting rights to themselves, but most leave this to the banks. The fact is - the New York banks control American industry by voting the stock held in their trust. In this way the banks control American industry and how America's industry spends its money. This allows them to control the rest of America. This is why industry-endowed colleges employ only liberal teachers, why only certain charities get money, why there is no difference between the political parties, and why every word written by newspaper chains or spoken by their TV media is filtered first.*

---

* A rare UP article which appeared in the Arizona Republic, Jan 7, 1974 revealed that "Chase Manhattan Bank in 1972 held....stock....in 28 broadcasting firms (while) Morgan Guarantee used 13 'nominee' names'....which cloaked....the fact that Morgan Guaranty was among the top 10 stockholders of 41 different utility companies."

In 1928 most corporations had no debt at all. Today, with the control of corporations in the hands of lending institutions, corporate debt is predictably large.

Here is the debt of a few of America's corporations:

	Long Term Debt
AMR Corp	$1,532,000,000
Duke Power	$2,753,000,000
S. Cal Ed	$4,194,000,000
Detroit Ed	$3,505,000,000

Banks are in the business of lending money. American banks control American corporations. American corporations must borrow money when their masters tell them to. Human nature is self serving. An investigation could quickly show if the corporations borrow from the same banks that control them.

This is important. If corporations are forced into bankruptcy because of the huge amounts of money controlling banks require them to borrow, a jury may find those banks responsible. The responsible banks could then be found liable for losses incurred.

America's corporations have been treated like cows. Once the halter has been placed about their necks by bank trust departments, they have been fattened to giant size by massive feedings of debt. Then the interest is milked from them. As a result, a large part of America's industry is oversized, over-staffed, and over-mortgaged. This does not benefit the corporations or the stockholders if it results in the corporation's bankruptcy. It does benefit the banks that lent the money.

Corporations build incredibly expensive skyscraper offices in New York costing hundreds of millions of dollars. It is assumed by many that these business blunders were made so that the controlling bank could profit from the loans.

The next Penn-Central type bankruptcy may force the answer to this question in court.

The few independent family-owned newspapers, TV, and radio stations stay in business by advertising. Corporations do the advertising. The corporations that do the advertising are controlled by bank trust departments. The media please the banks - or they don't get advertising. If they don't get advertising, they go out of business. It's that simple.

This has led to the rapid growth of "alternate media" newsletters, small newspapers, books (such as this one), and periodi-
cals. People are attempting to gain news not present in today's
media, since most of today's media carries corporate advertising
and has been "bought" while trying to keep that advertising.

In a political contest, corporate donations and media coverage tend to go to the candidate who pleases the New York banks.
It is virtually impossible to reach the top rungs of the political ladder without going by this rule. Frankly, the banking
industry would be foolish to support their enemies. For this
reason it must be assumed that any candidate endorsed by the
media is also pleasing the New York money interests.

The banks control the nation's corporations through their
ability to vote stock held in trust. The corporations controlled
by the banks in turn control politicians, colleges, and media
with their donations and advertising. These in turn reflect the
opinions of their masters. This results in liberal politicians,
liberal colleges, and liberal media being against almost everything Christian America is for.

Banks & Bank Stocks

The foregoing shows how usury-banks have grown - through
good times and bad. It would seem that this is the one foolproof
investment that will guarantee a profit in the days ahead. It is
easy to sit back and dream about becoming one of the rulers of
the West by buying into one of the stronger New York banks and
hoping IT will emerge the grand winner in the "bank eat bank"
period ahead.

Don't count on it. The odds may be worse than you think for
the following reasons:

1. A fog of uncertainty will fall over the entire banking
    industry in the days ahead as farmers, corporations and
    countries default.

2. It is virtually impossible to know which bank owns strong

loans and which owns weak ones; therefore, it is virtually impossible to guess the survivors.

3. The greatest cloud over the interest-banking industry has just now begun to rise and overshadow all else. It's name? Reform!

Solutions - Reform or Conquest

In the past, to alleviate the suffering of their nations caused by interest-banking, rulers in Greece and Rome in the ancient world, and Austria, France, Portugal, and many other nations in the modern world, have been forced to nullify debt. This is the STATE acting in a financial crisis.

The traditional position of the Christian Church on the subject has been to condemn usury-banking. The recent position of Pastor Sheldon Emry is typical:

"'And thou shall number...forty and nine years. Then shalt ...the trumpet of the Jubilee to sound...and ye shall return every man unto his possession.' Leviticus 25:8-10

"...this is a year of cancellation of all debts and the return of all foreclosed properties to the rightful owner. This is what can, what must, and what will be done in America.

"Debts, such as mortgages on homes, farms, businesses, automobile loans, the Federal debt, and all state and local bonded debts are all illegal under God's law and since they have been obtained by the money-lenders through violations of the law and Constitution of the United States, they must be canceled."[1]

Others quote Revelation 18:2-18

...Babylon the Great is fallen...she shall be utterly burned with fire...that mighty city! For in one hour is thy judgment come...For in one hour so great riches is come to nought. And every shipmaster, and all the company in ships...cried when they saw the smoke of her burning...

---

1. Sheldon Emry, P. O. Box 5334, Phoenix, AZ 85010 is one of the most outspoken Christian ministers in America on the subject of Bible Law. He has an information newsletter and an excellent tape ministry available for a modest donation.

184

Certain Christian leaders are calling New York - the center of world usury - the "harlot", as if she were modern day Babylon and the above scriptures were to be fulfilled tomorrow! These words - these opinions - have not been spoken with such fervor for generations.

Not caring whose toes they step on, more and more ministers are raising the banner against interest. Worsening economic conditions could quickly mushroom it into a tidal wave. This is a force transcending and sweeping away economic theory. It has historical precedent.

The West outlawed interest for over 1,000 years and instituted interest-free banking in obedience to their religious teachings and to protect unsophisticated debtors. The present rising demand to return to that form of banking was triggered by the resurrection of Arab interest free banks which are presently in operation.

If neither the State nor the Christian Church causes the demise of interest-banks in the days ahead, the time will inevitably arrive when there will be only two super banks left. One will take over the other. Since the borrower is servant to the lender, whoever rules the surviving bank will also rule the world.

*   *   *   *   *

African Colonization

In 1921 the unemployment rate reached 22%. Blacks had the highest rates. Many were desolate and hungry. Word was received from their kinsmen in Africa, who had been repatriated more than 100 years before, that there was plenty to eat there. "Back to Africa" movements sprang up overnight.

The largest and best known was the Universal Negro Improvement Association. This six million member organization was founded by a remarkable black genius named Marcus Garvey.

Garvey's organization spread over North, Central and South America. He distrusted whites - with good reason. White liberals did everything in their power to stop blacks from leaving America. Marcus Garvey despaired of getting help. He decided to go it alone.

He sold shares of stock to buy ships for his all-negro Black

Star Line. "An 'all white' court deemed Garvey's efforts visionary, impractical and partaking of fraud. He was sentenced to five years in a federal prison."[2] When he was released he was deported as an undesirable alien.

As soon as the Garvey movement was put down another one arose - the Peace Movement of Ethiopia. In 1933 a petition signed by 2 million blacks was sent to President Roosevelt requesting that their relief money be put in a fund to help them to return to Africa.

Roosevelt had been put into the White House by the Northeast lending interests. His job was to force Americans to borrow money into existence to get the country out of the depression, and also turn a profit for the banks. He couldn't allow millions of debt-free potential borrowers to leave. He refused to see the black delegation with the petition.

In 1939 Senator Bilbo introduced the Greater Liberia Bill supported with a petition signed by two and one-half million blacks. The bill was quietly sent to committee to die. Mrs. Gordon, President of the Peace Movement of Ethiopia, spoke strongly against the attempt to kill the bill. She was charged under the sedition laws and jailed for two years in a federal prison.

In 1949 Senator Langer presented the Langer Bill to aid blacks who wished to return to Africa. It was backed by many black organizations. It was referred to the Committee on Foreign Relations and never heard from again.

As discussed earlier, in a usury society slaves are freed to borrow money into existence and for no other reason. The ex-slave has freedom only to borrow money into existence. He does not have the freedom to remove himself from the society.

The only hope the black has of returning to his ancestral home is for the return of the Christian Economic System. If once the system of interest is done away with - the compelling need to keep the black in America will also be done away with. There will be no more need for "equal employment" to make sure the black has sufficient funds to float large loans. The need for "equal voting rights" will die when the need for minority housing

2. Earnest Sevier Cox, Teutonic Unity, Richmond, Virginia 1951. His "White America" is in print and may be purchased from The Noontide Press, P.O. Box 76062, Los Angeles, California 90005.

dies. The "block busting laws" will die when the need to push whites into new areas to borrow money for new houses dies. Forced race-mixing in schools and neighborhoods will live only so long as usury lives. When it dies blacks will be able to return to Africa if they choose. There will be no reason to stop them."*

1923 A total of 18,718 businesses failed. My father, Dr. John H. Hoskins, was a physician in Hazard, Kentucky. His patients were miners. Coal prices peaked in 1920 and started down. He had plenty of patients, but the patients had no money. Dad couldn't meet expenses and lost his hospital. There was a radical change in the nation's economy between 1920 and 1923.

In the 1920s it was the banks that sold most of the stocks traded on the exchanges, not the brokerage firms. They sold stocks on 10% margin and lent 90% at high rates of interest. Fantastic sums were borrowed for this purpose.

1925 Washington state municipal defaults started, including Tacoma and Spokane. Two percent of the banks failed. The stock market climbed.

1926 Mussolini regulated pimps, whores, and usurers to a fixed place of business. Fifty-five municipalities went into default in Washington state. Two percent more of the banks failed. The stock market was still strong.

1927 Four percent of the banks fail. Stock market soars. Florida defaults started again joined by Arkansas municipal defaults. Since this subject of municipal defaults is of more than passing interest to a number of readers, Portfolios Investment Advisory has consented to the publication of Issue #94 on Municipal Bonds in the next chapter.

---

* Abraham Lincoln supported the African Colonization Program. This is the other reason in addition to his issuing "greenbacks" which is given by some for his being shot.

Chapter 33

CYCLES OF MUNICIPAL BOND DEFAULTS

Municipal debt requires taxes. In hard times people feel taxes to be oppressive. The combination of high taxes and big mortgage payments overwhelms a large portion of the population. They rebel. Municipalities default.

The Municipal Railroad Bond

The 1830s and the 1840s was a time of tremendous expansion in America. Cities needed money for all sorts of improvements; docks, ship channels, streets, and railroads. Railroads were the big thing. If you had a railroad, you would grow. If you didn't, you wouldn't. The railroad promoters told this story to the city fathers many different ways.

To get money to build a section of a railroad, the cities issued "municipal bonds". These municipal bonds were cities' IOUs promising to repay the face value plus interest.

First Muni Defaults

The Great Commodity Inflation of the 1st Cycle peaked with the end of the Napoleonic Wars in Europe and the end of the "War of 1812" in the United States (1814). Commodity prices started down as debts came due and bankruptcies removed money from circulation. Toward the bottom of the depression (1843) massive urban unemployment plus business bankruptcies caused city revenues to evaporate. Municipal bonds started defaulting.

The first recorded default in the United States was Mobile, Alabama in 1839. King Cotton put her on her feet again in the 1840s. The next was Detroit, Michigan in 1841. Then Bridgeport, Connecticut defaulted a railroad bond in 1843, the first of many many railroad bond defaults. In 1847 Little Rock, Arkansas defaulted a general purpose bond.

The reason there weren't more municipal defaults in these early years was that there weren't many municipal bonds in existence. Municipal bonds were brand new inventions. They were looked upon as being highly speculative.

There were a few more scattered municipal embarrassments after 1847. In 1857 came two big ones which so dislocated the Northern economy that they helped bring on the War Between the States. The first was Chicago, the "miracle of the West," followed closely by Philadelphia.

In 1857, Philadelphia was looked upon in much the same manner as today we look upon the United States government itself. Philadelphia was sound, the Mistress of the new country. She had had no real problem with her finances since 1841. (In 1841 the 2nd Bank of the United States failed which disclosed the fact that foreigners controlled the largest block of stock of that bank.)

Banking troubles brought on the municipal problem in 1857. The Bank of Pennsylvania failed, and the city couldn't get its money to pay its bond holders. A short time later several other banks including the Girard suspended specie payments. This trouble with the banks played havoc with businesses that had payrolls and notes due on certain dates. One newspaper reporting the scene printed the following picture:

"Business of all kinds was prostrated and the people, thrown out of employment, formed idle mobs in the streets. ...on November 12, ten thousand people met in Independence Square, and demanded that the city give them work. A number of public undertakings were embarked upon and thanks to these measures...the distress did not reach the proportions which had been anticipated."

The following year Philadelphia picked up payments on her indebtedness, but this early default points out the dependence of municipal debt on the banking system itself. Banking crises can produce drastic and immediate consequences.

Muni-Default Chart

In the 1870s and 1920s there were large numbers of banking failures. The chart on the next page shows that there were also large numbers of municipal failures occurring at the same time.

The chart also shows a flurry of municipal defaults between 1858 and 1870. These were mostly in Ohio, Wisconsin, Iowa - areas formerly belonging to Virginia or settled by Virginians.

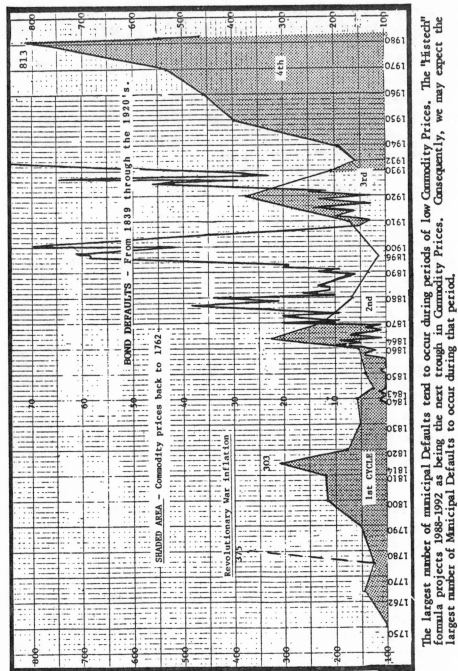

BOND DEFAULTS FROM 1839 INTO THE 1930s

The largest number of municipal Defaults tend to occur during periods of low Commodity Prices. The "Histech" formula projects 1988-1992 as being the next trough in Commodity Prices. Consequently, we may expect the largest number of Municipal Defaults to occur during that period.

Trade from the South was cut off by the War. This severely impacted this area causing the defaults. There were also a number of defaults for the same reason in western Pennsylvania including Pittsburgh. Practically all were railroad bond defaults.

Post War Defaults 1870 - 1890

The next wave of municipal defaults seemed to come from everywhere. Much has been made over the fact that many of them were in the South. This has been used to point out southern fiscal irresponsibility. The southern defense has been that the whites could not vote. Blacks had control of southern legislatures and were instructed by their northern banking masters to vote money into existence for anything and everything including princely salaries, lavish parties, and to buy the homes of their former owners. This argument seems irrelevant when the facts indicate that there were almost as many municipal defaults in the North as there were in the South.

It serves no useful purpose to fill column after column with hundreds of names of defaulting cities and counties. Instead, a few of the better known defaults within this 20-year period are listed with the type of bond defaulted. The results are interesting.

1870 - 1890 Defaults

Des Moines Co., Iowa - RR (1870)
San Antonio, Texas - RR Aid (1870)
Mobile, Ala. - RR (1871)
Pittsburgh, Pa. - RR (1871)
Battle Creek, Mich. - RR Aid (1872)
Wilmington, N.C. - Civil War Aid (1873)
Topeka, Kansas - Aid to Manf. (1874)
Memphis, Tenn. - RR (1874)
Montgomery, Ala. - Plank Road Aid (1875)
New Orleans, La. - RR (1875)
Houston, Texas - Gen. Imp. (1875)
Savannah, Ga. - Gen. Pur. (1876)
Shreveport, La. - Public Util. (1877)
San Antonio, Texas - RR (1877)

Alexandria, Va. - Gen. Pur. (1877)
San Diego, Cal. - RR (1878)
Elizabeth, N.J. - Gen. Imp. (1878)
St. Albans, Vt. - RR (1878)
Toledo, Ohio - Gen. Imp. (1880)
Rahway, N.J. - Gen. Pur. (1881)
Roanoke Co., Va. - Civil War Aid (1881)
Duluth, Minn. - Gen. Pur. (1882)
Baton Rouge, La. - RR Aid (1884)
Columbia, S.C. - RR (1884)
Charleston, S.C. - RR (1884)
San Francisco, Cal. - Sp. Assess. (1885)
Chicago, Ill. - Waterworks (1886)
Santa Cruz, Cal. - Waterworks (1887)

This list presents the tip of the iceberg. In many states conditions were simply terrible. It is reported that of the 300 municipalities in Illinois, 1/3 were in default, and that during the "debtors' revolt" in Missouri, 9/10s of the municipalities defaulted. In Arkansas repudiation was almost unanimous.

Nashville - First Receivership

Nashville, Tennessee has the distinction of being the first municipality to be placed in receivership.

This unique event took place in 1869. The city was on the verge of collapse facing hundreds of thousands of dollars of short term unfunded debt of 30 days or less. The town had been systematically looted by its black/carpetbagger coalition for years. Matters were desperate.

The non-voting white taxpayers persuaded a lower equity court to appoint a receiver - thereby ridding themselves of the parasites who had been tormenting them for so long.

1896 The War Phase of the 3rd Cycle started and the fresh influx of newly borrowed money caused municipal defaults to slow. By 1910 they had declined to three defaults recorded in that year.

Good times caused by borrowing money into existence for wars don't last. The War Phase ended in 1920 and as the chart clearly shows, municipal defaults again started.

Municipal Defaults - 1920-1930

The 1920s period was excellent for the stock market. Lower
commodity prices and lower wages helped companies' earnings. It
was, however, a bad time for municipal bonds. There were numerous defaults but no particularly "big name" defaults.

The highlight of the period was the tidal wave of defaults
from Washington state. These started in 1922 and by 1926 comprised a large proportion of the totals. There were 19 reported
in 1926 and 40 reported in 1927! The following short list gives
an idea of the widely scattered areas in which defaults occurred:

> Spokane, Wash. - Loc. Imp. (1921)
> Tacoma, Wash. - Loc. Imp. (1922)
> S. Sioux City, Neb. - St. Imp. (1923)
> Dallas Co., Texas - Levee Dist. #2 (1925)
> Roanoke, Va. - Gen. Pur. (1926)
> Vancouver, Wash. - Loc. Imp. (1927)
> W. Palm Beach, Fla. - Spec. Assess. (1928)

Florida Defaults

The Florida debacle started in early 1920s with the real
estate crash. After that there were two destructive hurricanes,
two killing frosts which decimated the fruit crop, a string of
bank failures with 56 of them belonging to a chain headquartered
in Atlanta. In 1929 there were eleven more reported defaults.
The flood of Florida defaults came in the 1930s and were so
numerous that it seemed like fruit falling from a tree.

Unknown Defaults

In the first hundred years of municipal bond history there
are over 800 known defaults. It is believed that only about 1/3
to 1/5 of the defaulting municipalities have been reported. Most
defaults have been recorded by the tedious method of locating
litigated court cases. Usually when a municipality goes broke,
it is obvious to everyone and no legal action is taken. Consequently, no record of the default is made.

Technicalities Leading To Defaults

Technicalities of the law have been used extensively to avoid payment of bonds. Whichever side was the more politically powerful was the one that usually ended up being right legally. This was especially so during the great "Granger Debt Revolt" in the last part of the 19th century. At that time it became a matter of religious principle among a large part of the American population not to pay usury demands.

Outrageous stratagems have sometimes been used to avoid payment. School District #5 of Sherman County, Nebraska refused to elect officials in order to defeat the bondholders. In the case of State & Short vs. Board of Commissioners of Sherman County (1891) 31 Neb. 465,467 it was alleged:

"Officers elected in 1874 have removed from said county, and the organization of said district, so far as possible, has been abandoned and no school has been held in said district, and that for the purpose of avoiding payment of its indebtedness said district refuses to elect new officers."

This is amusing, but it is not so amusing if you consider the terrible suffering of the taxpayers during that period. This default was another influenced by the Granger debt nullification movement. Variations of this movement appear every time hard times return.

High Coupon Bonds

High coupon rates determine probability of a bond's being paid. High coupon rates are acceptable only when interest rates generally are high. When interest rates decline high coupons are then considered unjust. A large percentage of defaults seem to stem from the fact that taxpayers are reluctant to pay high coupons during periods of low interest rates.

Once defaulted, many bonds were redeemed at a later date. Others were adjusted. This was done by "scaling" the coupon rate up or down or reducing the amount paid. Too often municipalities simply walked away from the obligation. It is reported that before 1930 about 40% of the general obligation bonds in default were held void.

On the other hand, the fact remains that most municipalities have honored their municipal obligations - sometimes at a great sacrifice to their own citizens.

1930 - To Date
The flood tide of municipal defaults resulting from the great depression of 1929 numbers over 4,700 cases. It serves no useful purpose to go into endless lists. The lessons of history are already clear to those willing to see.

Bond Defaults
The purpose of any economic research is to try to gain knowledge which may help profit and avoid loss in the future. It is with a certain confidence that we try to predict the next tidal wave of municipal defaults. These defaults will stem from hard times among debtors and will cause hard times among bond holders as money is defaulted out of existence. The following are conclusions which may be drawn:

Most municipal defaults occur close to the bottomside transition year. (See for yourself on accompanying chart.)

a) 1843
b) 1896
c) 1932

The next bottomside year is expected to occur sometime between the years 1988-1992. The majority of future municipal bond defaults may also be expected to occur near that time.

The Solon Syndrome
The biggest unspoken danger to municipal bond debt is the repetition of the Solon Syndrome. In 600 B. C. Greece was impacted with the same debt problem we have in the West today. Their solution was to cancel most of the debt outstanding.

Hard times cause people to turn to religion. The United States is a Christian nation. This religion of the Christians prohibits interest, just as the Mohammedan religion does.

This is a compelling argument for desperate men such as today's farmers. It gains teeth when Christian ministers throw

in scriptural arguments. The creditor is branded as an "extor-
tioner" and "usurer". The debtor is the "victim" who is supported by Divine Scripture. It may turn out that the debtors
will become the hunters and the creditors the hunted. It has
happened in the past.

The depression of the 1870s-1890s gave birth to the well
publicized James Gang that preyed on creditors. They were whole-
heartedly supported by the people. There was also the "Granger
Movement" to nullify debt. As a result, hundreds of municipalities defaulted. Only a dreamer can separate these events. The
1920s-1930s brought a revival of these same phenomena. It even
got certain state legislatures to hold moratoriums on foreclosures and reduce taxes. In places like Texas laws were passed
saying that lenders can't foreclose and sell homes, regardless of
the need for taxes to pay municipal debt. The coming hard times
should see a revival of everything that has gone before, except
more widespread, more violent, and more political.

It is almost certain that one of our present aspiring young
politicians will become a modern-day Solon who will try to please
the voters and put matters straight. Preachers will again raise
the banner against debt and interest just as the Arabs have done.
Debt will be wiped out with a stroke of "Christian" pen - or the
edge of a "reformer's" sword. Those who own someone else's IOU
will be wiped out - monetarily, physically, or both. Then the
whole thing will start all over as money is borrowed into exist-

---

Note: Researching defaulted municipal bonds has been a very difficult task.
Countless phone calls to government agencies on the subject produced a complete
blank. Twenty phone calls to brokerage firms produced the same. The biggest
help was the fact that many years ago in my ignorance I sold bonds for Francis I.
du Pont. The stories I heard from the "old timers" in the trade were not the
stories I got from the sales literature.

There are supposed to be some tracts, articles, and other works on the
subject, but the excellent local lending library, which is in contact with other
libraries all across the country was able to round up only one, "The Postwar
Quality of State and Local Debt", by George H. Hempel, New York, National Bureau
of Economic Research, Columbia University Press, 1971.

Fortune smiled by bringing me in contact with the scattered pages of an
unfinished and unpublished manuscript of A. M. Hillhouse, of the Municipal Finance Officers' Association of Chicago dated almost half a century ago. Raw
material is to be found mostly as a by-product of other historical research.
There is limited information available in the "Weekly Bond Buyer," the "Commercial & Financial Chronicles," "Nuveen," and "The Blue Lists". Most important are
the litigated law cases.

Other than the above listed and the few out of print items there is little
information available and it is likely to remain this way since it is not to the
advantage of the usury bankers to turn up old skeletons.

ence to get us out of the coming depression and into the War Phase.

Recommendation

It is recommended that those few individuals who have not done so may find it prudent to liquidate their municipal bond holdings. A municipal bond rally in the period ahead may produce the best and perhaps the last opportunity to do so.

*   *   *   *   *

Bottomside Transition Year - 1932

1928 The United States Government took action against the rising prices on Wall Street. Three percent of the banks failed. Stock market marched to new highs.

1929 By this time over 8,000 U.S. banks had failed. In spite of everything the U. S. economy had held up under it all - until September. Austria's Bodencreditansalt Bank got into trouble and was merged with Credit Ansalt. Credit Ansalt had been borrowing from her conquerors to pay them tribute. When her conquerors refused to lend her more money she was forced to default. The next day, September 24th, the New York Times Averages peaked, signaling that something had gone wrong. If the economists and politicians didn't know the economy had come unglued - the stock market did. The total number of dollars being borrowed into existence slowed to a trickle. Those already in existence were being paid into banks as interest faster than they could be borrowed into existence.

On October 24th the market broke 31 points. It all happened so fast - in less than a month! This is why you must go by the rules. No debt, and invest in no and low debt stocks. If you are caught you will have to make do with your existing situation.

1930 Florida was in a panic with business limited to a cash basis. Five percent of the banks failed. The stock market was lower.

1931 Germany defaulted. She had borrowed from the United States

to pay the U.S., England, France and Italy. Seven percent
of the banks failed. Stock market was lower.

1932 By now, sixty Florida municipalities had defaulted. Thir-
teen percent of the nation's banks had failed. The Commodity Price Index bottomed out. The Peace Phase ended as the
last drop of misery was wrung from a whimpering, bewildered
world. The stock market reached the level it started from
in 1920 and it too started up into a super bull market.

Chapter - 34

1932 - 1980 WAR PHASE

The latest War Phase has been so recent that it would be
senseless to delve deeply into things that the reader is familiar
with. A quick bird's-eye view will suffice.

In the early part of the phase many who were fortunate
enough to have jobs earned 10¢ an hour. Malnutrition was a fact
of life. In 1933 the Roosevelt administration embarked on pump-
priming projects. The National Recovery Administration, FDIC,
Civilian Conservation Corps, NRA, AAA, and Civilworks Administration provided work for the jobless; HOLC for homeowners;
FHA for potential home owners; TWA, etc. Farm prices improved
markedly.

A friend of mine, Mr. Milner Noble, had an uncle who sold a
12,000 acre plantation near Powhatan, Virginia for $6,000 and
felt fortunate to get out from under the taxes. The father of
another friend bought 10,000 acres for $3,200, or 32¢ an acre.
He bought it as it was being sold at auction for taxes. There
was just one bid made - he made it. He was a banker. My father
paid $14,000 for a house which had cost more than double that
price just three or four years earlier. Lots of fine homes in
Farmville were selling for under $1,000.

1935 On March 26th, second "Plebiscitary" election gave
10,000,000 votes for the Italian Fascists vs. 15,000 votes
against. Italy moved into Ethiopia on October 3rd and freed
the slaves. In 1931 the Italian government bank took con-

trol of the common stocks of manufacturing companies held in trust by private banks and ended their control of Italy ... this was a very "anti-bank" gesture that caused the banks world-wide to blacklist the government of Italy.

1936 Anti-Communist Pact was signed by Japan and Germany to check the spread of Communism by the Communist International. This violated the Christian Law:

> **Be ye not unequally yoked together with unbelievers. II Corinthians 6:14**
>
> **Thou shalt make no covenant with them, nor with their gods. Exodus 23:32**
>
> **...If thou has stricken thy hand with a stranger (zûwr), thou art snared...Prov. 6:1-2**[*]

In 1937 Italy signed the same Anti-Communist Pact. All three signed a military alliance in September, 1940. This was their doom. This violation of the Law was one of the things that made possible the horrible World War II in which millions upon millions of Christians died. The U.S. and England had fallen into the same trap and were allied with the USSR and China, other non-Christian lands.

1940 Christian Germany invaded the Khazarian ruled Slavic nation of the USSR. The International banks' rule over the USSR and its "Gosbank" was at risk. To bring America into the war to protect the loans required finesse since Germany refused to be provoked.

Roosevelt cut off oil and steel to Japan and caused the Dutch government in London to cut off the Dutch East Indies oil from the Japanese. The Japanese were then ordered to withdraw from their war in China and do the bidding of the U.S. Roosevelt correctly guessed the Japanese mind. They would fight. They attacked Pearl Harbor. Because of the 1936 treaty that violated Biblical Law, Germany and Italy

---

[*] Traditionally, this has been taken to mean ALL treaties, whether political, commercial, cultural or social. ALL agreements of any kind.

were forced into the war with the U.S. The military manufacturing contracts went out. Happy days were here again.

Common Interests

The 1929 Depression Psychosis has given birth to the "Hoskins First Rule of Interest" agreed upon by both borrowers and
lenders. It is simply this:

THE MONEY SUPPLY MUST BE EXPANDED TO ALLOW DEBTORS
TO PAY INTEREST ON THEIR DEBTS - UNTIL JUBILEE TIME.

In other words, the debtor who has borrowed $10 must be
allowed to come up with the 11th dollar or the system breaks down
- bankrupts - with consequences hard to deal with for both borrowers and lenders.

Government Historical Tables

The following table from the Historical Statistics of the
United States shows the three times since 1916 that the total
debts of the nation did not increase to allow people to pay the
11th dollar interest.

NET PUBLIC & PRIVATE DEBT*

by Major Sectors: 1916 - 1970

(In billions)

1970	-	1854.1	1950	-	486.2	1930	-	192.3
1969	-	1735.0	1949	-	445.8	1929	-	191.9
1968	-	1682.5	1948	-	431.3	1928	-	186.3
1967	-	1438.7	1947	-	415.7	1927	-	177.9
1966	-	1338.7	1946	-	396.6	1926	-	169.2
1965	-	1234.6	1945	-	405.9	1925	-	162.9
1964	-	1151.6	1944	-	370.6	1924	-	153.4
1963	-	1070.9	1943	-	313.2	1923	-	146.7
1962	-	996.0	1942	-	258.6	1922	-	140.2
1961	-	930.3	1941	-	211.4	1921	-	136.3
1960	-	874.2	1940	-	189.8	1920	-	135.7
1959	-	833.0	1939	-	183.3	1919	-	128.3
1958	-	769.6	1938	-	179.9	1918	-	117.5
1957	-	728.3	1937	-	182.2	1917	-	94.5
1956	-	698.4	1936	-	180.6	1916	-	82.2
1955	-	665.8	1935	-	175.0			
1954	-	605.9	1934	-	171.6			
1953	-	581.6	1933	-	168.5			
1952	-	550.2	1932	-	175.0			
1951	-	519.2	1931	-	182.9			

* Historical Statistics of the United States, Colonial Times to 1970. U. S. Dept
of Commerce, Washington D. C. 20402.

The first was 1929. We all know what happened then. Next was 1938 when Roosevelt tried to "balance the budget". This would have denied debtors the 11th dollar to pay interest and the country almost went back into the depression. At the last moment dollars were borrowed into existence to bail the debtors out. Once more in 1945 the country hovered on the brink of a depression but was saved by borrowers returned from the army and defense factories who used savings and borrowed enough new money into existence to tide the country over. This confirmed the Hoskins "Second Rule of Interest":

IT DOES NO GOOD TO HAVE UNLIMITED FUNDS IN BANKS - THE MONEY MUST BE IN CIRCULATION WHERE DEBTORS CAN GET IT TO PAY INTEREST.

When interest is paid back into banks it disappears from circulation and must be taxed or borrowed away to get it circulating again.

Lord Keynes - Spokesman

Lord Keynes gets a lot of bad press today. This is really undeserved since he was merely trying to use common sense to make the unworkable Usury System work as long as possible. In this effort he stands first.

Keynes' first big hurdle was to discredit what was then considered "common sense". At that time a carryover from earlier days said that it was wise to balance the budget and pay debts. Most people refused to pay interest or receive interest because of the Bible's prohibitions. In early days one could pay one's debts, balance the budget and matters went on in a relatively smooth manner.

This wisdom only held true as long as there was no "interest". When people borrow $10 and agree to pay back $11, they will bankrupt if they do not borrow and borrow and borrow.

Keynes further felt that when the people were no longer able to obtain money to pay interest and the economy showed signs of slipping into a depression, it was the duty of the government to help debtors and make money available. There were three ways to do this:

1.   Public Works, or "Monument Building" as it is sometimes
     called. Money is put into circulation for the debtors
     at public expense.

2.   War! - costly in lives - true, but the best of all
     excuses to borrow money into existence. If people can
     be persuaded to save their money until after the war
     instead of squandering it, there should be an extended
     period of prosperity following the end of hostilities.

3.   Last - a Tax Cut. If it appears that a 1929 is immi-
     nent a tax cut can push fresh funds into circulation
     immediately. This will atlow the 11th dollar to be
     paid until something more lasting can be arranged in
     the nature of one of the other solutions or variations
     thereof.

Korea

Federal Reserve inventive genius came into play with the
first of the "modern wars" - the Korean War. This was a war
whose objectives were twofold - the military objective was
stalemate, the financial objective was to borrow the 11th dollar
into existence. The fly in the ointment was General MacArthur
who tried to win the war and was fired for his effort. It does
no good to win a war if by so doing it ruins one of the major
reasons for the war in the first place: to borrow the 11th dollar
into existence. MacArthur was a good man but he didn't understand economics.

Vietnam

The Vietnam War was a vast improvement over the Korean War.
It had everything good as these wars go - and little bad. There
were great expensive air raids on vague military targets in the
jungles with the heartland of the enemy country placed "off
limits". Loud-speaker warnings were given the enemy prior to
ground attacks so that they could remove themselves from points
of danger. Great offensives well covered by the media ran bus-
ily, noisily, and expensively in circles, requiring hundreds of
billions of new money to be borrowed into existence which helped
the economy back home.

America never had it so good. There was not only money to pay interest but money left over to spend on other things. It is quite possible that the war would still be going on except that the cannon fodder objected and the war became politically unpopular. When this happened it was brought to a close within a week by mining the North Vietnam harbors - something which could have been done years earlier if there had been a single good economic reason for doing so. Once the war ended the big question arose: should the United States "win" the war or "lose" the war?

One of the purposes of the war in the first place was to "foreclose" the heavily indebted French planters who had nothing left to mortgage and to create a new relatively debt-free borrower - the communist government. These objectives could not be obtained by winning the war and leaving the land in a "status-quo" situation. If the South Vietnamese had been allowed to win the war, Vietnam would have been worthless to the banking system. There was nothing else in the country that could be mortgaged. A large part of the "fruits of war" would have been lost to the usury banks.

There is still talk of blaming those responsible for the Vietnam Giveaway. This will be difficult to do. Those who profit are usually those responsible. While the usury-banks profited most, there is not one person whose eyes read these lines who did not benefit economically from these wars - from politician to war widow. Morally they were reprehensible - economically they were a smashing success.

War On Poverty

The War on Poverty was brilliant in concept. It did everything a hot war does but did it without bloodshed. It was, however, hard to sell. After the first few score billions were borrowed and spent, voters who didn't understand that the money was really being borrowed to keep The System operating came down hard on the politicians who were then forced to moderate their zeal considerably and turn to other things.

Blockbusting

Whites won't live with blacks. When blacks move in, whites move out. This fact of life has been used by the New Economists

to keep the building boom going for 30 years.[3] Whenever the
economy slows and people have trouble paying interest on their
debts, strong civil rights laws have been passed which force
blockbusting. This is the Federal Reserve's method of "foreclosing". The "debt-nullification" movements of the last century
denied the usury-banks a great amount of profit. While whites
historically often stand and fight injustice from banks, they run
from living in close contact with blacks. The refugees from
blockbusted areas borrow money into existence to buy or build
elsewhere. Twenty refugee families can borrow one million -
20,000 refugees can borrow a billion. This is BIG BUSINESS!

The Blockbusting War has probably done more to keep The
System alive and well than all the military wars together since
World War II.

It is virtually impossible to find anyone who is in debt and
who benefits from the flow of blockbusting dollars who will
seriously speak against it - politician, college president,
preacher, teacher, bank president, union leader, street cleaner,
all are in the same boat. They can't bite the hand of usury
which feeds them. They do, however, have the decency to cringe
when asked to practice what they preach.

The system of usury demands expansion; it will expand to
survive regardless of the cost. Blockbusting and busing will
stay as long as it expands the money supply and the electorate
doesn't revolt. There is almost no one who will protest since
everyone benefits except the refugees.

The Panama Canal

Panama had no way to repay a loan plus interest to one of
our big banks and threatened to default. The obvious choice
given the banking system was to foreclose by financing a
revolution within Panama, or give the Panamanians a means to pay
the interest. A way was found to allow Panama to pay her debts.
She was simply given the Panama Canal so that she would have a
source of revenue. The "Panama Giveaway" was made a "loyalty
vote" by the bankers and very few of our politicians had the
nerve to vote against it. "The borrower is servant to the lend-

---

3. God placed His Law in the hearts of His people. (Jeremiah 31:33) The Law
forbids living among aliens "lest they make thee sin against Me". (Exodus 23:33)
Flight is the Christian's natural reaction to integration.

er." Panama is servant to the New York banks - our government is also servant to them. A major default was stopped, a banking system will receive its interest, and 1929 was again averted.

Now The USSR

The USSR and her Slavic satellites owe the international banks billions upon billions. They too have no way to pay principal and interest. The main thing she produces which is really needed is oil and she needs that for herself. New discoveries are years away from the market.

Of course, she produces chromium which everyone needs, but the world price for chromium was kept low because Rhodesia, the world's largest producer, kept it low.

A way was worked out by the West's banking system. Rhodesia was forced to sell her chromium to the Soviets. This was done by having Western governments make impossible demands on Rhodesia. When she refused to comply she was boycotted, leaving her only one customer for her chromium - the USSR. The Soviets in turn took Rhodesian chromium and sold it at double price to the West. The Rhodesian Deal saved the Soviet economy and our own. For years the Soviets grasped this financial straw which allowed her to pay the 11th dollar to her creditors.

The Rhodesian Deal fell through when the Rhodesians did the unexpected. They gave in to the impossible demands made against them. When this happened the reason for the boycott of Rhodesian chromium vanished. Rhodesia was again allowed to sell directly to the West, and the Soviet's income vanished! Now she must find a new source of income to pay the 11th dollar on her debts. Remember, if the USSR bankrupts, many banks in Europe will also bankrupt. This will cause many banks of the Federal Reserve to bankrupt. The Federal Reserve has as great a stake in finding a source of income for the USSR as they do themselves. Without income, the Soviets can't pay interest on their debts.

South Africa

South Africa is one of the last places left in the world which is independent and has great natural wealth. It has been assumed by many that this country will be converted into the next source of Soviet income.

The acquisition of South Africa by the USSR would give them

the natural resources to mortgage and sell to the West for generations. It would make it possible for the "international bankers" to continue to expand their loans to the USSR indefinitely
as the Soviets modernize and build up their country. It would be
beneficial to the economies of both the U.S. and the USSR.

South African gold has already been banned for sale in the
U.S. This will force her to sell her gold to the Soviets and
Mexico who will in turn re-sell it to the United States and use
the profits against their debts. At the same time the bankers
are pursuing their plan against the Arab Petrodollar.

Arab Petrodollar War

Long ago Western Oil companies went to the Near East and
received agreements from the local Islamic governments that the
oil companies would be given rights to any oil found with the
local governments getting a specified cut.

Washington politicians thought it would be good politics if
they kept the oil price low by regulation. So, it was kept low.
Good politics - bad economics. The money supply was not growing
fast enough and the 11th dollar was getting short. The Vietnam
War had ended and there were no other "stalemate wars" which were
politically acceptable.

Into this gloom and doom of approaching economic woe came a
beam of light. The New York banks persuaded the Arabs to confis-
cate American oil properties in Arab countries and raise oil
prices. This forced stingy American merchants to borrow new
money into existence to pay for the increase.

All this was done without a murmur of protest from our
government, press, unions, or educators. There is no reason they
or anyone else should murmur when the 11th dollar was again being
created, thanks to our own American businessmen.

This oil price increase was far more creative than the
Vietnam War, War on Poverty, War on Racial Separation, War on
Rhodesia, etc. The new massive borrowing created new money in
sufficient quantities again to stave off the "Year of Jubilee" -
and in this writer's opinion it was at the time the only way left
in which this could have been done short of World War III.

All who value their pocketbooks and dread the return of
Depression Years owe a debt of gratitude to the unsung banking
genius who thought up this plan. The modern inconveniences of

increased oil prices far outweigh the disadvantages of 1929!

Yesterday's Solution - Today's Problem

Today's major economic problems are:

1) The USSR must get the dollars needed to pay her debts.

2) The Arab oil dollars must be circulated.

Both problems require immediate attention, but the problem of the Arab petrodollars is the most urgent. Something must be done to circulate the Saudi-Arabian dollars which are sitting idle in banks around the world.

The Saudis have done what they could to help; they have built steelmills, airports, cement plants, swimming pools and air-conditioned stalls for camels. They have run real estate prices sky high in England and their attempts to circulate their money in America have brought about a rash of state laws against the "alien ownership of America". They have forced the price of gold to lofty heights, but still they have hundreds of billions in the banks of the world where they sit idle and violate cardinal economic rule number two:

IT DOES NO GOOD TO HAVE UNLIMITED FUNDS IN BANKS. THE MONEY MUST BE IN CIRCULATION WHERE DEBTORS CAN GET IT TO PAY INTEREST.

The Arabs are nervous - and justifiably so. They see the handwriting on the wall. The Soviets desperately need Federal Reserve Notes. The Saudis have tens of billions of them they can't spend. The Fed needs the USSR and her satellites to get Fed Notes to pay her debts plus interest. There you have it.

It is not reasonable to assume that the world's usury banks will sit idly by and let the world's economy grind to a halt because they lack the unobtainable Saudi dollars. There is nothing to prevent THE SYSTEM from doing "its thing" again. After all, there are only a few million weak defenseless Arabs and there are hundreds of millions of people in America, Europe, and the USSR who would benefit if the Arab countries were turned over to the Soviets.

Once the Soviet Union and her satellites have the use of Arab oil income and the use of Arab money already in Western banks a worldwide business boom can develop. This might last into the 21st century as orders go out for hundreds of billions of dollars worth of improvements which are desperately needed in the Russian sphere.

Conclusion

It seems to be a reasonable expectation that THE SYSTEM OF USURY to survive will demand that the petroleum producing Arab World and its cache of Federal Reserve notes be turned over to the Eastern Bloc of Communist nations, or this money will be put into circulation by inciting expensive Arab civil wars. If either of these events fail because of some unforeseen diplomatic event, then South Africa may be turned over to the Soviets, or conquered by the U. S. and then turned over to the Soviets to achieve the same result. The alternative - 1929! or a return to the interest-free "Western System" of our ancestors.

Chapter 35

JOINT VENTURE FARMS
(A Solution To The Farm Crisis)*

The mobs of Rome were made up of bankrupt farmers. Rome was crowded. There was hardly a place to sleep or eat. The country-side was vacant. Food had to be imported.

In earlier chapters we saw how the Roman farmer was forced from the land. He was simply lent 10 denarii and was required to pay back 11. In 14 years he had to pay back 40. When he couldn't pay he was foreclosed and lost his farm equipment, his house, and his livestock, which passed into the hands of 2000 landlord/lenders. Roman bankers hounded the farmers off the land. Italy's farms grew up in trees. Grain was imported. When this stopped, Rome starved.

---

* Nineteen eighty was a Year of Topside Transition. Everything that happened in the prior "topside years" is again happening. One of the things that requires most immediate attention are the farms of America. This problem was covered in PIA newsletters #93 and #95 and is printed with permission.

The American Farmer

Three times debt has forced the American farmer from his land: 1814-1843, 1864-1896, 1920-1932, and now. There is no new land to move to and clear. When today's farmer is bankrupted and forced to move to the city, the land is turned into pasture for picturesque Angus cattle, or allowed to go into "tree farms". Fewer and fewer acres under cultivation must support more and more people. To increase production to meet his interest payments, today's farmer is forced to farm every acre and commit every insult to the land.

In many places in the Midwest, after a ten-minute shower the land looks like a gigantic lake stretching for miles. The rain won't penetrate the soil and stands on top. The reason is that weedkiller is poured on the land, a chemical similar to "Agent Orange" used in Vietnam. This toxic agent controls the weeds but kills all the earthworms and all other living things in the earth that are needed to aerate and recondition the soil. There is no way water can enter the sterile hard-packed ground. To break up this "hard pan" so that water can reach the seed a 300 h. p. tractor is needed.

Ordinary seed no longer thrives in such harsh growing conditions and so special hybrid seeds are used, seeds that won't reproduce themselves. The farmer has to go back to the same dealers year after year to buy these special costly seeds.

Next, expensive liquid fertilizer is poured on. The farmer hopes to reap a bountiful crop which almost - but not quite - pays his mortgage.

With everything coming out and nothing replaced, this sterile soil produces wheat that often yields only 3% protein, where 15% was the norm only a few years ago. Farmers fed this grain to their cattle. They got sick. It was diagnosed "protein deficiency". They went to cotton mills to get cotton seeds to feed to their livestock to build up their protein requirements. This is the wheat we get to eat today. Many farmers now know the score, but they can't stop what they are doing because the next mortgage payment is due soon.

The average American doesn't know that the eight-feet deep topsoil found a few years ago is now only six inches deep in places. The weedkiller and fertilizers have poisoned surrounding springs and streams so that water for humans and animals must come from wells 1000 feet deep. The American public now wonders why the country is suddenly afflicted with inexplicable rashes, cancer, allergies, and nervous disorders. The answer is that they are receiving giant doses of herbicides in their food.

The Broken Cycle

Farmers are under pressure to make the next mortgage payment or lose their farms:

"To get maximum yield they do what the Federal Government and State Governments through their land grant colleges tell them to do. That is, to use chemicals of the kind now being promoted for Agribusiness use that are potentially as dangerous to the existence of the human race as spent nuclear waste! The gross and frightening aspect of all this....is that these sophisticated chemicals are given to agricultural use by people who have no technical-chemical background... They are marketed under innocuous titles that do not suggest their lethal nature! Lack of funding to provide inspection...is resulting in many degenerative diseases, allergies, birth defects and cancer."[4]

This becomes our problem when we look at our plate of food placed before us at mealtime.

To compound this crime against nature the weedkiller which is sprayed by the ton on the land has broken the biological chain at point "A" on the accompanying chart. Each acre of truly fertile soil contains millions of nematodes, earthworms, bacteria, and other soil insects. The earthworm population of 5 million per acre can translocate 5 tons of soil each day. The weedkiller kills everything. The land is dead. Hybrid seed is dumped in, liquid fertilizer is poured on - the last goodness left in the soil by 5,000 years of the biological cycle of life is sucked out - leaving cold, sterile, lifeless dirt. If you once break the cycle, it is only a matter of time before every-

---

4. A. P. Thomson, Annual Letter 1982, No.1, Golden Acres Orchard, Rt. 2, Box 770, Bayard (Route 639), Front Royal, Virginia 22630.

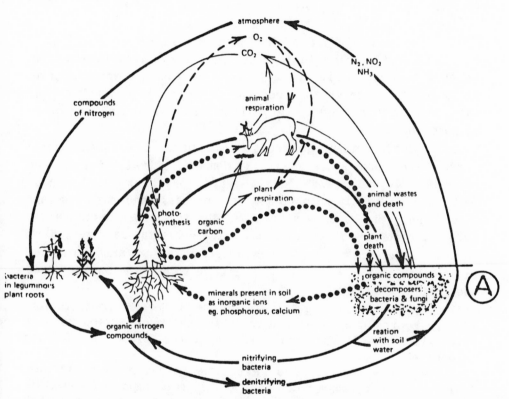

Annual Letter 1982, No. 1, Golden Acres Orchard, Rt. 2, Box 770, Bayard (Route 639), Front Royal, Virginia 22630.

THE BIOLOGICAL CYCLE OF LIFE

thing else in the cycle will also die.

It totally escapes some people that when the protein in perfectly ordinary looking wheat drops from 15% to 3%, it is possible to starve with loaves of bread in our kitchens. God warned us, "Ye have sown much, but bring in little, Ye eat, but ye have not enough" (Haggai 1:6). That is, of course, presuming that the poisons in the bread don't kill them first.

It Won't Cost The Taxpayers A Dime

Our first problem is to keep the farmers from bankrupting. We have to keep their production up so that we won't starve. We've got to clean up the food the farmers are putting on our plates so that we won't starve from what we are eating or be poisoned by it.

To do that we've got to get the banks off the farmers' backs. The bankers are presently demanding that a farmer who borrows $100,000 at 20% for 10 years, pay back a balloon of $619,173.62. This is extortion of the grossest and most flagrant kind. The grain buyer may make 5%, the fertilizer salesman may make 8%, the seed salesman may make 15% - but the bank gets 619%. No wonder they are bankrupting farmers and taking farms from them at the rate of 3,000 a month! It's time to get the banks out of the farming business.

Congress has the right to make money under the Constitution. All our representatives have to do is get together and vote it into existence. It has been done many times before (See Tallies chapter #9).

The farmers will also have time to clean up their act. Removing the pressure of having to make impossible monthly debt payments will allow them to plow the land under every 7th year to re-establish the biological chain (Lev. 25:1-7). They will also be able to afford to stop their present ruinous chemical warfare against their land and take care of it instead.

This is why the "PS LETTER"[5] writes, "Despairing of any successful solution to the continuing problems of high costs and low prices for products, the Farmers' Liberation Army, based in eastern Colorado and western Kansas, has decided on violence as the only possible alternative following the failure of peaceful methods."

---

5. P. O. Box 598, Rogue River, Oregon 97537

These farmers believe that to keep their farms they must fight, just as their grandfathers had to in the 1870s and 1880s. It seems a shame that matters have progressed to this point, but it is important to realize that they have indeed done so.

Our own interest is self-interest. If the American farmer is forced to stop production for any reason or is not allowed the time to reform his farming techniques - starvation faces America! It is foolish to say that we can't go back to proper, proven farming methods. As a matter of fact, there are profitable 1000-acre farms in Indiana that use no herbicides at all. Most of them are debt-free. These, however, are comparative rarities. We must now deal with the fact that the FARM CRISIS that everyone has been talking about is upon us.

Starvation

How can starvation be looking America in the face when she is the greatest food producer and exporter in the world? The answer is simple. Surplas food production may soon decrease to only 10%. This surplas must fill our grain elevators, cause storage problems, and furnish bargain sales to needy nations overseas.

Corporate farming (i.e. corporations combining farms of bankrupt independent farmers and operating them corporate-style) is not efficient. When the independent farmer is replaced by a hired manager, production drops off. At times it can be drastic. Russia was one of the largest food exporters in the world before their revolution. Their corporate style farming (communes) reduced food production 20%-40%. Today, almost 60 years after her revolution, she must still import food - or starve.

Most of the African nations were food exporters before their independence and adoption of the corporate farm system. Now most of these very same nations are finding their food in tight supply. This, in the richest farming area in the world.[*]

If the present rate of bankruptcies among farmers continues for another few years Americans will find themselves with a system of corporate farms owned by an alien banking system. It is possible that these corporate farms may cause food production to drop - anywhere between 10% and 40%.

---

[*] With the departure of the "adam" man (he who blushes), their blessing departed with them: "God give thee. . .the fatness of the earth, and plenty of corn." Gen 27:28.

Joint Venture Solution

JOINT VENTURE is the answer. There is no reason that the very same system used by our ancestors through interest-free banks won't work again. If a farmer has 30% equity in his farm, our own United States Government can MAKE - not BORROW - the 70% necessary to buy the lender's share.

The government will then own 70% and the farmer 30%. As in the past the farmer will get 30% of the profits and the government will get 70%. If the farmer has a good year he may be able to buy 10% more from the government and will then own 40% and receive 40% of the profits. It is hoped the time will come when he will own 100% of the farm.

We must persuade the government to MAKE money and use it to buy the mortgages of the American farmers. History shows that governments are often more compassionate "partners" than lenders who are too often interested only in "interest" and the profits from foreclosures.

The idea of a "corporate farm" replacing the individual farmer is a product of the USSR and has no place in America.

Laws should be passed to protect the land. Instead of paying farmers not to grow crops, we should require that the use of poisons and liquid fertilizers be terminated. Land should be plowed under and allowed to rest every seventh year. Reserve

Note: I am sure to be lambasted by Bible believing Christians who quote not only the Biblical prohibitions against debt and usury, but also the Canon Law. I am aware of the parts of the Canon Law which teach "The usurer was bound to make restitution, and those who paid usury could always claim it because they had suffered an injustice." Medieval Studies Vol. II, Pontifical Institute, p. 13, Toronto. And again....in every case the borrower may demand restitution of usury paid because of the sinful agreement upon which the payment is based. Not only is the usury not owed, but the usurer may not receive or retain it without committing sin. Summa, De Usuris, n.10 fol 375v. I am also aware of the argument being made for a return of all interest paid, which in most cases would fully pay for most of the presently debt-ridden farms. I believe, however, it is important to first save the farmers, and then wait for a Christian revival to terminate the interest system. If it is not terminated, the entire nation will again be owned by the usurers in a few short years.

Recommended reading: Acres USA, Raytown, Mo., $12/Yr., Natural Food And Farming, P. O. Box 210, Atlanta, Texas 75501, $12/Yr.; and a book, Your Apple Orchard, A. P. Thomson, Rt. 2, Box 770, Front Royal, Va. 22630. $3.95.

land must be brought back into cultivation to make up the loss of production while resting the land and bringing it back to life.

Right now American farmers make up less than 2.7% of the total American work force. They are skilled professionals. They cannot be allowed to leave the land. A "joint venture" ownership operation with the government as a partner will make lenders angry, but the survival of our source of food is more important than anyone's profit through interest and foreclosure.

The infusion of "hot" government money into the banks will be a temptation for them to inflate the economy. This can be nipped in the bud by increasing the reserve requirements of those banks that have this "hot" money. Surplus cash can easily be adjusted by taxation. This is the traditional way, and it works.

The Banks Get Help

It is an "obvious sham" to have $11 trillion in IOUs coming due world wide and only $493 billion in Federal Reserve's M-1 money supply with which to pay. Many of the usury banks that brought this situation about are now themselves being caught in their own nets. Many of their foreign victims are unable to pay the 11th dollar that does not exist and are defaulting.

We are told that if the banks lose this money that our entire economic system will collapse. To protect the banks our government has been ordered to "guarantee" these foreign loans so the banks won't lose. Today if a bank is to take a loss from a foreign loan guaranteed by a foreign government - Uncle Sam will make up the difference.

Why are the banks being protected and the farmers not being protected? What is sauce for the goose should be sauce for the gander. If it is fair to bail out the usury banks, it is fair to bail out the bankrupted farmers, the victims of these very same usury banks.

The Human Tidal Wave

Americans have lived in complete safety for so long that they cannot imagine that this condition will not continue for-ever. The present wave of black Jamaicans, mixed-breed Cubans and Mexicans that numbers in the millions is the harbinger of things to come.

The world is short of food. Much of it is already starving.

The point is that the world is starving while being supplied with massive shipments of grain from the United States. This grain comes from the vanishing surplus of our farms. If "corporate-farms" are allowed to replace our bankrupting farmers, and food production is reduced 10%-40% as a consequence, then our country will be critically short of food and the rest of the world will starve.

America's business of furnishing grain to a starving world is more than just a business. It is also a ransom. Much of the food is never paid for. In spite of this ransom, millions of aliens are still not getting enough to eat and are so desperate that they are risking their lives to sneak into our country. We have surplus food to offer them, and the bankers like new debt-free aliens who help their loans with their borrowing. They wink at this invasion and pass laws legalizing their trespass.

If the American farms are allowed to go out of business, our present food surplus will soon become a food shortage. Famine will stalk this formerly bountiful country. Aliens outside our borders and their brothers inside will no longer be welcome. There will no longer be enough for all.

Alien peoples will then have a choice. They can sit and starve - or "crash the gate" and take what they need to survive. There are alien nations aplenty who are now being armed that will be happy to furnish hordes of armed men for such a desperate enterprise. All they need is a strong nation that seems capable of winning to lead them. This leader now exists. These people are already at our doorstep. Their advance agents swarm in every American city as soaring crime statistics attest. They hate the "Saxon" - they always have. Starvation will be the spur that may send scores of millions of the world's starving but armed and desperate aliens to our shores. Their hope? To loot "the breadbasket of the the world" so that they can survive.

Chapter - 36

EURODOLLARS

The variety and effects of usury are endless. Once the door has been opened an endless succession of "schemes" march in. One of the biggest is the "Eurodollar" scheme.

Suppose there is no money in the world. You walk into a bank (that has no money) and ask to borrow $1,000.

You give the bank your IOU and the bank gives you credit for $1,000. You can either write checks on this credit or you can take cash. If you want cash, the banker can go into the back room and print 10 one hundred dollar bills and give them to you (which used to be done - but is now illegal), or he can phone the nearest Federal Reserve Bank and they can send over $1,000 in paper money which has already been printed.

Let's recap. Before you walked into the bank there was no money in existence. You gave your IOU and the bank gave you credit (or bills) for $1,000. Your IOU is the backing for the money now in existence. One minute there is no money, the next minute there is $1,000.

You can take the $1,000 and go shopping and spend it. The merchants are happy to see you come. Or you can bring the $1,000 back to the bank and exchange it for your IOU. You tear up your IOU and it disappears. The money returned to the bank also disappears from circulation. The merchants never suspected that the $1,000 you were flashing around was created by you in the first place and backed by YOUR IOU.

There are several lessons to be learned from this illustration. First, people like YOU borrow money into existence. Next, money is backed by YOUR own IOU. Third, if you pay off YOUR IOU - money disappears.*

---

* Governments were excluded from above example on purpose. They have the right and the power to "make" money and spend it into existence. The Soviet and Chinese governments do this. The Western and 3rd World governments are not allowed to. In order to make their bankers rich these governments go to the bank - just as you do - leave their IOUs just as you do - and walk out with a check or with cash - just as you do. They pay unnecessary interest to the banks - just as you do. In fact, in the United States the government is rather small potatoes in this entire transaction. Two dollars are borrowed into existence by individuals and corporations for each dollar borrowed into existence by the government.

This illustration is simple enough and easy to understand. In fact, almost everything about money is simple. It works the same way at the corner bank and in the big city. It works the same way for corporations as it does for governments. It works the same way everywhere.

If you need money while in England, just pop into a bank. If you have the proper collateral you will be allowed to borrow American dollars into existence.

If you are in Hong Kong or Paris and you need money, with the right contacts and the right collateral you can borrow Federal Reserve notes into existence there, too. It's no big deal. People do it all the time.

The big Soviet bank "Moscow Narodny" in London was one of the first to start lending American Fed notes into existence in a big way. If a customer walked in the front door and asked for dollars - fine. He would sign his IOU, leave his collateral, and walk out the front door with either a check or a fist full of Fed notes.

The London merchants knew that Moscow Narodny was good for a few dollars and so they accepted checks on that bank with no questions asked.

If the borrower wanted dollar bills instead of a check, any one of a hundred London banks would be glad to lend Moscow Narodny Federal Reserve notes to hand to the borrower in exchange for the borrower's collateral. After all, if the borrower defaulted, the collateral could be sold for American dollars, and everyone would be paid.

Moscow Narodny started lending American dollars into existence in a small way after World War II. After a while it was lending hundreds of millions of American dollars into existence.

If Moscow Narodny could lend American dollars into existence, why couldn't any of the other foreign banks? There was no reason at all they couldn't. Thus was born the world Eurodollar market. Some dollars were actually sent from the U.S. to Europe, but most of these dollars borrowed into existence in foreign lands have never seen America. If the U.S. were to sink into the sea, the Eurodollar market would continue on and on.

The world's trade is conducted in Eurodollars. When Russia does business with China, it is in Eurodollars. You can go to almost any bank in the world and borrow dollars into existence.

It is the one international currency that everyone understands.

Following are a few quotes from the Federal Reserve Bank of San Francisco, S.F. Weekly Letter, July 27, 1979:

"What are Eurocurrencies? Eurodollars are simply dollar-denominated deposits at banking institutions outside the United States...Eurodollar deposits probably constitute about three-fourths of the total of all Eurocurrency deposits. One of the earliest depositors in the 1950s was the Soviet-controlled Banque Commerciale Pour L'Europe, whose code name 'Eurobank' provided the inspiration for the name of the market.

"...In the Eurodollar and other Eurocurrency markets, however, the proceeds of loans are not automatically redeposited in the system. Most of the proceeds of Eurodollar loans are converted into foreign currencies for purchases or investments abroad, or transferred into transaction balances in the United States for purchases or investments in this country."

Don't let the "banker talk" throw you. In the statement above you can get a lot of good information. The word "deposit" means "money borrowed into existence". You borrow money into existence and "deposit" it in your checking account in the bank rather than carry it around in your back pocket.

Next, the article says that about 3 out of 4 Eurodollars are borrowed into existence right there in Europe - or wherever. Only about 1 dollar in 4 is brought in from the U.S.

The kicker in this comes next - "Most of the proceeds of Eurodollar loans are converted into foreign currencies...". Most Frenchmen or Germans need their own currency to do business in their own countries. They take these dollars to the bank and exchange them for their own currency.

This leaves the French central bank or the English central bank with a load of dollars. What are they going to do with them? They buy American Government securities. This is why Europe is loaded with U.S. government securities.

Many Americans are irate that just anyone can borrow U.S. dollars into existence. Unfortunately, the only thing that can be done about it is to change the system and require the U. S. Government to create money. Failing that, there is no way the government, or anyone else, can stop foreigners from borrowing American dollars into existence. In other words - our government has no control over Federal Reserve money.

Backing For The Eurodollar

Who backs this vast market of Eurodollars? The foreign nations say that they don't. Every dollar borrowed into existence anywhere in the world inflates the world's dollar pocketbook. Every time some banana republic or iron curtain country pays off part of their debt, it deflates the world's dollar pocketbook. The worry is that some sort of Polish or Mexican Eurodollar default will plunge us into a 1929.

To prevent this from happening the banks have made our government pass the "Monetary Control Act". This requires the U.S. government to monetize any foreign default guaranteed by a foreign government. This is the reason for the rush of foreign governments to take over their private banks, as has recently taken place in France, Mexico, and El Salvador.

Will it work? Will this keep us from 1929? The answer lies in history. The many government monetary precautions in the past have not kept the world from stumbling into one depression after another. Something always goes wrong when using the usury system.

Pulling The Plug

There is one more item that our media is very careful not to mention - the real purpose of the Soviet banks in the West.

We are told that these banks help trade. They do help trade. They help their government with politics and travel. They also do more. They allow borrowers to borrow dollars into existence. How much? No one knows.

It is supposed that these Soviet banks have lent billions upon tens of billions of dollars into existence ... much of it lent to very shaky borrowers.

From time to time the demise of a single bank in the United States threatens the entire dollar banking structure of the world. If a single bank can do this, just imagine what would happen if all of the Soviet banks in Britain, France, and the Far

East call their loans at the same time.

In an instant the borrowers would grab the floating supply of dollars to honor the call for dollars. The floating supply of dollars could disappear in a flash. Money could cease to circulate. Business, transportation, and communication would grind to a halt. While we try to cope with this paralysis we could receive one last shock. This will be spoken of in the last chapter.

Chapter 37

YEAR OF JUBILEE

We all know that the Scriptual Law requires that land be returned to its true owners every 50 years.[6] Man has ignored the law. Massive changes in ownership of land, however, take place every 50 years whether man likes it or not. Everyone has a "reason" for this 50-year "catastrophe" but no one is quite sure just why it happens every 50 years instead of say 100 or 200 years. The explanation most often given is this: in 50 years all mortgagable property has been mortgaged and consequently there is none left to mortgage in order to borrow money into existence. Therefore, the system collapses. The usurer takes newly foreclosed property and lends money to a new debt-free borrower to enable him to buy it. "The borrower is servant to the lender." There is a new generation of slaves who bend their knee to Baal and serve a new master.

Note in the following chart how the commodity prices have risen and fallen four times since the country has been founded. Overlaid you will find a hypothetical 50 year of Jubilee Cycle. Matching the tops and bottoms as well as possible, we find that the next hypothetical Ybottom points to 1988 as being the next time the commodity index will reach bottom thus bringing to an end the present Peace Phase and beginning the War Phase of the

---

6. Leviticus 25:10

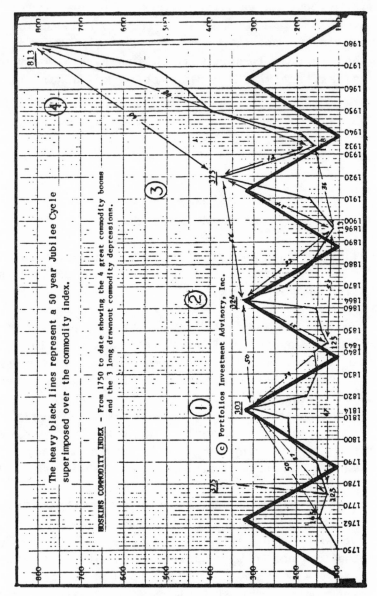

The heavy black lines represent a 50 year Jubilee Cycle superimposed over the commodity index.

HOSKINS COMMODITY INDEX - From 1750 to date showing the 4 great commodity booms and the 3 long drawnout commodity depressions.

(c) Portfolios Investment Advisory, Inc.

YEAR OF JUBILEE

next cycle.

In other words, the next "Bottomside Transition Year" should be 1988. Since there is margin for error, let us say that there is a very good likelihood that the bottom will be reached sometime during the period 1988-1992.

SECTION XI

USING HISTORY TO MAKE MONEY

Chapter - 38

MAKING MONEY IN THE PEACE PHASE

Natural Resources - Peace Phase

In the War Phase commodity prices rise to fantastic heights. At some point prices peak and plunge downward ushering in the Peace Phase. Today (1985), commodity prices are rushing downward. The last things one should own are commodities. The very things that increased in value so much in the War Phase are now rapidly losing value in the Peace Phase. Gold, silver, lumber, coal, oil, land, real-estate - all commodities tend to lose value.

Land - Peace Phase

As noted earlier, land sold for $300 an acre at the top of the 1st inflationary War Phase, $500 an acre in the 2nd, $625 in the 3rd, and $800 in the 4th.

Later, at the bottom of the 1st Peace Phase, the very same land sold for $25 an acre, $1.25 an acre in the 2nd, $50 in the 3rd, and your guess is as good as mine how low prices will go in the present 4th. For this reason land purchases should be delayed until after 1988.

Bankruptcy Sale Purchases - Peace Phase

Bankruptcies blossom in the Peace Phase. Most purchases should be limited to your own field of expertise. There will be few prices obtained at bankruptcy sales which will not be lower after "Bottomside Transition Year" has been reached.

Bank Defaults - Peace Phase

Bankruptcies of individuals and corporations will cause extreme difficulties for some banks. Many will do as they did in the 1920s - be backed to the wall and taken over by stronger banks. Usually the announcements of such mergers will be in such a manner as to leave the impression that this is the best business deal ever made. Will your deposits be safe in such banks?

No one knows. Every bank account is insured, but the insurance is limited to a set amount. One large New York bank failing could use up the entire insurance fund. Will the government come to the rescue? To the rescue of a private banking system for which they have no responsibility? Again, one can't say. They came to the rescue of one big bank. No one knows what some future government will do. The government has responsibility for its own debt, not the debt of the privately owned Federal Reserve System.

Rather than take a chance that the government will not pick up the tab on a defaulted Federal Reserve bank, it may be better to keep your cash money in a Treasury Bill. Treasury Bill Money Market Funds may also be a good parking area for your money, but the direct obligation of the U.S. Government - the T-Bill - is the best spot.

"Cash" is the thing many Pennsylvania farmers prefer. If you put your money in a bank lock box, will you be able to get it if the banks close? You could in Lynchburg during the last depression when they closed the banks. In other cities I have heard that people were not allowed access to their lock boxes. I believe that the answer to this question depends on the locality in which you live.

Chapter - 39

BUYING A HOUSE
(Peace Phase)

"Park Avenue" has been hired by the lenders to nurture carefully the feeling among young people that owning a home is a necessity. I say "nurture carefully" advisedly, because this is a relatively new concept in America. Earlier generations did not feel this way.

In a usury society, the ownership of anything that can be taxed poses a drawback to ownership. Millions of acres of land in our country have changed hands many times simply because former owners could not produce the required taxes. This problem with taxes is compounded when property is being "bought on time".

At the top of the business cycle a house might be worth $100,000. If you "buy" and contract to repay in 10 years at 20% you may be able to carry the payment load only if your business prospers.

A farmer is a commodity producer. His business suffers from the moment the "Topside Transition Year" is reached and commodities decline in value. As his income suffers, his ability to make payments also suffers.

A manufacturer uses commodities. His business prospers as the price of commodities declines and labor costs stabilize. Both the farmer and manufacturer suffer together when the "Bottomside Year of Transition" is reached and all business slows to a trickle and prices are at their lowest.

In many cases the income of both the commodity producer and manufacturer declines to only 20%-30% of former levels. At the very time when income has dropped to its lowest level, the price of real estate also drops. The $100,000 house may now have a market value of only $20,000 but will still require the legally contracted yearly payments of $23,190.72, and this does not count utilities, upkeep and taxes. The myth of "home ownership" entices foolish young people to ruin themselves in quest of "the American dream" which never in fact existed. They forget that our grandfathers rented until they could afford to buy. Study the following table to grasp the impossibility of the situation:

Payments On $100,000 At 20% For 15 Years

$100,000 borrowed			total repaid
21,075.60 payment year 1			21,075.60
21,075.60 " " 2			42,151.20
21,075.60 " " 3			63,226.80
21,075.60 " " 4			84,302.40
21,075.60 " " 5			105,378.00
21,075.60 " " 6			126,453.60
21,075.60 " " 7			147,529.20
21,075.60 " " 8			168,604.80
21,075.60 " " 9			189,680.40
21,075.60 " " 10			210,756.00
21,075.60 " " 11			231,831.60
21,075.60 " " 12			252,907.20
21,075.60 " " 13			273,982.80
21,075.60 " " 14			295,058.40
21,075.60 " " 15			316,134.00

If the buyer misses a payment the house can be thrown on the market for what it will bring. The chances are it may not bring as much as a single year's payment. That will mean that the owner is still liable for the remainder of the mortgage. The rest of his possessions may be attached and sold to satisfy the insatiable demands of usury.

Unemployment associated with the downturn in commodity prices forces hundreds of thousands of couples to abandon their houses and double up with their parents. This throws tens of thousands of other homes on the market adding to the housing glut. There are just as many people as before, but they are living in fewer houses. The prices of homes plunge. Many of these houses are rented to allow them to produce some sort of income. This tends to force "rent" levels lower and lower - a real boon to those who must rent.

The prudent who have lived by the Law and who have not owed - and who have lived modestly and prudently - are now in position to be rewarded for their patience. They may awake one day to find the $100,000 house of their dreams thrown on the market for $10,000 or $15,000. The "big spender" who was making the $23,190.72 payments each year may have bankrupted. His house will go for whatever people will pay for it.

In short, the young couple who wishes to own a house in the Peace Phase should plan carefully. They should rent modest accommodations or move in with their parents. They should save. They should continually shop the housing market to stay familiar with prices. No purchases need be made until commodities have bottomed and started up. There should be a long period of many months in which to purchase desirable property. In due time the seller will be most reasonable when approached by a potential buyer with cash in hand. The usury system is made to order for buyers who keep their values straight, who are patient, and who have money.

Conditions In The Last Depression

After the "1929 Crash" money disappeared. There was no money anywhere. Let's say that again. THERE WAS VIRTUALLY NO MONEY IN CIRCULATION.

The grocer had groceries. The car dealers had cars. There were houses for sale everywhere. There was a plentiful supply of trained labor willing to work for 15¢ to 20¢ an hour but there was no money to pay them! Where did all the money go?

The small floating supply of ready money that always circulates went to pay maturing debts and vanished into the banks. No new money was borrowed into existence to replace it. The reason that new money is not borrowed into existence is that once all property has an IOU attached, there is almost nothing left to mortgage on which a bank will lend money.

One morning a man goes to the grocer and pays him a dollar for food. That afternoon the grocer takes the dollar to the bank and pays it against his debt. The $1 credit cancels out the grocer's $1 debt and the dollar vanishes. "Poof"! Just like that. In the morning there was $1 in circulation - that evening it had disappeared. There is $1 less. In the deflation part of a 50 year cycle a money vacuum always develops.

How then can people get money to buy groceries? How will employers pay workers, and how can renters pay rents, and how can farmers buy seed? This was the big problem faced in the 1930s.

Ignorant people answer that "the government will print money". This would be nice, but it would violate the agreement made with the bankers. It is the bankers who control the monetary system not the government.

In the 1930s after a lapse of a great many months, the government borrowed money from the commercial banks in the Federal Reserve System to pay for "make work" programs. This put money into circulation to the benefit of interest bankers. If the people had waited for the government to do something, they could have starved to death.

Scrip-Tally Saved The Day

In desperation the people of America made their own money. Just as their ancestors made "tallies" - they made and issued money.

Cities across America printed and issued paper "scrip". This scrip was a "Tax Credit Certificate". It was good for the payment of taxes in the city that issued it. This gave it value. City policemen, firemen and other city employees were paid with this money. It was acceptable at the grocery store and had value.

Tired of waiting for the "politicking" politicians to do something to start the wheels of commerce rolling again, many large corporations also issued their own "scrip" redeemable in merchandise from their own factories. It was a piece of paper which could be exchanged for a washing machine, cast iron pipe, or cases of food. The scrip had value. The grocery store would accept it, too.

Across America counties issued "scrip". Cities issued "scrip". Long needed local municipal projects were undertaken and paid for in "scrip". The scrip was retired from circulation as it was tendered for taxes. The municipal "scrip-system" that grew up in the '30s left no lasting debt as a bad aftertaste.

From the complete absence of money which had caused commerce to grind to almost a dead stop, there emerged a super-abundance of different kinds of money. In the large cities, the local grocery stores were receiving 15 or 20 different types of "scrip" money in addition to the occasional Federal Reserve note.

Local businessmen met to bring order out of confusion and determined which kinds should be accepted. The public turned against debt. No one wanted to do business with the banks. The banks demanded repayment in nothing but their own Federal Reserve notes. Interest rates dropped as low as 1% to 2%.

America's usurers were not about to lose control of the

monetary system if they could help it. In spite of the national destitution brought on by their usury-banking, their banks refused to accept "scrip" in payment against the mortgages. Why should they accept "scrip" when they were foreclosing those who did not have Federal Reserve notes to pay on their IOUs? They also saw to it that nothing but their own Federal Reserve note could be received for Federal taxes.

When all property had been foreclosed that was going to be foreclosed, they ordered public works programs started. This would "prime the pump" and give the people enough Federal Reserve notes to start a new inflationary cycle.

Local municipal scrip was good locally. By law Federal Reserve notes were acceptable EVERYWHERE and were good for payment of Federal taxes. With the Federal Government's backing the Federal Reserve notes won out over local scrip - but it was close.

The day will come once more when lending will stop. New money will stop coming into circulation. Interest payments will quickly eat up the floating supply. Money will disappear from circulation just as it did before.

You will need groceries. The grocer will have groceries. Just like the 1930s there will be no way to make the transfer other than barter. The grocer will quickly get as many grandfather clocks and vacuum cleaners as he will want and will demand something better.

That "something better" is municipal "SCRIP". There is no reason it should take more than 48 hours for a city government to have it printed and paid into circulation. The present breed of local politicians may never have heard of it. Those who control the local usury banks and those on their payroll will automatically oppose it. It will slow their foreclosing and taking over mortgaged property. It will be up to YOU - the reader of this book - to get the ball rolling.

Talk to your local politician. Let him read this chapter. Tell him to do as his grandfathers did - pay the garbage man, policeman, fireman and the rest of the public payroll with "scrip" - redeemable for taxes. IF YOU DON'T - people may starve before anything is done about the problem.

Debtors Take Bankruptcy - Peace Phase

The subject of personal bankruptcy is a painful subject. "Our Law" tells us that we must be honest in our dealings and that we must "Owe no man anything but love." "The Law" also tells us that while we are allowed to charge interest to "strangers" (Heb. zûwr), we are not to charge interest to our own "strangers" (Heb. gêr), and that we are to "release" our debts every 7 years and not to enslave permanently one of our own since "the borrower is servant to the lender."

The Usury System which has been placed over us results in slavery in one degree or another for everyone entangled in its net. The farmer who was ignorant of the Law and who bought land for $800 an acre on credit in 1919 still had to make yearly payments of $125 an acre in the depths of the depression in 1941; but in 1941 the market value of this same land had dropped to only $65-$75 an acre. This selling price was significantly less than his buying price and even less than his yearly payment toward ownership. Because he had "given his word", however, he lived through impossible privation and forced this privation on his loyal wife and family. He became work worn, a wrung-out husk of a man, and his wife's face showed the privations. His children used cardboard to cover the holes in their shoes. I knew these people. I went to school with their children. This is slavery! The worst sort that has ever stalked any land.

All the debts can NEVER be paid in a usury society. There are more IOUs than there is money to pay. It was designed that way to trap people. The people who run the debt-system know precisely what they are doing.

Since we are dealing with the "Babylonian System" or the "devil's system", and since there is no way out for most who are caught in its net, I have this word of advice for its victims:

BANKRUPT IMMEDIATELY!

If you were ignorant of the law of usury; if you went into the usury contract innocently; if there is no way the contract can be fulfilled without undue suffering for you and your family; don't wait, bite the bullet and bankrupt immediately. Straighten out your life and your finances. Don't worry about your "credit rating", it's something you shouldn't have and don't need. Promise that you will never again return to the mire. With God's help doors may open to you in the future and you may gain back all that you may seem to lose today. In the meantime you can live as a "free" man. "Go and sin no more."

For those of you who knew God's Law, but with eyes open violated His Law, you are in the hands of the living God. He deals with His own. I have no words of advice.

The 4-Year Cycle - Buying Stocks

Look at the facing page. This is a picture of the stock market going back to 1926. Today you see copies of this chart everywhere. It is said that "imitation is the most sincere form of flattery." The author was the first to create and publish this chart many years ago. You will note that the vertical bars mark off 4-year cycles. The arrows mark off election day. Every four years the stock market bottoms. Two years later near election day it peaks. Just knowing that gives you a whopping edge.

Pump money in to make things look good and after the election cut it off. Observe the years 1978, 1974, 1970, 1966 ... on back to 1926. What do you see? Market bottoms! Every four years - market bottoms! In the interest-free system of our ancestors there was no such thing as booms and busts such as you see here. But in a usury system where the usurers manipulate the economy to elect their hand-picked politicians, you have inflations and deflations to coincide with elections.

You can see with your own eyes that this is no theory but an historical fact. In addition to the four-year bars at the lower part of the history chart, four-year election arrows have been placed at the top. These arrows represent election day. Congress appropriates money. The president spends it at the time most advantageous for him, just before election. This causes the stock market to rise making voters happy on election day.

With the money all spent, after the election the stock market crashes. A new four-year election cycle then starts all over again. If you didn't know this, you may have been fooled into selling at the bottom when others were buying, or buying at

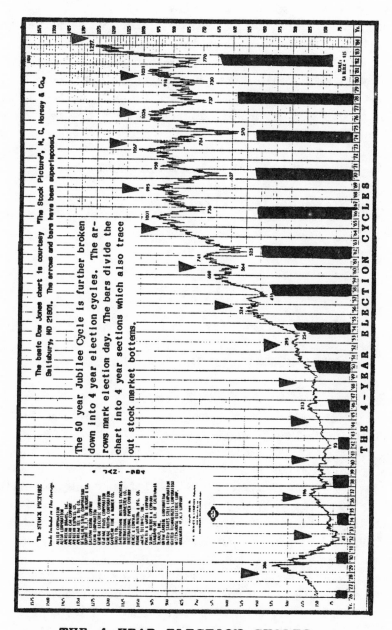

THE 4-YEAR ELECTION CYCLES

the top along about election day when others were selling. This knowledge is called "Historical-Technics" or "HISTECH". This is the author's specialty - the attempt to identify the place where we are on the current 4-Year Presidential Cycle and coordinate it with the place we are on the longer 50-Year Jubilee Cycle.

If the reader would like to receive a free issue of the author's newsletter showing what he believes to be the present place in the cycle, send a self-addressed envelope to the following address:

PORTFOLIOS INVESTMENT ADVISORY
P.O. Box 997
Lynchburg, Virginia 24505

Chapter - 40

MAKING MONEY IN THE WAR PHASE

War - War Phase

War! There will be war ... many wars, including a big one. No one knows the timing of the big one, but it will come.

There has to be war to make the usury system work. The lack of money to carry on business will cause the misery of the people to be intense. The government will NOT print money to relieve the suffering. The only way they will allow it to come into existence is for it to be borrowed into existence from the banks of the Federal Reserve System and their sister usury banking systems throughout the world.

It can be borrowed into existence faster if the government is made to borrow money to buy an expensive airplane (costing 50 million dollars each), than if the government has to go to the trouble of contracting for 1,000 - $50,000 houses one at a time. Then too, the plane will be obsolete in five years and will have to be re-ordered, a never ending source of business. The cheaper houses will be around for a long time.

World War II didn't get started until six years after the "War Phase" started ... usually it's sooner. In the past, the major war of the War Phase has not been a "brushfire" war, it has been something "serious."

Buy Natural Resources - War Phase

The present Peace Phase will end when commodity prices decline as far as they are going to decline. Mines will be closed. Lumber companies will have been shut down. This will cause raw materials to become scarce. In time a war will be started to force people to borrow money into existence. As a result prices will start up again. The "Downside Transition Year" is behind. When this happens one may buy any natural resource virtually risk-free. The next "Downside Transition Year" commodity buying time is expected to be approximately 1988.

Gold - War Phase

Inflation again raises its head. The people welcome it. The price of gold starts to rise. If the price of gold is "pegged" at a certain level by government decree, inflation will quickly drive gold out of circulation as people hoard gold coins. If the government confiscates gold for itself or for a private banking system, people will not notice price increases as rapidly. But "gold confiscation" causes such an uproar that Western governments try to keep a free market in gold if they feel that confiscation will cause problems. While prices are low, this is the time to buy gold or shares in gold mines.

Stocks - War Phase

Since commodity prices are starting to move up, it is now time to buy stock in companies that produce commodities. Manufacturing stocks will do well in the first part of the stock market rise, but commodity stocks such as metals, oils, lumber, etc., should put on a stellar performance. The manufacturing companies had their day in the Peace Phase of the last cycle. In the War Phase, the commodity stocks will have their day.

Real Estate - War Phase

Real Estate prices should theoretically bottom at the same time commodity prices bottom. The tremendous inventory of land for sale, however, tends to hold the lid on prices. It is a case of "special situation". Half way through the War Phase land prices start to edge up - faster in some areas than others - then rush to the top.

Houses - War Phase

This is the time to shop for houses. There is no rush. The mobs of unemployed, generations doubling up, and continuing bankruptcies tend to ensure that the price for houses will stay relatively low for some time. The commodity bottom was reached in 1932. House prices did not start to rise a great deal until after 1940.

Suppose Things Just Don't Happen That Way

Suppose - just suppose - these plans to cope with the usual sort of Cycle just don't work out ... that plans to buy houses, businesses, and profit by the next depression don't materialize the way they have in the past.

Few of our people believe that these are normal times. Most believe that events are in a countdown for something. Crime, rape, venereal disease, child molestation, homosexuality, and blasphemy greet our nation with each sunrise, and it gets worse and worse - WHY?

The reason why was written long ago:

Thine own wickedness shall correct thee ... thou hast forsaken the Lord. Jer. 2:19

There you have it. Things are getting bad because our people are being led to ignore the Laws of God. Conditions will continue to get worse until "thine own wickedness shall correct thee." If our people are hard-hearted enough, it is possible that we may reach a point of unspeakable misery. When will our Lord lift this burden from us? What is it He wants of us? This is what He wants, and this is what He will get:

Thou shall love the Lord thy God with all thy heart.
$$\text{Deut. 6:5}$$

And how are we to express this "love"?

If you love me keep my commandments. John 14:15

We have not kept God's command in regards to usury and matters have developed just as He said they would. In fact, matters have progressed farther than many realize. The history given in this book should enable the reader to grasp the true condition of today's society. At the risk of being repetitious, here is the present situation summarized:

Forty-five percent of the stock of all corporations in America is held in trust at bank trust departments. The banks vote this stock to elect directors of corporations. The directors tell the corporations whom to support and make grants to. In this way banks control:

o National Media: Every TV network, newspaper chain, or radio chain that has stock outstanding is almost certain to be controlled. To look into the TV is to see into the soul of its master.

o Small Media: If local radio, TV, or newspapers support Bank interests they get advertising. If this advertising is withheld, they are forced out of business. Small media must also be liberal.

o Alternate Media: Certain nationally known newsletters and newspapers claim to be conservative but receive favorable national media coverage. Almost without exception they support bank policies. Those that oppose bank policy receive national media blackout and loss of subscribers and loss of revenue.

o Education: Liberal Colleges receive grants from corporations. Corporate directors are placed on their board of visitors. Consequently, few colleges have conservative professors. Fewer colleges are conservative. They can't be if they expect to receive grants.

o Politicians: To receive media coverage for election most politicians must be liberals or "secret" liberals. Support-

ers of bank policies receive media exposure and donations.
Opponents of bank policy receive "media blackout" and are
not re-elected.

o Small Town Politicians: Public officials in even the smal-
   lest villages tend to owe their election to media exposure,
   just as their big city cousins.   It is possible to have 90%
   of the electorate in a small village conservative and still
   have liberal politicians. They will be the only ones given
   media exposure.

o Police: Liberal politicians control the police. The higher
   one goes the more complete the control. The most tightly
   controlled are the armed services, CIA, FBI, Federal mar-
   shals; next, city police, and county sheriffs. With few
   exceptions they all enforce policy indirectly dictated by
   New York banks - or lose their jobs.

o Other Nations: "The borrower is servant to the lender".
   Most nations in the world are in debt to the U. S. banks.
   As a consequence most nations of the world are servants to
   the 10 for 11 system of the U. S. banks and will do their
   bidding.

There you have it!   Media, politics, education, police, and
foreign nations.   All earthly AUTHORITY is in the hands of those
who rule the world's money system. You cannot look to any of the
above for help.

Suppose that instead of dropping atomic bombs the Soviets
are instructed to call their Eurodollar loans, or just default.
Or, suppose 3rd world nations refuse to borrow money into existence to pay interest.*   Dollars would immediately evaporate from
circulation causing massive shutdowns of business, transportation, communication and power.

Trucks and trains would stop running. There would be no way
to pay the drivers and engineers. There would be an immediate
shortage of food since supermarkets carry only a 3 day supply on
their shelves. The U. S. "food shortage stories" bandied about
by the survival letters ten years ago could develop rapidly.

This food shortage would be more than just the difficulty of

---

* The other side of the coin is for the international banks to make virtually
interest free loans to 3rd world nations. The 3rd world nations can invest the
loan money in U. S. government bonds and receive the interest. This bond interest can then be paid to the lending bank. In this way the U. S. taxpayers pay
foreign 3rd world debts, the banks take in billions, and America is bled white.
The end result is the same.

getting the food from farm to market. There would be an actual shortage. From 1/4 to 1/2 of America's farmers will soon be bankrupted off their land. The world is fed with our vanishing surplus. The Soviet Union and China will be short also.

It is not logical to assume the Soviet Slavs and the hundreds of millions of Orientals would sit still and starve while food is still being grown in America. They would be forced to take it to survive. The only way they can take it is to come HERE to take it.

Combine this situation with the reports over the past several years stating that the Soviets and their surrogates have trained and armed alien wetbacks before sending them into our country. If these zûwr strangers make common cause with the rest of the strangers in our midst, what need is there for a massive missile attack? The country would be at a standstill. Nothing moving. No food, no power, a hostile armed and belligerent crowd of zûwr strangers in our midst controlling finance, government, armed services, the media, while their wilder brethren rule the streets.

If, in spite of all, our people do rise to overthrow their oppressors, the foreign armies of our enemies would be ordered to enter our country to protect them. There would be no need for a massive assault. Since we would not deal with our enemies at a distance according to Law, we would have to deal with our enemies HERE, face to face, according to the Law. Savage enemies that are as countless as locusts - all united against their traditional foe.

Can this situation be avoided? Certainly. God forbids the usury system. We allow it. As a natural consequence our defenseless farmers are bankrupting. A food shortage is on the way. To keep from starving our enemies must try to take our land and our food; we own the world's breadbasket. They are being drawn to us as if they had hooks in their jaws. Since our leaders are doing nothing to put our people in compliance with the Law - these events will continue to unwind. Only instant, absolute obedience to the Law can stop them.

This frightening condition was foreseen long ago when our fathers still lived in Israel. The promise made to Abraham was that;

"...tell the stars, if thou be able to number them...so shall thy seed be." Gen. 15:5

If God said it would happen, it would happen. Abraham's descendants numbered only a few million in the tiny land of Palestine. This was not the hundreds of millions God had promised.

In the year 1000 B. C., while our people were still living in Palestine and before they were taken away into captivity, God remembered his promise and said;

I will appoint a place for my people Israel, and will plant them, that they may dwell in a place of their own, and move no more. II Sam. 7:10

He did. God gave us a land big enough to hold us, a land which had always been waste, but which became a rich, bountiful land, and blessed as no other land has ever been blessed. This land is ours. We are to move no more. The black cloud threatening this country and its people was foreseen down to the last detail. It was long ago foretold that;

"Two parts therein shall be cut off and die, but...I will bring the third part through the fire." Zech. 13:8.

Because of false priests and false leaders our land is rapidly filling with strangers. They now number almost half. Soon they will number two-thirds. In the face of this, we have God's promise that the third part will come through the fire! Our nation will live as long as there is a sun and a moon. This is not open to question. We have His Word.

The Last Chapter

Many Christians have the feeling deep inside that it is time for great things to happen in this world. There is a feeling of expectation in the air. It just may be that the time has arrived at last for our God to unfold the last chapter in his master plan for us. If this is that time, the future will be exactly as written in the Bible:

"And there came one of the ... angels...saying ... I will shew unto thee the judgement of the great whore that sitteth upon many waters: With whom the kings of the earth have committed fornication ... and I saw a woman sit upon a scarlet colored beast...And the woman was arrayed in purple and scarlet color ... and upon her forehead was a name written, MYSTERY, BABYLON THE GREAT ....

"And the angel said unto me ... I will tell you the mystery of the woman ... The waters which thou sawest, where the whore sitteth, are people ... these shall hate the whore ... and the woman which thou sawest is that great city (system), which reigneth over the kings of the earth.

"... And he cried ... Babylon The Great is fallen, is fallen ... for all nations ... and the kings of the earth have committed fornication with her ... and I heard another voice from heaven, saying, come out of her, my people, that ye be not partakers of ... her plagues....

"And the merchants of the earth shall weep ... for no man buyeth ... fine flour, wheat ... and chariots, and slaves, and souls of men... The merchants ... shall stand ... saying, alas, alas that great city ... for in one hour so great riches is come to nought ... and a mighty angel took up a stone ... and cast it into the sea, saying, thus with violence shall that great city Babylon be thrown down, and shall be found no more at all." Rev. 17 & 18.

"And the word of the Lord came unto me, saying, Son of man, set thy face against Gog ... And say, Thus saith the Lord God; Behold, I am against thee, O Gog, the chief prince of Mesheck and Tubal:... I will bring thee forth, and all thine army, horses and horsemen, all of them clothed with all sorts of armour, even a great company ... Persia (settled in part by Arabs and Turks who spread to southern Italy, Spain, and Central and South America), Ethiopia (now scattered throughout the West) and Libya (traditional enemy of Christendom).

"Gomer, and all his bands (Including Ashkanaz - Gomer's son) the House of Togarmah ... in the latter years thou shalt come ... against the mountains (nations) of Israel, which have been always waste ... Thou shall ascend and come like a storm, thou shalt be like a cloud to cover the land, thou, and all thy bands, and many people with thee ... and thou shalt think an evil thought:

"And thou shalt say, I will go up to the land of unwalled villages; I will go to them that are at rest, that dwell safely, all of them dwelling without walls, and having neither bars nor gates, To take a spoil, and to take a prey; to turn thine hand upon the desolate places that are now inhabited, and upon the people that are gathered out of the nations which have gotten cattle and goods....

"Therefore, son of man, prophesy and say unto Gog, Thus saith the Lord God; In that day ... thou shalt come from thy place out of the north parts, thou, and many people with thee, all of them riding upon horses, a great company, and a mighty army: And thou shalt come up against my people of Israel, as a cloud to cover the land; it shall be in the later days, and I will bring thee against my land, that the heathen may know me, when I shall be sanctified in thee, O Gog, before their eyes.

"... And it shall come to pass at the same time when Gog shall come against the land of Israel, saith the Lord God, that my fury shall come up in my face ... And I will call for a sword against him throughout all my mountains (nations), saith the Lord God: every man's sword shall be against his brother.

"And I will plead against him with pestilence and with blood; and

I will rain upon him, and upon his bands, and upon the many people that are with him, an overflowing rain, and great hailstones ... I will be known in the eyes of many nations, and they shall know that I am the Lord ... I will turn thee back, and leave but the sixth part of thee ... Thou shalt fall upon the mountains (nations) of Israel, thou, and all thy bands, and the people that is with thee ... I will give unto Gog a place there of graves in Israel...and there shall they bury Gog and all his multitude...

"Then shall they know that I am the Lord their God ... I have gathered them unto their own land ... Neither will I hide my face any more from them: for I have poured out my spirit upon the house of Israel, saith the Lord God." Ezek 37:21-39:29.

*   *   *   *   *

It will be worth your time to read the last few pages again. Events will unfold in just this way because God said they would. It is the result of all that has gone before. God forbade usury. His people have ignored the prohibition. In so doing they have allowed Babylon to rule them and inflict hurt on them generation after generation.

The author believes that the destruction of the forbidden usury system (not the end of the world) is at hand. Babylon will be destroyed according to scripture - "with violence".

In the days ahead it will be foolish to count on help from bankers, industrial leaders, media, elected politicians, armed services, police, or apostate religious leaders. A great many individuals in these organizations are secretly for you and will help you any way they can, but most of the leaders have been carefully selected through control and voting of corporation stock. Most people are already involuntary servants, but nevertheless obedient ones, through the system of lending 10 for 11 (the borrower is servant..). Face it, son of man, you are defenseless against the forces of Babylon. The only shield left to you is your God. He planned it this way.

You must now study more on your own. Seek the Truth about the Babylonian usury-banking system which endlessly demands War Cycles of blood and Peace Cycles of poverty. God will help you find it, and will tell you what to do (Zec. 12:8-9). In His hands you are safe.

THE END

THE AUTHOR

Dick Hoskins is a veteran of the Korean War serving with Air Force Intelligence. In 1952 he fired with the Air Force pistol team at the Nationals. Ten years later he was called to service again and served as an aide to the commanding general of the 100th Airborne division.

A native Virginian, he was educated at Hampden-Sydney, William & Mary, and Lynchburg College, receiving a degree in History. He has also taken special courses at several other colleges.

He joined the Wall Street firm of Francis I. DuPont in 1959 and was trained in all facets of the brokerage business with special emphasis on portfolio work. He has been married to the same wife for almost 30 years and is a father and a grandfather.

On April 28, 1965, at 4:00 in the afternoon, in the green rocking chair on the front porch of his home he professed belief in Jesus Christ as his Savior.

In 1973 he started his newsletter "Portfolios Investment Advisory" which was initially sent only to customers whose portfolios he managed. Later it was offered to the public and has since been distributed all over the world.

The 10th generation in this country, his family has participated in every war cycle with its blood letting and every peace cycle with its unspeakable misery since 1615. His military service, study of history, first hand experience in the field of economics, family tradition, and Christian perspective makes him uniquely qualified to write on this subject.

INDEX

APPENDIX 1

H O S K I N S   7   R U L E S   O F   I N T E R E S T

1. The money supply WILL be expanded to allow debtors to pay interest on their debts - until Jubilee time.

2. It does no good to have unlimited funds in banks. The money must be in circulation where debtors can get it to pay interest.

3. When money expansion stops   interest rapidly eats up the floating supply causing monetary strangulation and crash.

4. Interest will destroy any obstacle to its expansion and survival.

5. Interest requires a heavy tax rate so that money will not be hoarded but circulated to pay interest.

6. All users of the interest system - both debtors & creditors - become involuntary servants of the system.

7. Never will the usurer - or his hireling - show mercy to his victim.